Reference Without Refer

Reference is a central topic in phi
been the main focus of discussion about how language relates to the world. R. M. Sainsbury sets out a new approach to the concept, which promises to bring to an end some long-standing debates in semantic theory.

There is a single category of referring expressions, all of which deserve essentially the same kind of semantic treatment. Included in this category are both singular and plural referring expressions ('Aristotle', 'The Pleiades'), complex and non-complex referring expressions ('The President of the USA in 1970', 'Nixon'), and empty and non-empty referring expressions ('Vulcan', 'Neptune'). Referring expressions are to be described semantically by a reference condition, rather than by being associated with a referent. In arguing for these theses, Sainsbury's book promises to end the fruitless oscillation between Millian and descriptivist views. Millian views insist that every name has a referent, and find it hard to give a good account of names which appear not to have referents, or at least are not known to do so, like ones introduced through error ('Vulcan'), ones where it is disputed whether they have a bearer ('Patanjali') and ones used in fiction. Descriptivist theories require that each name be associated with some body of information. These theories fly in the face of the fact names are useful precisely because there is often no overlap of information among speakers and hearers. The alternative position for which the book argues is firmly non-descriptivist, though it also does not require a referent. A much broader view can be taken of which expressions are referring expressions: not just names and pronouns used demonstratively, but also some complex expressions and some anaphoric uses of pronouns.

Sainsbury's approach brings reference into line with truth: no one would think that a semantic theory should associate a sentence with a truth value, but it is commonly held that a semantic theory should associate a sentence with a truth condition, a condition which an arbitrary state of the world would have to satisfy in order to make the sentence true. The right analogy is that a semantic theory should associate a referring expression with a reference condition, a condition which an arbitrary object would have to satisfy in order to be the expression's referent.

Lucid and accessible, and written with a minimum of technicality, Sainsbury's book also includes a useful historical survey. It will be of interest to those working in logic, mind, and metaphysics as well as essential reading for philosophers of language.

Mark Sainsbury is Professor of Philosophy at the University of Texas at Austin.

Reference Without Referents

R. M. SAINSBURY

CLARENDON PRESS · OXFORD

OXFORD
UNIVERSITY PRESS

Great Clarendon Street, Oxford OX2 6DP

Oxford University Press is a department of the University of Oxford.
It furthers the University's objective of excellence in research, scholarship,
and education by publishing worldwide in

Oxford New York

Auckland Cape Town Dar es Salaam Hong Kong Karachi
Kuala Lumpur Madrid Melbourne Mexico City Nairobi
New Delhi Shanghai Taipei Toronto

With offices in

Argentina Austria Brazil Chile Czech Republic France Greece
Guatemala Hungary Italy Japan Poland Portugal Singapore
South Korea Switzerland Thailand Turkey Ukraine Vietnam

Oxford is a registered trade mark of Oxford University Press
in the UK and in certain other countries

Published in the United States
by Oxford University Press Inc., New York

© R. M. Sainsbury 2005

The moral rights of the author have been asserted
Database right Oxford University Press (maker)

First published 2005
First published in paperback 2007

All rights reserved. No part of this publication may be reproduced,
stored in a retrieval system, or transmitted, in any form or by any means,
without the prior permission in writing of Oxford University Press,
or as expressly permitted by law, or under terms agreed with the appropriate
reprographics rights organization. Enquiries concerning reproduction
outside the scope of the above should be sent to the Rights Department,
Oxford University Press, at the address above

You must not circulate this book in any other binding or cover
and you must impose the same condition on any acquirer

British Library Cataloguing in Publication Data

Data available

Library of Congress Cataloging in Publication Data

Sainsbury, R. M. (Richard Mark)
Reference without referents / R. M. Sainsbury.
  p. cm.
Includes bibliographical references and index.
1. Reference (Philosophy) 2. Language and languages—Philosophy. I. Title.
B105.R25S23 2005 121'.68—dc22 2004029392

Typeset by SPI Publisher Services, Pondicherry, India
Printed in Great Britain
on acid-free paper by
Biddles Ltd., King's Lynn, Norfolk

ISBN 978-0-19-924180-4 (Hbk.) 978-0-19-923040-2 (Pbk.)

1 3 5 7 9 10 8 6 4 2

For Victoria

Preface

There is a single category of referring expressions, all of which deserve essentially the same kind of semantic treatment. Included in this category are both singular and plural referring expressions ('Aristotle', 'The Pleiades'), complex and non-complex referring expressions ('The President of the USA in 1970', 'Nixon'), and empty and non-empty referring expressions ('Vulcan', 'Neptune'). Referring expressions are to be described semantically by a reference condition, rather than by being associated with a referent.

These are the main theses of this book. Special emphasis is placed on the unity among empty and non-empty referring expressions, summarized by the title *Reference without Referents* (RWR). The first chapter is intended for readers with little background in philosophy of language. Its final section (1.6) summarizes the main claims to be made in the book; for many readers, this will be the best place to start reading. The second chapter describes the framework within which the rest of the discussion takes place. In particular, it sketches the logic that is taken for granted (negative free logic, or NFL). The next three chapters consider specific kinds of referring expression: proper names (Chapter 3), pronouns (Chapter 4), and complex referring expressions (Chapter 5). RWR gives very straightforward answers to the more tractable issues about existence and fiction, and these are set out in Chapter 6, along with some less tractable ones, which are problematic for all theories. The final chapter considers mental reference, suggesting that this, too, is appropriately treated in the RWR way. Accepting this would lend strength to the theses of RWR about linguistic reference; but these theses could consistently be accepted even by someone who rejected the admittedly more speculative theses about thought.

My principal institutional debt is to the Leverhulme Trust, which awarded me a Senior Research Fellowship in 2000–2, during which most of the work for the book was completed. In the current state of Humanities Departments in the United Kingdom, with enormously increased demands of teaching and, especially, administration, research has become dependent upon special grants from charities and organizations like the Leverhulme Trust, AHRB, and the British Academy. These grants have accordingly become an essential part of academic development, and I feel privileged to have received one. Yet the importance of the grants to the work of UK Humanities departments shows that the Universities are not supporting research as they should. Adequate time for research should be built into the contract of every academic, rather than being available only to a privileged few who are fortunate enough to receive outside funding.

In addition to the Leverhulme Trust, my thanks go to other institutions: King's College London, which permitted me to take up the award, and the University of Texas at Austin which provided a hospitable place for research as a Visiting Scholar during part of my tenure of the award.

Many individuals have helped with comments on drafts of this material, including the following: Nicholas Asher, Roberta Ballerin, José Bermudez, Dean Buckner, Tyler Burge, Jack Copeland, Tom Crowther, Josh Dever, Maite Ezcurdia, Victoria Goodman, Mark Heller, Jim Hopkins, Ruth Kempson, Max Kölbel, Fraser MacBride, Cynthia Macdonald, Graham Macdonald, MM McCabe, Stephen Neale, David Papineau, Hanna Pickard, Diane Proudfoot, François Récanati, Gabriel Segal, David Sosa, Jason Stanley, Scott Sturgeon, Mark Textor, Mark Turner, Michael Tye (my apologies to those whose names I have inadvertently omitted). I am also grateful to two referees for Oxford University Press, whose comments on what I had thought was the final version led to many changes.

I owe a special debt to Keith Hossack, Anthony Savile, and David Wiggins, who have helped me not only through specific comments on these topics but also by their intellectual acumen and their friendship over many years.

Acknowledgements

Some parts of Chapter 4 originally appeared in 'Reference and anaphora', J. Tomberlin (ed.), *Philosophical Perspectives, 16, Language and*

Mind, (Malden, MA: Blackwell Publishing 2002), 43–71. Some parts of Chapter 5 originally appeared in 'Referring descriptions' in Marga Reimer and Anne Bezuidenhout (eds.), *Descriptions and Beyond*, (Oxford: Oxford University Press 2004), 369–89. Some parts of Chapter 7 originally appeared in Italian in 'Graziozi topi rosa: allucinazione e contenuto percettivo' in Claudia Bianchi and Andrea Bottani (eds.), *Ontologia e significa*, (Milan: FrancoAngeli 2003), 173–87. My thanks to the publishers and editors for permission to reuse the material here. The present text corrects mistakes in these earlier publications.

Contents

1 A short history of theories of names — 1
2 Framework issues — 47
3 Proper names — 86
4 Pronouns: anaphora and demonstration — 125
5 Complex referring expressions — 170
6 Existence and fiction — 195
7 Mental reference and individual concepts — 216

References — 255
Index — 261

Detailed Contents

1 A short history of theories of names 1
   1.1 J. S. Mill 2
       1.1.1 Connotation and denotation 2
       1.1.2 Lack of denotation; sameness of denotation 6
   1.2 Gottlob Frege 8
       1.2.1 Frege's puzzle 8
       1.2.2 Identity 10
       1.2.3 Idiosyncrasies of sense 13
       1.2.4 Sense without a referent 16
   1.3 Bertrand Russell 19
       1.3.1 'Logically proper' names and knowledge by acquaintance .. 19
       1.3.2 Russell on ordinary proper names 24
   1.4 Saul Kripke 27
   1.5 John McDowell 33
       1.5.1 Understanding and truth theories 33
       1.5.2 Axioms for names 35
       1.5.3 *De re* senses 41
   1.6 The Road Ahead 44

2 Framework issues 47
   2.1 Truth theory 48
   2.2 Russellian propositions 60
   2.3 Negative free logic (NFL) 64
   2.4 Ontology 75
   2.5 Rigidity and the essence of reference 76
   2.6 Notions resembling rigidity 81

3 Proper names 86
   3.1 Prima facie considerations in favour of intelligible
       empty names 86
   3.2 Names name 91
   3.3 Evans and Russellian names 94
   3.4 Alternatives to RWR 97
   3.5 Baptism 106

xiv   DETAILED CONTENTS

3.6	Transmission	111
	3.6.1 Initiation	113
	3.6.2 Continued participation	116
	3.6.3 A referent is forever?	119
3.7	Vagaries in name-using practices	122

4 Pronouns: anaphora and demonstration   125

4.1	Anaphoric dependence	125
	4.1.1 Some kinds of dependence	125
	4.1.2 Dependent unbound pronouns are referring expressions	130
	4.1.3 Evans's proposal	132
	4.1.4 Intention, speaker's referent, and salience	136
	4.1.5 Evans's account amended	139
	4.1.6 Understanding dependent pronouns	143
	4.1.7 Interpretation and individual concepts	146
	4.1.8 Interpretation and truth conditions	150
4.2	Non-linguistic dependence	153
	4.2.1 Introduction	153
	4.2.2 Understanding and identification	154
	4.2.3 Understanding and theories of meaning	157
	4.2.4 Conditional truth conditions	158
	4.2.5 Object dependence	163
	4.2.6 Understanding without identification?	163
	4.2.7 Understanding empty demonstratives	166
4.3	Main themes reviewed	169

5 Complex referring expressions   170

5.1	Compound names	170
5.2	Definite descriptions	174
	5.2.1 Introduction	174
	5.2.2 Examples of referential axioms	176
	5.2.3 Intentions	179
	5.2.4 Donnellan and the referential/attributive distinction	188
	5.2.5 Plural and mass descriptions	191

6 Existence and fiction   195

6.1	Existence and scope	196
6.2	A second-level approach	198
6.3	A simple RWR account of fiction	202
6.4	Fictional characters	209

7 Mental reference and individual concepts — 216
7.1 Development and individual concepts — 217
7.2 The nature of individual concepts — 221
7.2.1 Concepts and information: addition and subtraction — 222
7.2.2 Information and sortals — 224
7.2.3 Individual concepts and discriminating knowledge — 226
7.2.4 Concepts and recognition — 229
7.2.5 Principles governing the reference of individual concepts — 232
7.2.6 Individual concepts without a referent — 235
7.2.7 The value of individual concepts and of the mechanisms which produce them — 238
7.2.8 The determination of reference — 238
7.2.9 Acquaintance versus description as ways of thinking of objects — 240
7.3 Perceptual content — 242
7.3.1 The issue — 242
7.3.2 Problems for 'generalism' (the view that all perceptual contents are general) — 246
7.3.3 Hallucination and two kinds of singularism: DR (direct reference) and RWR — 252

References — 255
Index — 261

I
A short history of theories of names

Proper names like 'Aristotle' and 'London' are paradigms of 'referring expressions', expressions which refer to something, or at least are supposed to refer to something. In this chapter I will review some famous discussions of proper names within fairly recent history. It is debatable whether or not this recent history covers the full history of reference. Discussions of the relation between words and world go back about as far as philosophy itself, and are detailed and sophisticated in Aristotle. The debate is whether just any relation between words and world counts as the reference relation. Some hold that it is constitutive of reference that it should be a relation distinct from that between a common noun and the things of which it is true. Some hear it as trivially false that 'man' *refers to* Socrates, among others, as opposed to merely *denoting* or *suppositing for* each man. If this is right, it will be natural to focus on proper names and to regard them as paradigm possessors of reference, a focus which would be hard to find in ancient, mediaeval, or early modern discussions. Indeed, if this view about what constitutes reference is correct, then as far as I know there are no discussions of reference before Frege: the history of the topic is short indeed.[1]

There is no way to say where the history of reference should begin without saying what reference is, and this is something I do not wish to prejudge at this point; rather, I wish a view to emerge over the course of the book. So I will be guided by pragmatic considerations, discussing authors who are generally considered to be major contributors to the subject of reference as it is currently understood. These

---

[1] Thanks to Dean Buckner for making me aware of the problems of accurately describing the history of the topic.

include Mill, Frege, Russell, along with Kripke and some other philosophers closer to our times. I will take it for granted that whatever reference is, proper names are good examples of referring expressions. Except when my authors demand otherwise, I will not ask such questions as what the criteria are for being a proper name. (For example, I will not ask whether proper names always have to be one word, or whether they can be many, like 'George Bush Jr.', or whether there is one word 'Aristotle' with many bearers, or, rather, many words which look and sound the same as 'Aristotle', each having just one bearer.)

A useful initial idealization is that recent history can be divided into two streams. One stream starts with J. S. Mill and consists of theories according to which a proper name's contribution to language is exhausted by its referent. Understanding a name consists in knowing what it refers to. The other stream, sometimes held to derive inspiration from Frege, is descriptivist: according to descriptivist theories, the meaning of a name is given by or is equivalent to some body of associated information, and the referent of the name is whatever this information is true of, if anything. Understanding a name is linking this body of information with the name. The damaging crudity of this classification is one of the themes of this book, but for expository purposes it is not without value. Many arguments for theories belonging to one stream consist in demonstrations of difficulties besetting theories belonging to the other; the implicit assumption is that all theories can be assigned to one or other stream. Much debate has consisted in unproductive oscillations between Millian and descriptivist theories; my theme is that the best theories cannot be happily classified as belonging to either camp.

1.1 J. S. Mill

1.1.1 *Connotation and denotation*

In presenting his account of logic, and in particular inductive logic, in *System of Logic* (1843) Mill begins by stressing the importance of language. 'Logic is a portion of the art of thinking' (1843: 17) and language is the normal vehicle of thought. So without 'a thorough insight into the signification and purposes of words' one cannot hope to have a clear view of logical relations. Mill goes on to take an even more language-oriented position, holding that logical relations hold primarily between propositions, where a proposition is, in effect, a declarative sentence: 'discourse in which something is affirmed or denied of something' (1843: 19).

'Every proposition consists of three parts: the Subject, the Predicate, and the Copula. The predicate is the name denoting that which is affirmed or denied' (1843: 19). In 'Gold is yellow' the predicate 'yellow' denotes the quality *yellow* which is affirmed of gold. This corresponds to the 'first grand division of names': there are general names, fit to serve as predicates, and individual or singular names. 'A general name ... is capable of being truly affirmed ... of each of an indefinite number of things. An individual or singular name is only capable of being truly affirmed ... of one thing' (1843: 27).[2] Examples of individual names are 'John' (Mill notices and effectively brackets the point that many people are called by this name) and 'The present queen of England'. We see here no sign of that asymmetry between the way proper names and common nouns relate to the world which some take to be constitutive of reference. Mill's denotation is a property as much of common names as of proper names. If the asymmetry is constitutive of reference, Mill's account is not a contribution to our subject. The fact remains that his position has been constantly cited as a source of contemporary 'Millian' or 'direct reference' theories.

If Mill is really trying to capture the functional difference between a subject expression and a predicate, the approach in terms of how many things are denoted will not work, for there are predicate expressions (= general names?) which are true of just one thing ('natural satellite of the earth', or, at a certain moment in history, 'dodo') and subject expressions (= individual names?) which are true of more than one thing, like 'Plato and Aristotle'). Moreover, 'yellow' can be truly affirmed of something in a sense in which a subject expression

---

[2] Nathan Salmon suggests the following interpretation of Mill (1986: 196 n. 10): 'Mill held a complex theory of information value, according to which the information encoded by a sentence like "Socrates is wise" has at least two components: (1) the proposition about Socrates that he has the property of wisdom, and (2) the metalinguistic proposition about the expressions "Socrates" and "wise" that the individual referred to ("denoted") by the former has the property "connoted" by the latter and is therefore among the things "denoted" by the latter.' Mill does not write very carefully by the standards of our times, and I would not myself think that this is his considered view. Even if it is, its historical importance has been minimal.

typically is not: in affirming that gold is yellow we use 'yellow' to affirm something of gold, but we use 'gold' to pick something out in order to affirm something of it, rather than to affirm anything of anything. The difficulties associated with being accurate on issues like this do not impede Mill's development of the aspects of his theory which have been influential in our area.

Mill goes on to divide names into concrete and abstract: 'Man is a name of many things', so concrete, for things are concrete; 'Humanity is a name of an attribute of things' and so abstract (1843: 29). He then introduces his best-known distinction among names, between connotative and non-connotative:

A non-connotative term is one which signifies a subject only, or an attribute only. A connotative term is one which denotes a subject, and implies an attribute.... Thus John, or London, or England, are names which signify a subject only. Whiteness, length, virtue, signify an attribute only. None of these names, therefore, are connotative (Mill 1843: 31).

By contrast, 'white' is connotative: it denotes all white things, and implies the attribute *whiteness*. The implied attribute determines the denotation: 'white' denotes paper in virtue of paper's possession of the connoted attribute of whiteness, and ascribing 'white' to paper signifies that this is so. 'Proper names', Mill says, 'are not connotative: they denote the individuals who are called by them; but they do not indicate or imply any attributes as belonging to those individuals' (1843: 34). We may have had a reason for calling something by one name rather than another. We may call a man 'John' because that was his father's name, and we may call Dartmouth 'Dartmouth' because it stands at the mouth of the river Dart.

But it is no part of the signification of the word John, that the father of the person so called bore the same name, nor even of the word Dartmouth, to be situated at the mouth of the Dart. If sand should choke up the mouth of the river, or an earthquake change its course, and remove it to a distance from the town, the name of the town would not necessarily be changed.... Proper names are attached to the objects themselves, and are not dependent on the continuance of any attribute of the object (Mill, 1843: 34).

The thesis for which Mill argues is that proper names are not connotative; he just assumes that they are denotative (no doubt in part because there was no other option within his taxonomy of how names are significant), and we will return to that assumption shortly. The argument just displayed falls short of establishing the general conclusion of non-connotation: at most it establishes that 'John' does not connote *having a father called 'John'* and 'Dartmouth' does not connote *situated at the mouth of the River Dart*. Perhaps the names connote other attributes. In the case of 'Dartmouth', a more promising candidate would be *having been built at the mouth of the River Dart*. This attribute 'continues': if ever possessed, it is always possessed, and so Mill cannot show that 'Dartmouth' does not connote it by showing that the name might continue to denote a town which comes to lack it. But it is not difficult to extend Mill's idea to this case: perhaps the original builders thought they were building it at the mouth of the Dart when they were not; this would not imply, absurdly, that 'Dartmouth' denotes nothing (or some other town). Or the builders may have known quite well that they were not building at the mouth of the Dart, as was the case with the founders of Dartmouth, CT. It seems that Mill's idea that names are not connotative points to some important feature of their use.

Mill expressed the non-connotative character of proper names by saying that 'these have, strictly speaking, no signification' and that 'a proper name is but an unmeaning mark' (1843: 36, 37). This does not mean that they have no role in language: they permit us to identify the denoted objects and so 'we may connect them with information previously possessed' (1843: 37). But the proper name as such supplies no information.

If there are counterexamples to Mill's claim that proper names do not connote, they are of a rather special nature. The two best candidates for a name's connotation can be constructed by using this pattern: 'Dartmouth' connotes *being Dartmouth* or *being called 'Dartmouth'*. The first is ineluctably linked to the denotation: setting equivocation aside, there cannot be a case in which the denotation of 'Dartmouth' lacks the attribute of *being Dartmouth*. It could lack the attribute of *being called 'Dartmouth'*, as we know from the history of Leningrad, but presumably it must be being called 'Dartmouth' by a speaker at the time of the use of the name 'Dartmouth', so one could not envisage the denotation of a use of 'Dartmouth' on a given occasion failing to have the attribute of being called 'Dartmouth' by that speaker on that occasion. It would seem that either attribute could play the role that *whiteness* plays in determining the denotation of 'white': this word denotes snow, because it connotes whiteness and snow possesses the attribute of whiteness; 'Dartmouth' denotes Dartmouth because it connotes *being Dartmouth* and Dartmouth possesses this attribute; 'Dartmouth' denotes Dartmouth because it connotes *being called 'Dartmouth'* and Dartmouth possesses this attribute.

Mill did not discuss such attributes (if attributes they be). Intuitively they perhaps do not undermine his claim that when we use proper names we do not 'convey to the hearer any information about' their bearers, for neither *being Dartmouth* nor *being called 'Dartmouth'* intuitively counts as an item of information about Dartmouth.[3]

1.1.2 *Lack of denotation; sameness of denotation*

Mill's only official resources for describing the functioning of expressions are connotation and denotation. If he is right that proper names lack connotation, he faces two problems: (1) What is to be said about those proper names which lack denotation, like 'Santa Claus' or 'Vulcan' (as used of the supposed heavenly body postulated to account for some features of the orbit of Mercury)? If they lack both connotation and denotation, then presumably we should conclude that they have no intelligible role in language, which seems surprising. (2) What is to be said about proper names which have the same denotation, like 'Hesperus' and 'Phosphorus', distinct names for the planet Venus? These are alike in connotation (none) and denotation (Venus), and so alike in all the ways that Mill has the resources to describe. Yet intuitively they do not have the same meaning. One sign of this is that if they did, 'Hesperus is Phosphorus' would have the same meaning as, and so be as trivial and uninformative as, 'Hesperus is Hesperus'. Yet it was a significant astronomical discovery that Hesperus is Phosphorus.

Mill does not have much to say in answer to these questions. In connection with the first, the claim that 'All names are names of something, real or imaginary' (1843: 27) suggests that every name

---

[3] Especially for the second case, it would be hard to justify this intuition.

denotes, so that the question asked in (1) does not arise.[4] This view has been revived recently (cf. Salmon 1998). But, given the widespread use of names in fiction, and our natural disinclination to believe that our world contains other than real things, it is clearly a controversial one.

In connection with the second question, Mill does discuss some cases of identity: Sophroniscus may also be referred to as the father of Socrates, and we may usefully point to a city and say 'This is York'. The first does not raise our problem, as 'the father of Socrates' is a connotative individual name, by Mill's reckoning, and not a proper name. The second does raise the problem if we assume, as seems plausible, that pronouns used demonstratively, like 'this' in the present example, are also non-connotative. Although Mill does not raise questions like 'How could this remark be informative?', he does say something which is likely to be relevant to a correct answer: the use of the name 'York', but perhaps not the use of 'this', enables the speaker to bring to bear York-related information already in his possession. Even if proper names do not connote attributes, Mill at least hints that they can play an important role in organizing information, and that this role must be mentioned in a full explanation of how they function.

Problems of identity statements using names (recently illustrated by 'Hesperus is Phosphorus') can be deployed in more than one way in objecting to Mill's view. Here is Dummett's formulation of a problem with identity:

> If the sense of a name consisted just in its having a certain reference, then anyone who understands the name would thereby know what object it stood for, and one who understood two names which had the same reference would know that they stood for the same object, and hence would know the truth of the identity connecting them, which could therefore not be informative for him. (Dummett 1973/1981: 95)

Applied to our example, Dummett is committed to the view that if one knows what 'Hesperus' refers to (namely, Hesperus) and what 'Phosphorus' refers to (namely Phosphorus), then, given that Hesperus

---

[4] Mill's casual remark should not be relied upon to distinguish the controversial claim that there are imaginary entities which some names denote from the uncontroversial claim that we can well imagine, concerning names which in fact do not denote, that they denote.

and Phosphorus are identical, one can but know that 'Hesperus' and 'Phosphorus' refer to the same thing. By contrast, it seems clear that a completely rational person might know the individual facts about what each of 'Hesperus' and 'Phosphorus' refer to without knowing that they refer to the same. The point affects knowledge in a general way: one could know what Jack sees (namely Phosphorus) and what Jill sees (namely Hesperus) without knowing that they see the same thing. This feature of knowledge (or of 'knowing what') needs to be respected when using problems of identity against a Millian view. The feature is prominent in Frege's discussion of identity.

1.2 Gottlob Frege

1.2.1 *Frege's puzzle*

Frege (1892) distinguished between the sense (Sinn) and the referent (Bedeutung) of a name.[5] He thought that the value of the distinction could be seen by considering identity, expressed by two proper names which refer to the same thing. It struck him as evident that statements of the form '$a = a$' and '$a = b$' differ in 'cognitive value'. Statements of the former sort are knowable apriori, 'while statements of the form $a = b$ often contain very valuable extensions of our knowledge and cannot always be established apriori' (1892: 157). This difference, sometimes called 'Frege's Puzzle' (e.g. by Salmon 1986), calls for explanation. If the statements are true, they correspond in point of Bedeutung: the Bedeutung of 'a' is the same as that of 'b'. So it is natural to suppose that a name contributes more than just its Bedeutung; this something more 'I should like to call the *sense* (Sinn) of the sign, wherein the mode of presentation is contained' (1892: 158).

Frege's idea is that names are associated with ways of thinking of an object, or with ways (or modes) in which an object is presented.

---

[5] 'Bedeutung' is often (and in Blackwell publications always) translated 'meaning'. This may be the best English match for the normal German use of 'Bedeutung', but in my opinion it is a very unhelpful translation in the present semi-technical context. I shall use either the German word itself or else 'referent'. (I use 'reference' for the property an expression has which fixes whether or not it has a referent and, if it does, which object that is.)

Different names are typically associated with different ways of thinking, but they may have the same referent, for the same object may be thought of in different ways. For example, the Morning Star, Phosphorus, may be thought of as the last star to be extinguished at dawn by the rising sun, and the Evening Star, Hesperus, may be thought of as the first star to appear at dusk. These are the same heavenly body, the planet Venus, thought of in different ways. One could see Hesperus in the evening and Phosphorus in the morning without realizing that one had seen the same heavenly body twice. Frege is willing to describe this in terms of difference in modes of presentation or ways of thinking: different times of day, different times of the year and different parts of the sky. If a proper name like 'Hesperus' somehow 'contains' the evening-related 'mode of presentation', and 'Phosphorus' contains a morning-related mode of presentation, we may be able to account for the informative and non-trivial character of the claim that Hesperus is Phosphorus: the claim somehow links distinct modes of presentation, and it is not trivial or uninformative that this link obtains.

Although Frege introduced this problem as one of the challenges posed by identity, the issue is not confined to statements of identity. It seems possible for a rational person simultaneously to believe that Hesperus is visible but that Phosphorus is not. If Bedeutung alone mattered, it would be hard to see how there could be this difference. But if, in addition to Bedeutung, different names may be associated with different modes of presentation, we can perhaps make room for the possibility of rationally combining the beliefs in question. Frege's puzzle is as much a puzzle, and his introduction of sense as much a solution, wherever we have coreferring names; it is not confined to statements of identity.

Frege does not imagine that these rather vague reflections constitute any sort of proof of the existence of sense as well as reference. He just says that they make it 'natural to think' of there being a further aspect of expressions. There is no evidence in his texts that he thinks that difference of sense offers a direct explanation of the phenomenon. Rather, the notion of sense plays a number of roles. It marks a way in which coreferring names can behave differently, and connects this with understanding, with compositionality theses, with the apriori, and with reported speech. Difference in sense explains the possibility of informative identities only indirectly, by showing how this phenomenon is unified, through the notion of sense, with various others with which it might at first have seemed to have no relation.

As the article 'On sense and reference' progresses, Frege refines the notion of sense, by introducing and in some cases arguing for a series of claims, including the following:

- the sense of a name is grasped by everyone who understands it;
- expressions with the same sense have the same referent;
- expressions with different senses may or may not have the same referent;
- the sense and reference of larger expressions are determined by or built up out of the sense and reference of those of their parts which have sense and reference;
- some expressions have a sense yet no referent;
- the referent of a sentence (if any) is a truth value (the true, or the false);
- a thought is the sense of a sentence;
- in 'oblique' contexts, like those created by indirect speech reports, an expression refers to its customary sense.

To make a serious assessment of Frege's notion of sense, we would need to see how well it could describe or explain a wide range of phenomena, and that would be too large a project for the present context. Here I will follow three lines of enquiry: one (§1.2.2) concerns the Hesperus–Phosphorus puzzle, and how the notion of sense might address it; another concerns the difficulty for Frege that if we think of the sense of a name as a mode of presentation of the bearer, it seems hard to keep sense public and common to all who use the name with understanding (§1.2.3); the third (§1.2.4) addresses Frege's position on the possibility of sense without a referent.

1.2.2 Identity

Frege claims that identity can be discovered; such discoveries can be added to the stock of the things we know, things which can, as he says, be 'transmitted from one generation to another' (Frege 1892: 160). The earliest astronomers no doubt knew that Hesperus was identical to Hesperus,[6] but they did not know that Hesperus was identical to Phosphorus. There is something which they didn't know but which later came to be known: that Hesperus is Phosphorus. In general, there are publicly accessible items of knowledge whose number can be added to by further discovery. This makes no explicit mention of language, but only of 'things known'. It seems to me that any adequate theory must allow that this picture reflects some significant truth.

If we accept the picture in the most straightforward way, we will soon become converted to Fregean senses. The items of knowledge, in the Fregean picture, are thoughts, and thoughts are the senses of sentences. If knowing that Hesperus is Hesperus differs from knowing that Hesperus is Phosphorus, then the sentences 'Hesperus is Hesperus' and 'Hesperus is Phosphorus' must have different senses. If they had the same sense they would express the same thought. Given that senses of whole sentences are built up out of the senses of their parts, this means that the sense of 'Hesperus' must differ from the sense of 'Phosphorus'. One could have reached the same conclusion by applying the considerations to the possibility of knowing that Hesperus is visible in the evening without knowing that Phosphorus is.

To bring out what is controversial, let us suppose that items of knowledge are sets of possible worlds, and that discovery consists in shrinking the set of worlds compatible with what is known. There is then strictly speaking no discovery of facts of identity: to know that Hesperus is Hesperus is to know that Hesperus is Phosphorus, for these things obtain at just the same worlds. Likewise, there is strictly speaking no discovery of identity-dependent facts: if we already know that Hesperus is visible in the evening, we cannot discover that Phosphorus is visible in the evening. What we call a discovery

---

[6] Though 'Hesperus is identical to Hesperus' is most naturally read as expressing something trivial, this does not follow from the form of words alone. Since, in natural languages, distinct things can share a name, a name of something might be introduced to someone in two such very different contexts that he could reasonably suppose it to be a case of distinct things sharing a name. Kripke's 'Paderewski' cases are like this: Peter first encounters the name 'Paderewski' in a musical context, and by all ordinary tests comes to understand it. Later he encounters it again in a political context, and does not realize that it is the same name of the same person again (Kripke 1979). For such a person, 'Paderewski (the musician) is Paderewski (the politician)' could come as news. I assume that a Fregean must say that Peter understands the sense of the name, but fails to realize that all the occurrences of 'Paderewski' he has encountered have the same sense.

is better described as a rearrangement of the way in which our knowledge is presented. We improve the presentation of our knowledge but add no new knowledge. It may sound as if this rival view requires Frege's notion of a mode of presentation, applied now to knowledge. This is partly right, but the key difference is that the rival view need not suppose that there is anything shared about these modes of presentation, nor that these modes of presentation have a special connection with the understanding of language, so they will be quite unlike Fregean senses. The rival view can allow that different people think of Hesperus quite differently, even if they all use 'Hesperus' to think of it; *a fortiori* if some use 'Phosphorus' to think of it. This is enough to explain what discovery is within any individual thinker (each comes to realize that they were thinking of one thing in the two ways) without supposing that there is any common way of thinking imposed by mastery of the language. In short, we could have individual mental differences in ways of thinking without any public Fregean sense.[7]

A similar point can be made in a different way. Let us accept that Frege's puzzle shows that something more than Bedeutung is involved in a proper description of the relevant cases. Everyone in fact accepts this, for everyone accepts that, as usually described, the cases involve different expressions.[8] Why should this not suffice to explain the phenomena? Suppose you are writing an ordinary sort of computer program, and you expect that at some point in some calculation the same value may be assigned to distinct variables, x and y. To make use of this fact, the program must compare the values and deliver a special representation of the identity. Until this happens, although the computer 'knows' that $x=x$ it does not know that $x=y$. So computer programming languages need to incorporate a level of sense, as well as reference! This conclusion is absurd: nothing more than difference of variable is needed to explain the computer's 'ignorance'.

---

[7] A position of very roughly this kind is developed by Nathan Salmon (1986), and structurally similar positions abound. It would be deeply uncongenial to Frege: it would eliminate Fregean sense, doing no justice to any public difference in items of knowledge, and would leave only what he called 'associated ideas', subjective, idiosyncratic, and of no concern to logic.

[8] The qualification allows for Paderewski cases.

1.2.3 *Idiosyncrasies of sense*

Frege noticed a phenomenon which stands in the way of a theory of Fregean sense: it is hard to say what common and public way of thinking of an object is imposed by a grasp of a name for it. This may be masked with rather special examples like 'Hesperus' and 'Phosphorus', but in more ordinary cases it is conspicuous. Frege himself observed that

> In the case of an actual proper name such as 'Aristotle' opinions as to the sense may differ. It might, for instance, be taken to be the following: the pupil of Plato and teacher of Alexander the Great. Anybody who does this will attach another sense to the sentence 'Aristotle was born in Stagira' than will someone who takes as the sense of the name: the teacher of Alexander the Great who was born in Stagira.... such variations of sense may be tolerated, although they ... ought not to occur in a perfect language (Frege 1892: 158, n. 4).

Although Frege starts by expressing the matter as a difference of opinion about what the sense of 'Aristotle' is, as if there were a single correct opinion, there is no justification for not regarding the example as one of variation of sense, as it seems to become by the end of the passage, suggesting that Frege should qualify his official doctrine that sense is common across the linguistic community.

This qualification is explicit in some of his later work. Since an object may be thought of in countless different ways, we find ourselves forced either to say that a proper name has countless different actual or potential senses, or else to supply a principle which selects a unique candidate from among these ways to be the sense. Frege adopts the former option in 'Thoughts':

> with a proper name, it is a matter of the way that the object so designated is presented. This may happen in different ways, and to every such way there corresponds a special sense of a sentence containing the proper name (Frege 1918: 359).

The options are not logically exclusive: perhaps names have both many idiosyncratic senses and a single public sense. But the idiosyncratic idea is antipathetical to Frege's normal insistence upon the 'objectivity' of sense. Objectivity, for Frege, is sometimes a matter of not being dependent for existence upon being owned (1918: 361), and an idiosyncratic sense might be objective in this sense. But he also operates with the notion of a public language, for which objectivity is a matter of being shared. This may explain why, having admitted multiple idiosyncratic senses, Frege goes on to say that this must be done away with by stipulation:

So we must really stipulate that for every proper name there shall be just one associated manner of presentation of the object so designated (Frege 1918: 359).

This effectively abandons public sense as something usable to describe language as it actually is (for the stipulation has not yet been made for any proper name, as far as I know, and no one has the slightest idea how to make it or enforce it). It means that we cannot appeal to a public sense of names in describing how there can be such a thing as discovery of identities.

Mode of presentation, or way of thinking, is an appealing idea which may have a place in an overall description of language and thought, but it is much harder to find a place for such modes in the specification of the public use of expressions. It may be that Frege was too carried away by the metaphor. The main work which sameness of sense must do is make sameness of referent manifest; likewise the main work that must be done by difference of sense is to fail to suggest sameness of reference. Normally, though not always, when we reuse a name within a given context we offer a guarantee of coreference. (Exceptions are Paderewski cases.) Normally, though again not always, when we use two names within a given context we explicitly refrain from offering such a guarantee. (Exceptions include 'elegant variation'.) Successful interpretation requires recognizing the guarantee, when it is present. But this does not have any consequences for 'modes of presentation'. We could accordingly envisage a more or less Fregean philosophy of language containing senses but no modes of presentation, a 'minimal' Fregeanism.

If someone uses a name in such a way that it refers to an object, x, understanding what is said involves knowing that reference has been made to x. This last occurrence of x lies within an opaque context, and so raises difficulties of interpretation. The kind of Fregeanism that is vulnerable to the objection we have been considering tries to construe the knowledge in terms of shared mode of presentation; the objection is simply that for most names it appears that there are no shared modes of presentation, even though the names are used successfully in communication. A minimal Fregeanism, which accepts sense without modes of presentation, owes another account.[9] I think that the right thing to say is that the relevant knowledge is possessed by parties to a single name-using practice. The knowledge condition is in a sense 'external', given not just by the subjects' internal mental states but by those of their mental states in which they are related to their speech community. I argue for this position in Chapter 3. It is clearly some distance from Frege's own view, which, despite his attacks on psychologism, still operates within an individualist perspective, abstracting from social facts.

Minimal Fregeanism requires only sameness and difference of sense, and does not need senses as entities.[10] Sameness of sense makes coreference manifest, typically by using the same expression again. The manifestness it supplies cannot be guaranteed to have the right effect on the cognitive state of a competent interpreter, as Paderewski cases show. Moreover, simply reusing an expression is not always a correct way to manifest coreference, as indexicals show (I should not use 'I' in interpreting your use of 'I'). As Frege said, the identity sentence 'Hesperus is Phosphorus' does not make coreference manifest. It is because different names, like 'Hesperus' and 'Phosphorus', do not suggest coreference (if anything, they suggest the opposite) that we should not use one in the interpretation of the other. 'Hesperus is Hesperus' does make coreference manifest because, defeasibly, we rightly take the two occurrences to be of the same use of the same word. We take it that this is not a case of falsehood, like 'Aristotle (the philosopher) is Aristotle (the shipping magnate)', nor a case of a truth of the Paderewski sort, in which identity obtains but is not recognized. This picture seems to me recognizably Fregean even though it has not mentioned modes of presentation.

---

[9] Minimal Fregeanism is argued for (under the name 'pared-down Fregeanism') by Sainsbury (2002: Introduction).

[10] It also does not require infallible knowledge of sameness and difference of sense in the way that Dummett envisaged: 'It is an undeniable feature of the notion of meaning—obscure as that notion is— that meaning is *transparent* in the sense that, if someone attaches a meaning to each of two words, he must know whether these meanings are the same' (Dummett 1978: 131). A Fregean perspective without transparency is developed by Sainsbury (2004).

From this perspective, modes of presentation belong with an unsuccessful attempt to provide a psychological explanation of these facts about how sameness of reference is or is not made manifest. The unsatisfactory explanation would go something like this: objects are opaque, in that we may encounter the same object on different occasions while thinking it to be different, and encounter two objects on different occasions while thinking them the same. We explain this by introducing modes of presentation: when these are the same, we are assured that we have re-encountered the same object; when they are different, we have no such assurance. Suppose we could be exposed to the same mode of presentation on distinct occasions without realizing that the modes are the same: then modes of presentation are opaque, like objects, and what needed to be explained for objects now needs to be explained for modes. Suppose we could not be exposed to the same mode of presentation on distinct occasions without realizing that they are the same. Then modes are mental entities concerning whose identity we have infallible knowledge. No one wishing to offer an empirically serious explanation of a cognitive ability would dare posit such entities.[11]

The difficulty of finding modes of presentation which could be public, and which might perhaps even explain the phenomena concerning identity, accounts for much of the resistance to Frege's views about sense, which are widely acknowledged to be in other respects natural and attractive. For example, Kripke's attack on Frege consists in a rich development of this problem. Minimal Fregeanism promises a way of avoiding this difficulty, and it is supported by the account of Fregean sense offered by John McDowell (1977), as we will discuss in §1.5 below. The main feature of McDowell's solution constitutes a crucial part of the view I will be developing.

1.2.4 *Sense without a referent*

Frege admits this to be possible in unequivocal terms early in 'On sense and reference':

The expression 'the least rapidly convergent series' has a sense but demonstrably has no referent, since for every given convergent series, another

---
[11] This line of thought is indebted to Millikan 1991.

convergent, but less rapidly convergent, series can be found (Frege 1892: 159).

Gareth Evans has pointed out that many of Frege's subsequent discussions of the issue quickly introduce fiction, poetry, or, in general, non-serious uses of language. This led Evans to qualify the natural view that, for Frege, sense without a referent was straightforwardly an open possibility within the framework, even if one not often realized. As Evans put it:

Frege's later [i.e. post 'Über Sinn und Bedeutung'] apparent willingness to ascribe sense to certain empty singular terms was equivocal, hedged around with qualifications, and dubiously consistent with the fundamentals of his philosophy of language (Evans 1982: 38).

Evans in part justifies the last remark, about the consistency with Frege's fundamentals, by the observation that if sense is glossed as the way in which an object is thought about, it would seem that there could be no sense without an object thought about, and so no sense without a referent.

In 'On sense and reference', Frege's willingness to recognize sense without a referent does not seem equivocal or qualified. We have already noted the unequivocal remark about 'the least rapidly convergent series'. Frege himself used 'Eigenname' very widely to include definite descriptions and whole sentences, thus including semantically complex expressions as well as semantically simple ones. The possibility of sense without a referent takes a different turn for complex and simple expressions. Given Frege's attachment to compositionality principles, the sense of any complex expression ought to be built up out of the senses of its parts. If this associates the complex with a way of thinking about an object, well and good; but the sense of the complex is assured, on Fregean principles, by the senses of the parts and their manner of combination, whether or not the whole constitutes a way of thinking of an object. The same does not apply to semantically simple names, proper names in our use of the term: their only sense-investing feature, within Frege's framework, is their association with a mode of presentation of an object. If this is to be possible in the absence of an object, we need to understand 'mode of presentation of an object' on the model of 'picture of an object'. There can be a picture of a unicorn even if there are no unicorns.

We would need to allow that in some similar way there could be ways of thinking of an object, or modes of presentation of an object, even if there is no object.

Frege discusses a simple proper name, 'Odysseus', in 'On sense and reference', saying that it is doubtful whether it has a referent (1892: 162). The aim of his discussion at this point is to persuade us that a sentence has a truth value as its referent. He observes that if we take seriously the question whether or not a sentence is true, we take it for granted that each proper name it contains has a referent. Hence there is a special connection between the referents of the parts and the truth or falsehood of the whole; this suggests that since truth or falsehood is determined by the referents of the parts, truth or falsehood is what should be counted as the referent of the whole.

This discussion is predicated on the hypothesis that sentences as wholes have a referent, and is designed to reveal what, on this hypothesis, the referent would be. Frege says that if 'Odysseus' lacks a referent, then whatever the referent of a whole sentence containing it is will also be lacking, a remark which reveals his commitment to the compositionality of reference. A sentence like 'Odysseus was put ashore at Ithaca while still asleep', on the assumption that 'Odysseus' lacks a referent, lacks truth or falsehood. Hence we are invited to conclude that truth or falsehood is a sentence's referent, if anything is. Hence the invitation to think of the True and the False as objects, the former the referent or value of all true sentences, the latter the referent or value of all false ones.

Lack of truth value matters only if we are engaged in serious questions, and does not matter if our only concern is with 'aesthetic delight'. In the latter case, we can engage with thoughts, without considering whether they are true or false, for 'the thought remains the same whether "Odysseus" has a referent or not' (Frege 1892: 163; 1906: 191). Whatever one may think of the overall argument for truth values as the referents of whole sentences, there seems no equivocation in this discussion (nor in the 1906 discussion) about whether or not there can be semantically simple names which lack a referent.[12]

---

[12] The evidence that Frege equivocates comes from other passages, and I will not here reiterate what I believe is mistaken in Evans's interpretation (cf. Sainsbury 2002: 9–14).

1.3 Bertrand Russell

1.3.1 'Logically proper' names and knowledge by acquaintance

Russell thought that a proper name, 'in the narrow logical sense' (Russell: 1918–19: 201), is a simple expression which of necessity has a referent, and that one must be acquainted with this referent in order to understand the name. The following quotations (Russell 1918–19) show his commitment to these theses:

A name is a simple symbol... (244);

a name has got to name something or it is not a name (243);

you cannot name anything you are not acquainted with (201);

In order to understand a proposition in which the name of a particular occurs, you must already be acquainted with that particular (204).

At this time, Russell held that the only particulars with which one could be acquainted are sense data. He was quick to recognize that these doctrines mean that 'it is very difficult to get any instance of a name at all in the proper strict logical sense of the word' (1918–19: 201). The closest one gets in ordinary language are 'this' and 'that', and these are odd because they are 'ambiguous': they can be used to refer to different things on different occasions. Moreover such a name 'seldom means the same thing two moments running and does not mean the same thing to the speaker and to the hearer' (1918–19: 201). This is because the objects of acquaintance are fleeting and are not shared between distinct perceivers.

Russell took it to be a consequence of these theses that one cannot use this 'logically proper' kind of name in an intelligible affirmation or denial of existence, and that understanding a true identity sentence formed with such names would be sufficient for knowledge of its truth. It is therefore overdetermined that there are no logically proper names in natural language. Russell says that there are also none in the artificial language of *Principia Mathematica* (1910–13/1981: 201). Given all this, one would be hard put to say what justified Russell in thinking that logically proper names are important to logic.

Russell's conception of a logically proper name has been, and remains, highly influential. A common view is that it is on the right lines, but goes astray through taking too narrow a view of what counts as acquaintance. Russell's conception is intimately linked with his fundamental distinction between knowledge by description and knowledge by acquaintance; this distinction survives, and has proved attractive, even when the notion of acquaintance is liberalized so as to allow the possibility of acquaintance with the things which natural names name.

Russell says that we may know that the candidate who gets the most votes will win, yet not know who will win, because we do not know who is the candidate who will get the most votes. In his terminology, we can think of this person by description, but not by acquaintance. He explains the knowledge we lack in terms of names:

we do not know any proposition of the form 'A is the candidate who will get the most votes' where A is one of the candidates by name (Russell 1912: 53).

More recently, Gareth Evans has given this preliminary and intuitive account of the distinction:

[Philosophers] recognise the possibility, perhaps as a limiting case, of thinking of an object by description: as one may think of a man, some African warrior perhaps, when one thinks that the tallest man in the world is thus and so.... But, again... they cherish the idea of a more 'intimate', more 'direct' relation in which a subject may stand to an object (a situation in which the subject would be 'en rapport' with the object), and the idea that when a subject and his audience are both situated *vis-à-vis* an object in this way, there exists the possibility of using singular terms to refer to, and to talk about, that object in quite a different way—expressing thoughts which would not have been available to be thought and expressed if the object had not existed (Evans 1982: 64).

Evans reveals in this passage a commitment to an absolute distinction between knowledge by description and knowledge by acquaintance, or between thinking of something via a description and thinking of it 'directly', and a commitment to linking the distinction with the use and grasp of certain kinds of singular terms.

Consider the following example of the way in which knowledge 'by description' might modulate into knowledge 'by acquaintance'. You notice that the cheese in your larder is disappearing overnight.

You hypothesize that this is caused by a mouse. You imagine this mouse in some detail, which you reinforce by experiment: you leave sand near the cheese and confirm that it is a house mouse by its tracks; by similar methods, you discover where it lives when it is not raiding your larder. Your behaviour becomes a little obsessive: you dignify your mouse by the name 'Freddie'; you speculate, correctly in fact, that Freddie is the head of a large family of mice, and that he does not eat all the cheese he steals but takes some back as paternal investment in a recent brood; you get a camera and in the morning you replay scenes of Freddie's activities the previous evening. Then one evening you actually see Freddie eating your cheese. If the distinction between knowledge by acquaintance and knowledge by description is sharp, there is a precise moment at which your knowledge of Freddie, which uncontroversially begins as knowledge by description, becomes knowledge by acquaintance. What is that point? When you introduce a name? When you see Freddie on the video? When you see him for real? We should not take for granted that there is a sharp distinction, or even that there are two clearly disparate extreme cases.

In Russell's hands, the supposed distinction between description and acquaintance is between cases in which there is representation (knowledge by description) and cases in which there is not: in acquaintance, an object comes directly before the mind, without the intermediary of any representation. Seeing on a video would count as a case of seeing by means of a representation, whereas seeing for real would not. Russell himself thought that the objects of acquaintance were very restricted (sense data, universals and possibly oneself), but Russell's contrast between acquaintance and description is still influential, even when the notion of acquaintance is liberalized so as to include what we ordinarily count as objects of perception (mice, mountains, and so on). By contrast, I think (and in later pages will argue) that for an object to come before the mind, for example by being seen, is for it to be represented. There may be interesting differences among representations (perhaps some are of a kind that could not exist unless the thing represented existed; perhaps some represent by representing properties whereas others represent by representing individuals), but these are more nuanced than Russell's acquaintance/description dichotomy.

Acquaintance, for Russell, is essentially acquaintance with something, and matches his view that (logically proper) names need a referent. This is turn was part of a more general conception of meaning as essentially reference. For predicates, this seemed not to raise a problem: just as Frege thought there were no intelligible concept-words without a referent, so Russell thought that there were no intelligible predicate words that failed to mean a universal or property. This sounds like a substantive ontological commitment, but in practice Russell often wrote as if there was nothing more to a predicate meaning a property than its being intelligible, so the claim is essentially verbal. These ideas in more recent work combine to produce the notion of 'Russellian propositions', sequences of particulars together with a universal (as many particulars as the universal has slots), which are said to individuate the truth conditions of some natural language sentences. A sentence which expresses a (unary) Russellian proposition is true iff the particular in the proposition instantiates the universal or property in the proposition, and is false iff that particular does not instantiate that property. This conception has had a powerful hold, and has tended to render almost invisible the view that a sentence like 'Fido barks' is true iff 'Fido' refers to something which satisfies 'barks', and is otherwise false. The contrast is this: the mere intelligibility of a sentence which expresses a Russellian proposition entails the existence of the corresponding particulars (and universal), but this is not required by the alternative truth conditions just described.

Theorists who wish to rehabilitate Russell's picture of logically proper names try to show that some of its more striking supposed consequences do not really follow. Evans and others have urged, with good reason, that once the notion of acquaintance has been liberalized, names which satisfy the Russellian theses can be used in intelligible affirmations or denials of existence, and that one can without irrationality fail to know the truth of a true identity sentence composed of such names which one understands. I consider these issues in turn. The same material could be adapted to a defence of Mill.

Existence: If '*a*' is a name satisfying the Russellian theses, it has a bearer, and so '*a* exists' is true. It is necessary that a sentence so constructed should state a truth, though it does not follow that it states a necessary truth. Contrary to what Russell said, we do not have unintelligibility, for we have truth. However, present day Russellians have had to contend with a related non-modal problem, which is to explain how, for example, 'Vulcan exists' can be false. A defender of Russell's position has to say that there cannot be falsehoods of this form if the name functions straightforwardly as a Russellian one, that is, one which has a referent.

There is a related epistemic question, which quite likely moved Russell. He said: 'If "God" were a name, no question as to existence could arise' (1918–19: 250). Spelled out in more detail, there are two steps: if 'God' were a logically proper name, it would have a referent, so God would exist; so if we knew it was a logically proper name, we could thereby come to know that God exists. Russell probably assumed that any competent language user would be able to make correct classifications of the words they use. Everyone must admit that we might well use a word taking it to be a name even if it had no referent; Russell treats this as a further reason for thinking that names which satisfy his theses do not occur in natural languages. Contemporary Russellians will probably prefer to allow that one could be in ignorance about whether what one took to be a name was really one.

Identity: Russell argued that if 'Scott is c' is true (and both 'Scott' and 'c' are logically proper names) then the sentence is a tautology, and does not differ in meaning from 'Scott is Scott':

the name itself is merely a means of pointing to the thing, and does not occur in what you are asserting, so that if one thing has two names, you make exactly the same assertion whichever of the two names you use (1918–19: 245).

Intuitively, it is one thing to assert that Hesperus is Hesperus and another to assert that Hesperus is Phosphorus; one thing to assert that Hesperus is visible, and another to assert that Phosphorus is visible; one thing for the variables x and y in a computer program to have the same value, and another for this information to affect the program. If these intuitions are right, then the passage just quoted from Russell serves to exclude 'Hesperus' and 'Phosphorus' from the category of names. Indeed, since anything *could* have two names, the line of thought potentially renders the category of names empty: for any expression now in the category, a trivial stipulation (the introduction of another name for the object) could lead to a situation in which the expression would have to be excluded.

Contemporary Russellians can coherently deny that Russell's commitment to names having bearers, and their serving merely as pointers, entails commitment to there being no distinction between 'Hesperus is Hesperus' and 'Hesperus is Phosphorus'. One could know what each of two pointers point to without knowing that they point to the same thing. In front of the delicatessen counter you see among several other pointers one pointing to a pile of sandwiches and reading 'Ham: $3.50'. Walking around the back of the counter you see a pointer pointing to a pile of sandwiches and reading 'Push—these are really old'. You can know to which pile each pointer points without knowing that they point to the same one. Contemporary Russellians do well to reject Russell's view that names which simply point cannot occur in informative identities.

1.3.2 Russell on ordinary proper names

Russell was well aware that what we ordinarily call proper names will not satisfy the following condition for being a logically proper name: necessarily having a bearer with which all who understand the name are acquainted. He explained how ordinary proper names function in terms of their being 'truncated' or 'abbreviated' definite descriptions, expressions of the form 'the so-and-so'. If an ordinary proper name really abbreviated a definite description, it would be very different from a logically proper name:

- definite descriptions, like 'the man in the moon', do not owe their intelligibility to having a referent;
- one does not have to be acquainted with the referent of a definite description in order to understand it (it may not have a referent, and in any case understanding is ensured by understanding its parts);
- since a definite description does not have to have a referent, there is no reason to think that there is a special problem about 'the man on the moon exists' being false;
- since a definite description does not merely point to an object, but rather invokes properties or relations, definite descriptions

may refer to the same thing (perhaps 'the greatest ruler' and 'the wisest ruler') without this being something which one who understands both is thereby in a position to know.

It is a strength of Russell's own theory of definite descriptions that it does justice to these facts about them. One does not need to invoke that or any other theory in order to see that there are attractions in describing the functioning of ordinary proper names in terms of definite descriptions.

But how exactly? It is often assumed that Russell thought that each ordinary proper name has the same meaning as some definite description. Understood in a natural way, so that a good candidate for a synonym for 'Gödel' would be 'the first person to prove the incompleteness of arithmetic', this view is easy to refute: no description is associated with a name by all those who use it with understanding. Even if you and I associate that description with 'Gödel', his playmates at school certainly did not, yet intuitively they used the same name as we do, and with no difference in sense.

The easily refuted view was not Russell's, as the following passage makes clear:

Common words, even proper names, are usually really descriptions. That is to say, the thought in the mind of a person using a proper name correctly can generally only be expressed explicitly if we replace the proper name by a description. Moreover, the description required to express the thought will vary for different people, or for the same person at different times. The only thing constant (so long as the name is rightly used) is the object to which the name applies. But so long as this remains constant, the particular description involved usually makes no difference to the truth or falsehood of the proposition in which the name appears (Russell 1912: 54).

Presumably many proper names have a shared meaning, constant across users, and constant over time. So Russell is not saying that proper names have a meaning which is the same as some definite description.

He is saying something more interesting, and in effect promoting a view of a kind we have encountered already: from the point of view of contribution to truth conditions, all an ordinary proper name can supply is its referent; but from the point of view of the mental states of users of the name, we can find further material, notably definite descriptions, ones which may vary from speaker to speaker, or from occasion to occasion for a single speaker. These definite descriptions can explain how people can have different attitudes to names with the same bearer, and so to the same object named differently, and how one can think a true negative existential thought.

Let us watch Russell's view in action, by amplifying an example he goes on to give. Jill utters the words 'Bismarck was an astute diplomatist' and Jack hears and understands what she has said. Jill will associate 'Bismarck' with some definite description, for example 'The first chancellor of Germany', and if we wish to describe as accurately as possible 'the thought in her mind' in uttering those words, we should say that it was that the first chancellor of Germany was an astute diplomatist. This is her thought, but it may well not be what she is trying to communicate, for she will know full well that Jack may not associate this description with the name. Her communicative aims will be satisfied if and only if the description Jack does associate with the name refers to the first chancellor of Germany. Jack may have a different thought when he hears Jill's words. He will not assume that the thought he has was one which Jill was trying to communicate. Rather, assuming that communication has been successful, he will know that Jill was aiming to say something about whoever satisfies the definite description *he* associates with 'Bismarck', and that she speaks truly just on condition that this person was an astute diplomatist. What Jill intends to communicate is coarser than the unit of thought: she intends to communicate simply that Bismarck was an astute diplomatist, just as her words suggest, while she thinks something more fine-grained.

This view forms the basis of a solution to a number of difficulties facing generally Russellian accounts.[13] It can allow that, at least normally, a name contributes nothing more than its referent to the determination of the truth conditions of sentences in which it occurs, and thus avoids the problems encountered by the easily refutable view Russell is so often supposed to have held. Its disadvantages include the fact that it arguably makes successful communication unduly easy to achieve, and that it does not allow that a publicly available thought is expressed by a true negative existential sentence

---

[13] For further details on how Russell's account of the relation between names and descriptions can solve standard difficulties, see Sainsbury (2002: 85–101). For an account which is in some respects close to Russell's (though the similarity is not stressed) see Recanati (1993).

(for example, 'Vulcan does not exist'), even though, as Frege would say, there is intuitively a single truth which belongs to our common stock of knowledge. The view also faces difficulties in giving an account of reported speech; though this does not single it out from rival theories.

1.4 Saul Kripke

In *Naming and Necessity* (1972/1980) Kripke argues against theories which link names with descriptions. He refers rather casually to the 'Frege–Russell description theory' of names, and at times seems to suppose that these authors subscribe to the easily refuted view that each name has the same meaning as some description which is associated with it by all who use the name with understanding. In a later paper (Kripke 1979), he makes it plain that he takes it that a 'Frege–Russell description theory' will hold just for an idiolect, not for a public language. Frege, as we have seen, was disturbed by the fact that his view seemed to lead in this direction, for Fregean sense is supposed to be common to all speakers of a language. By contrast, Russell would not have found it disturbing that his views would hold only for an 'idiolect', for he was concerned not with language (he tells us) but with the idiosyncratic facts of judgement, the mental states of individual thinkers.

As Kripke stresses, one theory is that a definite description gives the sense of a name, another is that it fixes the referent. If sense determines reference, that is, if, necessarily, expressions with the same sense have the same referent, the former role entails the latter but not conversely.[14] It might be that some complex set of facts of language use conspire to determine that the referent of a name is the *F*. It does not follow that users of the name must know this. Kripke advances specific arguments against both versions of the theory, including these:

(i) The definite descriptions usually cited as senses have a different modal profile from names, and so cannot be or express the senses of names.

---

[14] A conception of sense which relegates it to giving an account of what goes on in the mind of speakers (an account constrained by making sense of their behaviour) might be one on which sense does not determine reference.

28   A SHORT HISTORY OF THEORIES OF NAMES

(ii) For many names, there may be no information which every user of a name associates with it.
(iii) One can understand a name without associating any uniquely identifying information with it.
(iv) The information one associates with a name may fail to be true of the name's bearer.

(i) *The definite descriptions usually cited as senses have a different modal profile from names, and so cannot be or express the senses of names.*
Kripke argued that the proper names we are accustomed to use are 'rigid designators':

Let's call something a *rigid designator* if in every possible world it designates the same object (Kripke 1972/1980: 48).

'Nixon' is a rigid designator, as revealed by the fact that when we come to ask for the transworld truth conditions of 'Nixon lied' we find that there is a single object, Nixon, such that whether the sentence is true with respect to a world depends on whether that object lied at that world. By contrast, it struck Kripke, and many others, that the analogue of this would not hold for 'The US President in 1970 lied'. On this view, a transworld evaluation of this sentence requires us to consider, with respect to each world, who was US President in 1970 at that world, and whether that person lied at that world. The relevant Presidents may differ from world to world.

The contrast grounds Kripke's claim that proper names and definite descriptions are unlike in modal profile, so that the former cannot be examples of the latter, and cannot have a meaning or sense given by the latter. The definite description in our example was supposed not to be a rigid designator: there are worlds with respect to which someone other than Nixon is designated by 'the US President in 1970', worlds, for example, in which Nixon never existed and in which (who shall we say?) Humphrey was US President in 1970. In reading the first published version of *Naming and Necessity*, one might be misled into thinking that Kripke took it that names differ in modal profile from all definite descriptions, and that this was the basis of the argument that no definite description could serve to illuminate the semantics of names. However, he himself cites rigid definite descriptions like 'the even prime', so this cannot be the intended argument.

The situation was clarified when the lectures first appeared in book form (1980). In the Introduction, he distinguishes between being a *de facto* rigid designator and a *de jure* one. In the case of *de jure* rigidity, 'the reference of a designator is *stipulated* to be a single object, whether we are speaking of the actual world or of a counterfactual situation'. This is contrasted with 'mere "*de facto*" rigidity, where a description "the *x* such that *Fx*" happens to use a predicate "*F*" that in each possible world is true of one and the same unique object...' (Kripke 1980: 21 n.). Definite descriptions are not stipulated to be rigid because they are not stipulated to be anything: their meaning arises in a compositional way from the meanings of their parts. So we now have the beginnings of a valid argument: proper names, but no definite descriptions, are *de jure* rigid designators, so no proper name coincides semantically with any definite description.[15]

The argument could be challenged in more than one way (see for example Sosa 2001). The main work is being done by the semantic simplicity of proper names: that is how their *de jure* rigidity is possible. An opponent who believes that names somehow are definite descriptions, or have their sense expressed by a definite description, will deny that they are really semantically simple: their semantic complexity is masked. He can agree with Kripke's modal intuitions, and allow that proper names designate rigidly, but will deny that their rigidity is *de jure*: it emerges from the *de facto* rigidity of the underlying definite description. An alternative objection is that we can properly extend the notion of *de jure* rigidity so that it does not trivially exclude semantically complex expressions. For example, one might say that an expression is *de jure* rigid if it is rigid thanks to containing an expression whose semantic role is stipulated in such a way as to ensure the rigidity of any referring expression in which it occurs. This still includes proper names (we allow that *occurring in* is reflexive), but would also include definite descriptions rigidified by the insertion of 'actually' or by the replacement of 'the' by Kaplan's 'Dthat', where both these expressions by stipulation ensure rigidity. A Kripkean modal argument would thus require more development.

---

[15] There is textual evidence against counting this as Kripke's argument. In the Introduction (1980) he says that he is happy to base the conclusions of the lectures on a notion of rigidity which does not discriminate *de jure* and *de facto*, though, he says, it was obviously the former that he had in mind when he claimed that proper names were rigid.

Even if no such argument succeeds, Kripke's other considerations provide good grounds for the desired conclusion that a name neither means the same as any definite description of the envisaged kind nor has its referent fixed by such descriptions.

(ii) *For many names, there may be no information which every user of a name associates with it.*

Concerning the name 'Aristotle', Frege admitted that 'opinions as to the sense may differ' (1892: n. 4). Taking the footnote as a whole, it seems he really should have been saying that what differs from person to person is the sense of the name, and not just opinions about it. The difference is illustrated by the different descriptions people associate with it. If Kripke is right about (ii), this will be the normal case: it may well be true of necessity that each speaker associates information with a name, but there need not be, and according to Kripke is not, any information which each speaker associates with it. When we think of the relevant information as of the kind which figures in Frege's example (the famous attributes of famous people), Kripke is surely right. Intuitively, most people keep the names they are originally given, and their names mean the same throughout their lives. Winston Churchill was so-called from his earliest days. It is absurd to suppose that the information that you or I would associate with the name, which would relate to the famous deeds of the mature man, would also have been associated with it by, for example, the schoolteachers of the six-year-old Winston. The point depends upon the assumption that the name is constant in its meaning (or Fregean sense). That this is so is shown by our immediate understanding of the name as it occurs, for example, in a teacher's diary. In the right context we have no need to fear that we misunderstand the teacher just because she could not then have associated famous deeds with the name 'Winston Churchill'. Moreover we unhesitatingly add the information we acquire about Winston's youth, presented to us by the use of the name, to the stock of information we hold true of the man.

If associated information consists in significant properties of the bearers of the name, the correctness of (ii) is suggested by the very function of names, which is to enable communication between people who do not share information. Communication across time, as in the example of the diaries, makes it specially clear that one cannot count on there being a common core of information (of the envisaged kind) shared by all who use the name in successful communication.

(iii) *One can understand a name without associating any uniquely identifying information with it.*
Kripke argues for (iii) by example:

> the man in the street, not possessing these [sophisticated identificatory] abilities, may still use the name 'Feynman'. When asked he will say: well he's a physicist or something. He may not think that this picks out anyone uniquely. I still think he uses the name 'Feynman' as a name for Feynman (Kripke 1972: 81).

It is striking how very willing we are (in our pretheoretical moments) to admit that someone understands a name. A corollary is how easy it is to introduce a name. As Charles Chastain said: 'The simplest way to introduce a proper name into discourse is just to start using it' (1975: 217). If I know you are not familiar with a name I am disposed to use, etiquette demands that I preface my use of the name by some qualifier: 'I'm having dinner with *my friend* Jill tonight', rather than 'I am having dinner with Jill tonight'. It would be absurd to suppose that the qualifier gives my hearer any very useful information (unless indeed I have the misfortune to have just one friend), let alone that it enables him to distinguish Jill from all other objects. Yet we do not think that my hearer has failed in understanding if he goes on to use the name 'Jill', for example, in asking 'Have you known Jill long?'

What Kripke draws attention to in the Feynman example is thus a quite general feature of our use of names, and one which deserves explanation. It is not a knock-down argument against theories which link names with definite descriptions. As Russell said, one can always generate a description uniquely true of an object named by a name, N, in a mechanical way: the thing called 'N'. Presumably a description of Feynman of this kind was available even to 'the man in the street'; and it might be used to rebut the suggestion in (ii) that it may be that no associated information is common to all speakers. Though most names have several bearers, we can rely on context to select the right use of 'Feynman' in the response 'the man/famous physicist called "Feynman"'. Being called 'Feynman' is a property Feynman has thanks to the activities of a large community of users of that name, so one cannot say that this information is trivial or insubstantive. Admittedly, problems of circularity might make it impossible for this information to be what holds the usage of each user of the name in place, but that is a distinct point: Kripke's aim in adducing the Feynman example was to show that people may lack any individuating information about the bearer of a name they understand. The objection shows that there is information expressible by a definite description which is in principle available to an otherwise pretty ignorant user of a name. It does not establish that such users in fact rely upon such information when they use the name, nor that information of this kind would suffice for understanding a name. Although we are generally undemanding in our requirements on understanding a name, the supposition that this could be mediated by a definite description of the envisaged kind would mean that any name NN we encounter is one we can understand, for we can all too easily come to know that NN names the person called NN.

(iv) *The information one associates with a name may fail to be true of the name's bearer.*

Kripke argues for this claim by using the Gödel/Schmidt example. Perhaps we associate the name 'Gödel' with the definite description 'the first person to prove the incompleteness of arithmetic'. But this association does not so much as fix the referent of the name, for we could well imagine that someone other than Gödel first proved incompleteness. This way of describing the imagined situation would be contradictory if the referent of 'Gödel' was fixed by the definite description 'the first person to prove the incompleteness of arithmetic'. The general phenomenon is that there is no upper limit to how much misinformation we can believe of a named object. Hence we cannot rely on information to fix the referents of our names. This seems to me a crucial point, and it means that every adequate theory of names must look elsewhere for an account of how their referents are fixed. Kripke's own account (or 'picture') was in terms of an initial baptism followed by a causally connected chain of uses: you refer to Churchill by your use of that name because your use is a link in a causally connected chain of uses which originated in a 'baptism': a bestowing of the name on a specific object, namely, Churchill. This account will be examined, and a similar but distinct version developed, in Chapter 3.

1.5 John McDowell

McDowell (1977) made two important claims. One is that we need not think of Fregean senses as descriptions; more generally, we need not suppose we can analyse them in any other terms; hence 'crediting names with senses . . . is not necessarily crediting them with anything like connotation or descriptive meaning' (McDowell 1977: 163). The other is that we can coherently form the notion of a *de re* sense, one which could not exist unless a corresponding referent existed, and that we can usefully apply this notion to a description of natural language. I agree with the first of these claims, which is crucial to this book's main thesis. It is no less important to the position advanced here that the second claim, at least as McDowell interpreted it, be rejected.

1.5.1 *Understanding and truth theories*

McDowell commends the Davidsonian idea that a roughly Tarski-style theory of truth for a language can serve as a theory of meaning, a theory which would enable someone who knew it thereby to come to understand that language. A theory of truth for a language will be finitely axiomatized and will, for each of its sentences, s, have a T-theorem, a theorem of the form '*s* is true iff *p*'. If the theory of truth is 'interpretive', that is, is one which can serve as a theory of meaning, for each T-theorem the slot held by '*p*' is filled by a translation into the metalanguage of whatever sentence is referred to by the expression in the slot held by '*s*'. Any theoretical statement of all the facts an interpreter needs to know will generate a theory of truth, though not every true theory of truth will be interpretive. These points largely mirror the fact that '*s* means that *p*' entails '*s* is true iff *p*', but the converse does not hold. McDowell suggests that an interpretive truth theory will serve as a theory of Fregean sense.

Truth-theoretic approaches to meaning are sometimes defended by claiming that they provide a detailed working out of the idea that knowledge of meaning is knowledge of truth conditions. This thought is potentially misleading. In one good sense, the conditions under which a sentence is true are just those situations which, if they obtained, would ensure that the sentence is true. This familiar idea can be idealized in terms of possible worlds: truth conditions in this sense are just sets of possible worlds. But possible worlds truth conditions alone do not provide an account of meaning, for sentences which differ in meaning, even in quite radical ways, may agree in possible worlds truth conditions. (All necessary truths agree in possible worlds truth conditions, but some differ widely in meaning from others.) In the context of truth theory, a truth condition is specified by what occupies the position marked by 'p' in any T-theorem of the form 's is true iff p'. It is considerably more plausible to suggest that knowledge of a truth-theoretic truth condition, as supplied by a T-theorem, is enough for knowledge of the meaning of the sentence involved. To avoid confusion, I will speak of 'possible worlds truth conditions' to mean sets of possible worlds, and 'truth-theoretic truth condition' to mean a condition specified by the right-hand side of a T-theorem. (It is not always possible to keep to the singular to mark this use, since if you have given the truth-theoretic truth condition of each of two sentences you have given two truth-theoretic truth conditions. However, the singular 'truth condition' in this book always abbreviates 'truth-theoretic truth condition'.)

We cannot straightforwardly identify understanding a sentence with knowing its truth condition as specified by any true truth theory. There are three kinds of reason. First, the relevant knowledge is supposed to filter down to individual sentences from knowledge of a total truth theory, one which supplies a truth condition for each sentence of the language (Davidson 1967). Secondly, not every true truth theory is interpretive (Foster 1976). Thirdly, even if one knows an interpretive truth theory, one arguably does not know enough to understand the relevant language unless one additionally knows that the theory is interpretive (Foster 1976). Bracketing the first and third issue, McDowell suggests that an interpretive truth theory is one which pulls its weight in enabling us to make sense of the lives of those who use the language. For example, if someone utters s with sincerity, a truth theory will supply a truth condition which we can identify as the content of a belief to which the speaker gave expression. Interpretive theories will do this in such a way that we find we can make sense of speakers' actions in terms of their beliefs and other attitudes:

We have not properly made sense of forms of words in a language if we have not, thereby, got some way towards making sense of its speakers. If there is a pun here, it is an illuminating one (McDowell 1977: 160).

In this perspective, truth theory is a component of a wider project of understanding people and their way of life, and an interpretive theory is one which associates utterances with contents in a way which maximally facilitates the wider project.

1.5.2 Axioms for names

An interpretive truth-theory derives its theorems from a finite number of axioms, which deal with the finitely many, semantically simple expressions of the language. These are assigned a property which plays an appropriate part in the derivation of a T-theorem for every sentence in which the expression occurs. In the case of proper names, McDowell suggests that appropriate axioms would specify the name's bearer on the following lines:

'Hesperus' stands for Hesperus (1977: 161).

This axiom will not differ in point of which thing it says that 'Hesperus' stands for from one like this:

'Hesperus' stands for Phosphorus.

Nor will it differ in this respect from the axiom for 'Phosphorus':

'Phosphorus' stands for Phosphorus.

Since Fregean sense was motivated by a wish to accord different sense to, for example, 'Hesperus' and 'Phosphorus', it might seem as if the approach McDowell commends cannot do justice to Frege: he suggests that it is enough to assign a referent, yet the same referent will be assigned to expressions which are supposed to differ in sense.

Dealing with the objection, McDowell points out an ambiguity in 'the reference of x'. It is equivalent to 'what x refers to' but this is ambiguous depending as 'what' is construed as a relative pronoun (equivalent to 'that which') or as an interrogative pronoun introducing an indirect question. Taken in the first way, to know what x refers to is to know an object (for example, to be acquainted with it); taken in the second way, to know what x refers to is to know how to answer the question 'what does x refer to?', and so is most naturally taken as knowing something propositional, for example, that 'Hesperus' refers to Hesperus. This opens the possibility that expressions with the same referent should be distinct in point of their reference according to the second interpretation, distinct, that is, in point of what constitutes a proper answer to the question: what does x refer to?

The aim of a theory of meaning is to describe knowledge which would enable someone to understand a language, an ability which includes being able to make accurate reports of what other speakers of the language say. One ought not to report someone's utterance of 'Hesperus is visible' as her having said that Phosphorus is visible, for this report might not enable one to attain the best understanding of that speaker. For example, the speaker might have made this utterance in the context 'Phosphorus is not visible but Hesperus is visible'. If the last part is reported as the speaker having said that Phosphorus is visible, and the first part is reported in the natural way, the total report will attribute to the speaker the saying of a manifest contradiction, that Phosphorus is not visible but Phosphorus is visible. Unless the speaker is engaged is some non-assertive use of language or has been victim of a sudden bout of insanity, there is no possible explanation of how she would say such a thing. It would thus be incorrect so to interpret her. An axiom ' "Hesperus" stands for Phosphorus' which leads to such an interpretation is therefore itself incorrect. In this way, McDowell suggests that a theory of truth whose axioms simply assign referents to names may be criticized for *how* they make the assignment, even if every name is assigned its referent. Getting the right referent is enough for the truth of a truth theory, but is not enough for the theory to be interpretive. Some ways of assigning reference may lead to an uninterpretive theory; perhaps only one way, in which the name itself is reused in the metalanguage, leads to an interpretive one.

For the purposes of an interpretive truth theory, not all ways of stating what a proper name refers to are equally good. Those who think that knowing what a name refers to is understanding it should therefore have no quarrel with McDowell's position (since his position identifies understanding a name with a specific way of knowing what it refers to). However, a common reaction to McDowell's position is that the knowledge in question is too easily acquired, in a way which reveals that it is insufficient for understanding. Might we not attain it merely on the basis of knowing that, for example, 'Hesperus' is a name with a bearer? Given this, we can mechanically write out ' "Hesperus" stands for Hesperus', and be sure that what we write is true.

Addressing this objection, McDowell points out (1977: §6) that knowing that a sentence is true does not entail knowing, concerning how it states things to be, that things are thus. You may tell me that a certain French sentence is true; since you are an authority, I may thereby come to know that it is true. But if I do not understand the sentence, I do not thereby come to have the knowledge it expresses. Likewise, I cannot move from knowing that the sentence ' "Hesperus" stands for Hesperus' is true to knowing that 'Hesperus' stands for Hesperus without understanding the sentence, and so without understanding 'Hesperus'. It would be a mistake to think that the knowledge in question is too easily acquired for it to be sufficient for understanding.

This point suggests a different objection: the knowledge cannot be what people have to know in order to understand 'Hesperus', since in order to have the knowledge they need already to understand the name; more exactly, they need already to know the meaning of some name with the same meaning as 'Hesperus', using which the relevant knowledge could be expressed. McDowell's position was not that the knowledge in question should be necessary for understanding, only that it should be sufficient. That it is sufficient is conceded by the form of the objection, which allows that one knows that 'Hesperus' stands for Hesperus only if one understands 'Hesperus' (or some synonymous name). What is no doubt behind the objection is really that the relevant knowledge doesn't seem usable in the right way: for example, it could not be used to teach someone how to use 'Hesperus', since the tyro would already need to know what 'Hesperus' meant in order to be able to possess the proffered knowledge. If we are thinking of the case in which the theorem is expressed in English, that is indeed so; hence one must distinguish between something knowledge of which would suffice for understanding, and something knowledge of which does not antecedently require, but does result in, understanding. One of McDowell's insights is that it is quite unclear that there is, in general, knowledge meeting both conditions, if the language of the theory in which this knowledge is expressed is essentially the same as the one it seeks to describe.

The most straightforward way to describe how a word functions without requiring a prior understanding of it is to supply an analysis. One does not need already to understand 'vixen' in order to acquire the knowledge that the word is, in virtue of its meaning, true of all and only female foxes. Having acquired this knowledge, it then seems that one can rightly be said to understand 'vixen', which one did not before. We cannot expect this style of statement for the typical words of our language: such statements are available only for redundant words, those which we could have done without (we could have kept to 'female fox', and done without 'vixen'). This approach is not available for expressions whose meaning cannot be analysed in other terms, and these are presumably the majority. Since names are not thus analysable (we here need to appeal to the refutations, by Kripke or others, of the view that every name is synonymous with some definite description), we cannot in general expect the more revealing kind of specification of what a name means, or of what it stands for, in an interpretive truth theory.

We can introduce a novice to a name by using a definite description. This sustains the intuitive view that one understands a name if one knows what it refers to. It does not sustain the view that a description which specifies what a name refers to, and thereby enables a novice to advance to mastery, provides a synonym. You ask me who John McDowell is, and I give a brief account of his current position and his main interests and writings; or I say simply 'The author of *Mind and World*'. Arguably, my response equips you with the capacity to use the name with understanding, but it is not intended to provide a synonym, and would not be understood as providing one. An axiom of the form ' "John McDowell" stands for...', where the dots are filled with either of the packages of information I envisaged, would not generally lead to correct interpretations, even if it states something coming to know which would result in the acquisition of understanding. It would not be right to interpret an utterance of 'That's McDowell's car' by McDowell's mechanic (whom we can presume wholly ignorant of McDowell's professional activities) as his saying that that is the author of *Mind and World*'s car.

We use names to associate information with their bearers, but we take it for granted that there is no guarantee that this information is correct. It is guaranteed that synonyms refer to the same thing if to anything. The way we treat typical information which enables us to come to understand a name shows that we do not treat it as supplying a synonym.

The doubts just considered about names, doubts which oscillate between the view that the relevant knowledge is too easy to acquire and the view that it is too difficult to acquire because it presupposes the very understanding it is supposed to describe, arise also at the level of whole sentences. A theorem of the kind of theory of truth that McDowell says can serve as a theory of meaning might be

(T) 'Snow is white' is true iff snow is white.

This may seem too easy to know, because it is indeed easier to know that (T) is true than to know what 'Snow is white' means. This does not show that it is inappropriately easy to know the fact (T) states, and indeed this knowledge is not possessed by the majority of mankind, who do not speak English. It is also true that understanding (T) presupposes understanding 'snow is white': that is, unless one already understands this sentence one will not be able to understand (T). This shows that theorems of this kind are not appropriate for teaching English to those who do not know it. This is consistent with such theorems providing a representation of facts knowledge of which would be sufficient for understanding.

In responding to objections of this kind, McDowell stresses the 'austere' or 'modest' character of theories of meaning, or theories of truth fit to 'serve as' theories of meaning. He makes much of what such theories do not profess to do, and in this way helps to defend them against those who approach them with higher expectations. They are not intended to state necessary conditions for understanding, they may well not be suitable as a means for introducing a novice to a language, and they do not attempt to analyse the meanings of individual words. What is the positive value of such a theory? Why should we be interested in stating something which, if known, would be enough for understanding? I think the answer is that this theoretical task gives us a check on our theoretical grasp of the compositional character of the language. Typical axioms, like the one for 'Hesperus', are 'homophonic': the contribution of the target expression in the object language is specified simply by using that same word in the metalanguage. 'Hesperus' stands for Hesperus, 'green' is true just of green things. The theorems, too, typically have this homophonic character, which is regarded as a virtue within this tradition. Those who believe that such axioms and such theorems cannot be deeply interesting are, in my opinion, right, though I do not see this as any kind of criticism. What is of interest is how, if at all, we can derive the theorems from the axioms. To the extent that we have difficulty, as with, for example, indirect speech, we still lack a complete theoretical grasp of the idioms which give rise to the problems.

If we view descriptive theories of names in the light of truth theories, there are two ways of developing the idea that a definite description gives the sense of a name. One is to exploit a notion of logical form governed by the view that the logical form of a sentence is what results from a pre-processing which transforms the sentence into something suitable to be an input to a systematic semantic theory (cf. Davidson 1970). On this option, the descriptivist view will be that, in logical form, any name will be supplanted by some definite description. The other option uses definite descriptions in the axioms for names:

n stands for the F.

Everyone would agree that for each name that has a bearer there is some such truth, and that many names are first learned through such truths, so it is not obvious how to use such truths to develop a controversial thesis.[16] One possibility is to see things in McDowell's light, so that an axiom of this kind will work its way into the T-theorems for sentences containing names. This involves the notion of a canonical theorem: it will be canonical that 'n is G' is true iff the F is G, but not canonical that 'n is G' is true iff n is G. We should exploit theorems of the former kind in reporting speakers and understanding their behaviour. We know from the discussion of McDowell that such a proposal could not be justified merely by the desire to assign different senses to distinct coreferring names.

Both options will seem wholly unmotivated in the present context. Taking the second option first: except in special cases, for example,

[16] It is plausible that every description can be rigidified by adding a suitable 'actually' operator, so that even the necessitation of the condition under discussion should be uncontroversial.

cases involving indexicals, the homophonic method of reporting speech can hardly be thought incorrect: we cannot be wrong in reporting one who utters 'Fido barks' as having said that Fido barks, though we might well be wrong to report her as having said that the largest dog on the street barks. Turning to the first option: most adherents of the methodology of logical form, including Davidson, feel happier when logical forms are as close as possible to surface forms; departures are justified by the difficulty of developing semantic theory otherwise. In the case of names, there are no such difficulties, and no justification of this kind for departing from the homophonic ideal.

1.5.3 De re *senses*

I have defended McDowell's conception of appropriate axioms for names against those who see the axioms as too easy to know (which they are not), or think that they cannot be used to introduce the name to a novice (which they cannot, but were not supposed to do). In short, I have defended McDowell's conception of sense as 'austere'. I now turn to his other main thesis, that on the austere conception the sense of a proper name is '*de re*': it essentially involves an object (indeed, essentially involves the very object it actually involves). This is connected with the fact that the axioms he envisages are correct only for names which have bearers, and affirming such an axiom commits the theorist to the existence of a bearer. Gareth Evans found himself in a similar position, which he makes very explicit. Speaking of the kinds of axiom McDowell envisaged for names, for example ' "Hesperus" stands for Hesperus' and ' "Phosphorus" stands for Phosphorus', he says:

These clauses *show* the different senses which the two terms possess, but at the same time they could not be truly stated if the terms had no referent. (Evans 1981: 296).

Given that the theorist is presenting his theory as something he himself knows (and knowledge of which would suffice for interpretation) the theorist is committed also to it being known that names for which such axioms are offered have bearers. Yet there seem to be names in natural languages which it is agreed lack bearers ('Vulcan'), and names concerning which it is disputed whether they have bearers ('Homer'). There could well be in addition a name which in fact has a bearer, though this is not known to the users of the name (even though, perhaps, they truly believe it). All these cases present problems for accounts which use axioms for names which require them to have bearers.

McDowell recognizes bearerless names as a 'complication', one 'which brings us... to the deepest source of the richer conception of the sense of names' (1977: 172). I shall argue that we need not depart from McDowell's modest or austere conception of the sense of names in order to do justice to names without bearers, or names not known to have bearers. So I will separate his general approach to what can be expected from a theory of meaning from his claim that proper names have *de re* senses.

McDowell argues that on his view a name with no bearer must be regarded as having no sense, since it cannot be dealt with by true axioms which specify what the name stands for. He contrasts this with what he takes to be Frege's view, one part of which is

that the sense of a name, if expressible otherwise than by the name itself, is expressible by a definite description (1977: 172).

The other part is that definite descriptions can have sense quite 'independently of whether or not objects answer to them'. The proffered contrast is between McDowell's view, which treats proper names without bearers as without sense, and Frege's view, which treats proper names as definite descriptions and thereby allows for proper names without bearers to have sense. There is 'the' (*sic*) non-Fregean view, which McDowell espouses, and the Fregean descriptive view. As I shall argue, there is a third alternative: a view which agrees with McDowell in being non-descriptive and aspiring to no more than modest or austere senses, but which also agrees with Frege in allowing sense without reference. This third alternative is the main topic of this book: I call it 'reference without referents', or RWR.

McDowell argues for his preferred side of the supposed dichotomy in two ways: he describes the way in which bearerless names relate to the general enterprise of making sense of speakers; and he casts aspersions on the motivations for the Fregean descriptive view. In the first connection he points out, incontrovertibly, that a speaker who uses a name with no bearer thereby gives rise to no 'transparent' ascription of a propositional attitude, for there is no object of which the speaker has said anything, or concerning which he has represented himself as believing something. But, he suggests, this does not make the speaker's use of an empty name something which cannot be exploited in interpretation, for 'we can indeed gather, from the utterance, that the subject believes himself to have a belief' (1977: 173), expressed by the sentence containing the bearerless name, and this false second-order belief can be used to render the speaker's behaviour intelligible overall. Let us apply this to an example.

A child is asked why he is so excited and replies, 'Because Santa Claus should be bringing my presents soon.' Naively, we might envisage an ordinary kind of explanation: the child is excited because he believes that Santa Claus will soon be bringing his presents. On McDowell's account, however, the explanation must take a different tack: the child expresses no belief by his words, since 'Santa Claus' is a name without a bearer; likewise, we theorists could express nothing, so in particular no explanation, by using this name. The child, by speaking these words, manifests a false second-order belief that they express a belief, and we are somehow to move from this to an understanding of why he is excited. McDowell does not explain how this move is to be made. There is nothing exciting as such about a belief to the effect that some words one has uttered express a belief. It is not enough to infer that the child believes that someone will be bringing his presents soon, for not any bearer of gifts is an intelligible source of excitement (not if the child had believed the presents were coming from a misguided aunt who gives only unreadable volumes of elevating sermons). McDowell's picture cannot provide a satisfying account of how to find a place for uses of names without bearers within the wider project of making sense of people.

McDowell disparages the Fregean-descriptive story for its 'suspect conception of how thought relates to reality' and, more generally, its 'suspect conception of mind'. On this conception, mind relates to reality only indirectly,

by way of a blueprint or specification which, if formulated, would be expressed in purely general terms: whether the object exists or not would then be incidental to the availability of the thought (1977:173).

Sense without reference is here closely linked to purely general sense, and this is a link I wish to unpick. McDowell allows that a name with a bearer can be used in a specification of its own sense, in the austere homophonic pattern. I shall argue that exactly the same goes for names without bearers. There is no justification at all for equating the view that there are intelligible names without bearers with the view that names supply blueprints or specifications in purely general terms.

McDowell is right to think that these issues lead to ones about the nature of the mind. In particular, one may be tempted, as McDowell is, to believe that if, when all goes well, a thought connects 'directly' with its object, then the object cannot simply be peeled off the thought, leaving behind something which could as well have existed even if the object had not. The 'directness' or otherwise of thought is one thing; whether thought essentially requires an object is another. According to RWR, referring expressions are rigid, so a name which in fact has a bearer has it necessarily (holding its meaning constant), though not all names have bearers. This is congenial to the claim that a thought which in fact has an object has it essentially, but not to the claim that, necessarily, every thought has an object.

1.6 The Road Ahead

The history of theories of names is dominated by oscillations between Fregean and Millian poles. Both poles have attractions. The Fregean pole promises explanations of how names can be learned and used, how there can be differences of cognitive value and informative identity sentences, how there can be intelligible names which lack bearers, how substitution of coreferring names may fail to preserve truth, and how sentences which seem to deny the existence of something can be true. The Millian pole does justice to the intuition that names pick things out without attributing information, that they are used in populations which do not share significant information about their bearers, and that they designate rigidly. The very merits of each pole are closely associated with their defects. For example, the Fregean pole seems to require that each name is associated with some special subclass of information which is shared among its users, and the Millian pole seems to make no room for the possibility of intelligible empty names. Many of the arguments for one pole consist in nothing more than pointing out problems with the other. This dialectic is unsound if, as I will suggest, there are intermediate positions.

The topic is polarized by two further distinctions. One of these is Russell's distinction between description and acquaintance, originally applied to thought or judgement. Its linguistic application distinguishes expressions which relate to reality in the manner of a descriptive thought, and expressions whose relation is 'direct' and non-descriptive, just as the relation between mind and object in acquaintance is 'direct'. The other distinction arises within a framework for approaching these issues shared by Russell and Frege, and which still exercises a powerful pull: the belief that the semantic mechanisms involved in the language of classical first-order logic are all the semantic mechanisms there are. This framework provides two possibilities for the semantic mechanisms of proper names in natural language: they resemble individual constants, giving rise to the Millian position, or they resemble Russellian definite descriptions, giving rise to the Fregean position. I aim to undermine both these distinctions, showing that a dialectic which depends on them will set up an idle oscillation.

Starting with logic, I take as my framework negative free logic (NFL) as described in Chapter 2.3. The crucial feature is that interpretations may or may not assign an entity to the individual constants of NFL languages. This immediately gives us something often overlooked: a model for how a non-descriptive referring expression can be intelligible yet lack a referent.

I have already given some reasons for dissatisfaction with Russell's distinction between thoughts which express knowledge by description and thoughts which express knowledge by acquaintance (in connection with Freddie, the cheese-eating mouse); these are amplified in Chapter 7.2.

My main target is the Fregean/Millian polarity. The essence of RWR, the positive view to be proposed here, can be put very simply: set McDowell's austerity within NFL. Austerity ensures that descriptivism is avoided, while NFL makes room for intelligible empty names. You have benefits from both Fregean and Millian poles, without the standard defects.

In more detail, RWR is partly defined by the following theses:

1. There are singular referring expressions (like many proper names) and plural ones (like compound names: 'Plato and Aristotle').

2. There are simple referring expressions (like many proper names) and complex ones (like compound names and various species of definite description).
3. Some intelligible referring expressions have no referents.
4. A referring expression without a referent may occur in a truth (e.g. 'Vulcan does not exist').
5. Semantic theory is governed by negative free logic (NFL) rather than by classical logic.
6. Reference is an absolute relation, and is not world-relative.
7. Referring expressions are rigid designators and constitute a uniform semantic category.
8. A singular referring expression meets the condition: if it refers to x and to y, then $x = y$.[17]
9. In semantic theory, referring expressions are associated with reference conditions rather than referents. An example:

    for all x ('Hesperus' refers to x iff $x =$ Hesperus).

10. Semantic theorems are often (and ideally) homophonic.
11. Coreferring expressions may be assigned distinct reference conditions.
12. Subject–predicate sentences are associated with Ockhamist rather than Strawsonian truth conditions. (*Ockhamist*: S–P is true iff S has a unique referent which satisfies P and is false otherwise. *Strawsonian*: S–P is true iff S has a unique referent which satisfies P and is false iff S has a unique referent which fails to satisfy P.)

The remainder of the book is designed to substantiate these claims. The first task is to say more about issues concerning the appropriate framework in which to discuss reference: truth theories, propositions, logic, and ontology. Readers willing to take these on trust, at least temporarily, might prefer to pass directly to Chapter 3, which applies RWR to proper names.

---

[17] For plural referring expressions, like 'Plato and Aristotle', the analogous condition is expressed using plural variables of quantification (ones which occupy positions fit to be occupied by plural referring expressions). I mark these with capitalized versions of singular variables, so the condition is: if the expression refers to X and to Y then $X = Y$. (I assume that '=' can stand for either singular identity ('is the same as') or plural identity ('are the same as').

2
Framework issues

This chapter is concerned with issues affecting the framework within which the views which follow are developed. I think that one of the main barriers to acceptance of RWR is a residual conception of content in a broadly Russellian tradition (see §2.2 below). Metaphysically, propositions are thought of as sequences of entities. Epistemologically, understanding is seen as involving some special relation to the entities in question. Logically and semantically, model theory is taken as the single right approach. By contrast, I find no use for propositions, I think of understanding as participation in a practice, and I see logical and semantical issues best addressed within truth-theoretic methodology.

The truth-theoretic approach has two major merits (see §2.1 below): it deflates semantic ambition, and it helps restrain *ad hoc* proposals. Semantic theory of the kind which underpins the approach taken here should not aspire to provide detailed analyses of the meanings of individual words. The appropriate 'austerity' (as McDowell (1977) has called it) is manifest in the acceptance of 'homophonic' theorems, in which truth conditions for the object language expression are specified by reusing these very expressions in the metalanguage. The systematic character of truth theory, requiring unambiguous expressions to be associated with a single contribution to truth conditions, a contribution to be made in all embeddings, prevents *ad hoc*-ery.

A crucial aspect of RWR is its use of negative free logic (NFL). Burge (1974*a*) argued that this is the species of free logic suitable for semantics, and gave a clear statement of the underlying philosophical motivation in a truth-theoretic setting. I have almost nothing to add to what Burge said, but since his work in this area has not been duly appreciated, and since the logic he clarified is a crucial component in the position I wish to develop, I spell out some details of NFL below (§2.3).

Reference inevitably raises ontological questions, like whether there can be reference to what does not exist. I state in §2.4 the very conservative assumptions I make in this book. I assume that everything exists, and that there are not (really) any fictional characters or other such controversial supposed entities. My strategy here is not to try to change the minds of those who have opposed convictions, but to show to all parties that this ontological conservatism does not bring with it any semantical or logical problems. If there are good arguments in favour of, for example, the existence of fictional characters, they do not consist in saying that we need their existence in order to account for the logic and semantics of fiction (see Chapter 6.3 below).

Like many others, I see the rigidity of names as a crucial feature; indeed, I regard rigidity as a feature of all referring expressions. There are various notions of rigidity in logical space. In §2.5 I describe the version I will use, and show that it is a notion which naturally embraces empty names. It is merely a myth, and one which helps to conceal the area of logical space occupied by RWR, that rigidity requires a referent.

2.1 Truth theory

Meaning, as McDowell (1976) said in a memorable phrase, is just what a theory of meaning is a theory of. He was introducing the reader to a Davidsonian approach to some problems in the philosophy of meaning, and separating the approach into two main features more firmly than Davidson himself had done. There is the idea, just mentioned, that we should think about meaning in terms of a *theory* of meaning, using 'theory' in a formal sense: a set of sentences closed under deduction, more particularly, a 'first-order theory' in the sense of Mendelson (1964). Then there is the idea, for which Davidson is more famous, that truth is what such a theory should address if it is to 'serve as' a theory of meaning. Both these aspects have merits, though the merits stem from different sources.

When we focus on a theory of meaning for a whole language, we raise our sights above the meanings of specific words or sentences in order to think about the structural or compositional aspects of language. Our linguistic knowledge is in one respect finite: our vocabulary is finite and we know only a finite number of ways whereby to fit known vocabulary together to form sentences. Yet in another respect our linguistic knowledge is infinite, or at least has no upper bound: however many sentences we understand, we can come to understand another (life and concentration permitting). A formal theory with finitely many axioms and infinitely many theorems mirrors these features of our understanding.

The mirroring may be taken a step further. Semantic information concerning the expressions and constructions involved in a given sentence is complete if the meaning of the sentence follows from this information by logic alone. A formal theory can in this way enable us to check the completeness of the semantic information we associate with subsentential elements of the language: the deductive closure relation needs to be enough to deliver sentence-related theorems on the basis of word- or construction-related axioms. We should also require that the theory be minimally sufficient to achieve its semantic task: it should contain no information not required for the purpose of associating each sentence with its meaning.

What is it for a theorem to associate a sentence with its meaning? Davidson's official answer (1967, 'Truth and meaning') is that a theory of meaning is a theory knowledge of which would suffice for understanding. This shifts the question to: what is it for a theorem to associate a sentence with something which suffices for understanding? Davidson (1973, 'Radical interpretation') addresses this question, and a slight variation on his position has been offered by McDowell (1977; see also Davies 1981): the association obtains if we can use the theorem to give a correct report of what one who uses the sentence to say something thereby says (likewise for questions, commands, etc.) If someone utters the English sentence 'Nothing travels faster than light', a theorem which associates this sentence with its meaning will enable us to report the speaker as having said that nothing travels faster than light.

Such an account of what it is to associate a sentence with a meaning renders the claim that there is a complete semantics for a language substantive, and in my view dubious. As has been stressed in much recent work at the boundaries of pragmatics and semantics (e.g. Davidson 1986, Sperber and Wilson 1995, Travis 1997, Neale 2004), interpreting another's utterance, and so attaining a position in which one could correctly report what they say, often, perhaps always, requires exercising quite general cognitive skills, ones which cannot properly be encoded in a specifically semantic theory. These are involved in, for example, determination of reference, resolution of ambiguity, and appreciation of which of two semantically distinct but like-sounding words has been uttered. Charles Travis (1996) suggests that even in the absence of ambiguity or any variation of fact, both 'Yes' and 'No' can be the right answer to the very same question, depending on the interests of the participants.[1] When we speak of the 'same question', we are individuating it semantically: the same words are used with the same meanings, and the same things are being referred to in the same way. If we recognize the correctness of distinct answers, we can avoid contradiction only by recognizing that questions can also be individuated more narrowly. This level of individuation is more detailed than what is typically thought to belong to semantics. It arises through appealing to what is normally regarded as non-semantic information, like the overall concerns of the questioner. If this narrower individuation is required by interpretation, then no amount of semantic information, as usually understood, will be complete.

A specific version of this view is that the ordinary 'meaning' of expressions falls short of what is required to determine truth conditions (even when indexicality and other well-recognized forms of contextual effect are bracketed). Identifying truth conditions is part of what is involved in interpretation. So if the completeness of semantics is to be tested by the provision of sufficient information to permit interpretation, there may be no complete semantics. I know of no general argument against such views. One has simply to examine the examples case by case. Yet even if semantics falls short of truth conditions, the truth-conditional approach constitutes a useful idealization, and the kind of phenomena that might make one think it inadequate in general have no role to play in the discussions

---

[1] A version of one of Travis's examples is as follows. The question 'Is the ball round?' is asked of a certain squash ball at a certain moment. If we think of the needs of a first-time spectator, wishing to know whether a squash ball is more like a rugby ball (ovoid) or more like a soccer ball (round), the right answer is 'Yes', even if the ball is at that moment ovoid through being squashed against the wall. If we think of the needs of a manufacturer of squash balls, who has fitted this ball with minute detectors to monitor its deformations and transmit the information to a computer, and the ball is at that moment squashed against the wall, the right answer is 'No'. For more discussion, see Sainsbury 2002: 201–3.

of this book. Even if a conception of meaning closely tied to the demands of interpretation turns out to require the exercise of general skills, rather than only of language-specific ones, I think the issues to be discussed here will not be affected.

Working under the idealization, an appropriate theory of meaning describes each object language sentence in a way which leads to a correct report of the speech of one who utters the sentence. According to Davidson, a radical interpreter, someone who is trying to understand a language from scratch, without the help of bilinguals, must view his interpretations as contributions to the larger goal of understanding the behaviour of the speakers he is studying on the basis of their beliefs and desires. A good interpretation of what is said by an utterance is one which leads to an attribution of belief or desire in the light of which the speaker's overall behaviour makes sense. As McDowell put it in a phrase quoted in Chapter 1, 'We have not properly made sense of forms of words in a language if we have not, thereby, got some way towards making sense of its speakers' (McDowell 1977: 160). At the base, behaviour is to include not mere motions of human matter through space, but simple actions, like coiling a rope, in which goals, intentions, and beliefs are manifest in a way that, on occasion, may be quite independent of the agent's use of language. At a later stage, we see certain actions as 'holdings-true' (on Davidson's version of this story) of linguistic items, sentences or utterances. Such actions, Davidson suggests, though language-related, can be identified independently of knowing the speaker's language. At a yet later stage, hypotheses about what the speaker's language means are brought to bear in describing actions (in uttering 'Curry for me' he ordered curry for himself), and the quality of such descriptions is to be assessed in holistic terms, involving other speakers and other occasions, and, for Davidson, the norm of rationality.

Not all correct truth conditions are fit to encode speaker understanding. Few would wish to deny the truth of Donnellan's claim:

'Vulcan does not exist' is true iff the history of the use of 'Vulcan' ends in a block (Donnellan 1974: 25).

This claim, though no doubt true, does not provide an account fit to describe what is said by an utterance of 'Vulcan does not exist', or of what is known when such an utterance is understood. The saying and the understanding need not involve the technical concept of a block, so in this respect the condition would be too demanding. On the other hand, saying and understanding do involve mastery of the use of 'Vulcan'. Since the condition only mentions this word and does not use it, it is in this respect insufficiently demanding.

Under the idealization, the output of a theory of meaning is to be judged in the first instance by whether it delivers the right account of what speakers have said, where this in turn is judged on the basis of how well this account of sayings integrates with the overall behaviour that speakers display, the integration depending upon the connection between what people say and their beliefs and desires. This is the feature to which we appealed in the discussion of McDowell in Chapter 1: the reason that a truth theory, serving as a theory of meaning, should not allow you to interpret one who has uttered the words 'Phosphorus is visible' as having said that Hesperus is visible is that this interpretation might not allow optimal understanding of the speaker, especially not if, for example, she were also to utter, in the same context 'and Hesperus is not visible'. Within this perspective, it is plain why homophonic interpretations have a special status: setting aside indexicality and related features, one typically cannot have a more accurate report of what a speaker said in uttering certain words than one which simply reuses those words. For example, in uttering 'Nothing travels faster than light' the speaker said that nothing travels faster than light. Whatever else one may think about this report, one could hardly suppose it was in the least degree incorrect or inaccurate.

The discussion so far concerns what we can expect from a theory of meaning and how it might be grounded in behavioural evidence, evidence from human actions. It is a distinct question what form the theory should take. A traditional idea is that meanings are entities which are 'grasped' in understanding. A distinctive feature of Davidson's approach is that it does not treat meanings as entities. This is not because he fears that meanings, along with all 'intensional entities', are 'creatures of darkness' (Quine 1956: 180) but because 'they have no demonstrated use' in a theory of meaning (Davidson 1967: 21). This contrasts with many contemporary views which, influenced by model theory, seek to describe the meanings of words in terms of 'semantic values'. Model theory was never originally designed to specify linguistic meaning (as opposed to formal logical relations), and the attempt to put it to work in semantics makes referring expressions which do not refer seem problematic. One may try to model such expressions by assigning them a 'null entity' or a member of the 'outer domain', an assignment designed to mark the fact that the expression has no referent. If there is only one such value, there is no way to mark the semantic difference between 'Vulcan' and 'Zeus'. Having different null entities for different expressions brings into prominence the misconceived basis of the enterprise: one cannot sensibly represent failure of reference in terms of successful reference to some special kind of entity.

By contrast, Davidson, inspired by Tarski (1933), suggested that a theory of meaning should take the form of a theory of truth: a finitely axiomatized theory with theorems ('T-theorems') of the form 's is true iff p', where 's' marks the position of the name of an object language sentence and 'p' the position of a metalanguage sentence. The sentence in the position marked by 'p' does not introduce a semantic value for the sentence referred to, but rather introduces a necessary and sufficient condition for that sentence's truth. I suggest that we should see the axioms for referring expressions in the same way: these expressions are associated with a reference condition which may or may not be satisfied, just as a sentence is associated with a truth condition which may or may not be satisfied. Roughly speaking, in model theory meanings are entities, whereas in truth theory they are conditions.

Not all true truth theories are usable for interpretation, so truth theories do not count as themselves theories of meaning, as Davidson stresses in many places. He hypothesized that if we consider just true truth theories devised using the procedures of radical interpretation, and if we confine ourselves to canonically proved theorems, the output of such truth theories will be of the properly interpretive sort (e.g. Davidson 1976: 37).

He gave various reasons for thinking that a theory of meaning should be based on a theory of truth, and I will not review these.[2]

---

[2] See Larson and Segal (1995) for a very detailed and sophisticated application of the truth-theoretic approach to the semantics of natural language. This book still marks the current state of the art of truth-theoretical semantics.

The crucial issue for present purposes is that because knowledge of a theory of truth would not in itself suffice for interpretation, the account of what knowledge would suffice must be expanded. The condition is not merely knowing the theory, but also knowing that it is the right kind of theory, the kind one can properly use in interpretation, and that one is using the right kind of theorem, one which is 'canonical' (see Davidson 1976: 37).

The homophonic ideal is natural when we consider sentences lacking any significant indexicality, but becomes in general impossible once the indexical aspects of language are incorporated.[3] As Davidson put it, indexicality is a 'very large fly in the ointment' (1967: 33). Considering demonstratives, he made the following suggestion:

> 1. 'That book was stolen' is true as (potentially) spoken by p at t if and only if the book demonstrated by p at t is stolen prior to t. (Davidson 1967: 34)

An instance is:

> 2. 'That book was stolen' is true as (potentially) spoken by Davidson at noon on 02/02/02 if and only if the book demonstrated by Davidson at noon on 02/02/02 is stolen prior to noon on 02/02/02.

The instance (2) is unsatisfactory because it cannot be used in interpretation.[4] Intuitively, it is never correct to report an utterance by Davidson of 'That book was stolen' as his having said that the book demonstrated by Davidson at noon on 02/02/02 is stolen prior to noon on 02/02/02. What Davidson actually said by those words does not involve the concept of demonstration, nor the conceptual apparatus used to specify dates. I think that the only way to achieve a correct description of what is said in such a case involves two parts. First, the scene is set by some such remark as 'Pointing to a copy of *Word and Object* at noon on 02/02/02 . . .'. This gives the background in which the original speaker used the indexical words, and also

---

[3] Davidson stresses that homophony should not be mindlessly applied: not, for example, to an utterance he envisages of 'There's a hippopotamus in the refrigerator' (1968: 100–1). He connects this with the indeterminacy of meaning.

[4] Davidson comments that 'there is no suggestion that "the book demonstrated by the speaker" can be substituted ubiquitously for "that book" *salva veritate*' (Davidson 1967: 34). He does not explain how (1) delivers interpretive theorems.

provides a background which the reporter can exploit in what follows, which might take the form: Davidson said that it [that book] had been stolen. Here 'it' is anaphorically dependent on 'a copy of *Word and Object*' used in the scene-setting part, and the tense of 'said' is dependent on previous tenses. When the two parts are put together, we have no need for the parenthetical '[that book]', and we have the following intuitively correct report:

3. Pointing to a copy of *Word and Object* at noon on 02/02/02, Davidson said that it had been stolen.

The reporter can use any devices and concepts he wishes in order to set the scene, even ones, as in this case a date and a book title, which were not overtly exploited by the speaker (and which may have been unknown to the speaker); these then bind the use of pronouns or tenses in the report, ensuring that they have the correct referent, without suggesting that the original speaker himself exploited them. The upshot is that there may be no self-standing sentence, corresponding to the position occupied by p in 's is true iff p', which the reporter can use to express the content of the speech he correctly reports. Success is achieved in the more complex two-part way.

Correspondingly, the truth-theoretic methodology must be modified. T-theorems usable by an interpreter will need to quantify over utterances rather than merely sentences, and we would expect axioms of the following sort:

4. For all x, if in uttering 'That is F' the speaker used 'that' to refer to x, her utterance is true iff x satisfies 'F'.

An instance might be:

5. For all x, if in uttering 'That is stolen' the speaker used 'that' to refer to x, her utterance is true iff x satisfies 'is stolen'.

If we are given that Davidson, in uttering 'That is stolen', referred by his use of 'that' to a copy of *Word and Object* we can infer that his utterance is true iff it [the copy of *Word and Object*] satisfies 'is stolen'. More generally, by supplementing truth-theoretic axioms with contextual information, one will be able to derive conjunctions like:

6. in uttering u the speaker referred to some object x and time t, and u is true iff ... x ... t ....

User instructions say something like: find out to what objects and times the speaker referred, and construct a report by first referring to these in your own preferred way, and, applying axioms like (4), make those referring expressions govern what replaces 'x' and 't' as they occur after 'iff'.

The recognition of indexicality has a substantial effect on truth-theoretic views. While homophony remains some kind of ideal, marking the fact that within this approach to meaning there is no attempt to reduce specific contents to others, it will rarely or never be achieved, thanks to the degree to which our language is indexical (tense is the most widespread indexical feature). A very general issue is raised about the determination of reference. In thinking about classical truth theories for names, one often brackets the fact that the same name is used of many different things ('Aristotle' is used of the philosopher and also of the tycoon) and pretends that reference can be determined in a context-free way within truth theory. Even if this degree of idealization can be justified for names, it would be quite inappropriate for indexicals. In the example in (4), the truth of the antecedent required there to be an object to which the speaker referred in using 'that', but no information was given about whether this was so and, if so, which object was referred to. Where might this information come from?

Language users are in practice pretty successful at determining the referents of referring expressions. Generally, a wide range of cognitive skills are employed: implicit knowledge of what is likely to be salient to a speaker, or is likely to be thought by the speaker to be salient to the hearer; knowledge of which of various people with the same name is likely to be at issue in the context, knowledge of how pointing and other demonstrative gestures work; and general knowledge of which objects in the shared environment have which properties. It is an open question whether these skills can be 'axiomatized': whether, that is, there is some way of representing them by a first-order theory. There is no bound on what information might be relevant in helping determine reference. An attempt to axiomatize what is involved would run into an acute form of the 'frame problem'. Rather than take a stand on whether axiomatization is in principle possible, I will consider each alternative.

Suppose that it is possible. Then there could be a first-order theory which, for an arbitrary event in which some speaker of a language used a referring expression, would deliver as output a determination of the referent, if any, of that expression in that use. We could imagine an utterance being delivered in the first instance to a parser which sorted referring expressions from others, and sent the former to the theory of reference which would pair each utterance with a sequence of referents. This pair would then be delivered to the semantic theory, say a truth theory, for interpretation. The semantic theory would in the first instance generate conditionals like (4), and would then use the referent supplied by the reference theory to establish antecedents of the conditional, and so arrive at full interpretations. On this picture, it is terminological whether we say that reference determination lies outside semantic theory, or whether we call the semantic theory the union of the reference theory with the kind of theory which produced merely conditional theorems like (4).

Now suppose (as seems to me more likely) that reference determination is not susceptible to axiomatization. Then reference determination must come from outside the semantic theory. The theorist could respond in one of two ways. She might leave the semantic theory as it is, with its merely conditional theorems, and say that applying the theory involves first determining the reference of referring expressions, an operation concerning which she has nothing to offer. Alternatively, she could embark on the task of recording each use of, for example, demonstratives, and assign them whatever reference her normal native speaker methods suggest. Starting work today, she encounters Davidson using 'that' to refer to a copy of *Word and Object*, and so enters the following axiom:

> In uttering 'That is stolen' at noon on 02/02/02, Davidson used 'that' to refer to the copy of *Word and Object* which Goldfarb had lent to Dreben.

The material about Goldfarb, Dreben and the loan is obviously extraneous to what Davidson said, but it can figure legitimately in setting up a scene in which a book is introduced, and the remark is registered as true iff it (that book) is stolen.[5]

---

[5] A nearby alternative is to be rejected: if the theorist introduces her own name for the referent, say 'That$_j$', she will not be able to use it in the content of an accurate report of what Davidson said (which

58   FRAMEWORK ISSUES

There is room for dispute about the class of referring expressions for which this approach is appropriate. Kaplan's 'pure indexicals' are defined in part as ones for which the approach is needless, since a semantic axiom can straightforwardly fix the referent for every context. A plausible candidate is 'I', for which many theorists have supposed that axioms along these lines would be adequate:

7. For all x, u, if x utters u and x contains 'I', that occurrence of 'I' refers to x.

Assuming that any hearer can identify the utterer of any utterance she wishes to interpret, (7) will supply all that is needed to identify the referent of an arbitrary use of 'I'.

As Kaplan is aware, such suggestions are at best partial truths. Because I have such a thick accent which I fear would confuse callers, I ask you to record the outgoing message on my voice mail. You utter 'I am not at home right now but please leave a message'. In this utterance the occurrence of 'I' refers not to you, the utterer, but to me.

At the other end of the scale, the height of 'impurity', there is almost nothing to be said about pronouns used demonstratively. In most languages, personal pronouns contain a mark of gender, and perhaps 'that' needs to be used for things in some sense more remote than those for which it is appropriate to use 'this'. Even if these indications belong properly to content, they evidently do little towards determining reference.

Proper names and definite descriptions are intermediate. Few definite descriptions are 'complete' in the sense of supplying a uniquely satisfied predicate; context is supposed to supply 'supplementary information' (Quine 1960: 183). Proper names may strike us as more context free: when we are using them, disambiguation of reference does not often arise as an issue. In the ancient philosophy seminar, there is no question about the reference of 'Aristotle', though there may be a question about the reference of 'the book'. It is unlikely that there is a deep difference between the cases.

Proceeding in the case-by-case way, in which the theorist simply adds a new axiom for every use, the task of semantic theorizing will

---

was not that that$_j$ is stolen). Likewise if someone says 'That is not Smarty Jones', using 'that' to refer to Smarty Jones, I do not report her speech correctly by saying that she said that Smarty Jones was not Smarty Jones. In such cases, the two-part approach is again required: Speaking of that$_j$, Davidson said that it was stolen; speaking of Smarty Jones, she said that it was not Smarty Jones.

never be completed. Even so, the theory at any given stage illustrates how we are to proceed in applying it to new cases, and in this way it mirrors our semantic competence. The fact remains that reference determination has eluded theory. This should raise wider anxieties: for referring expressions, reference is contribution to truth conditions; if, for a given class of expressions, that contribution eludes theory, why not for expressions in general? Might not the contribution which general terms or quantifiers make to truth conditions also be dependent upon context in a way which brings into play the wide range of cognitive skills which resists axiomatization? While this anxiety deserves to be explored, this is not the place. Truth-theoretic approaches, even if they involve a large dose of idealization, can still show why there is no need to think of meanings as entities, and, by their focus on compositional features, help deter *ad hoc* 'analyses'.

Subscribing to a generally Davidsonian approach may seem paradoxical in the present context, for Davidson appears to relegate reference to at most a minor role:

Reference . . . plays no essential role in explaining the relation between language and reality (Davidson 1977: 225).

Davidson's view is not that there is no such thing as reference, but only that it relates to truth theory rather in the way that posited microphysical objects relate to observed macrophysical situations: reference is empirically a derived relation, not a basic one, and is whatever relation makes the assignment of truth conditions to whole sentences meet the demands of proper interpretation.

I challenge this approach in Chapter 7, although the success of this challenge is not essential to the official theses of RWR. I think that non-linguistic and pre-linguistic animals can train their attention on individual objects, tracking them perceptually and in memory. This capacity for non-linguistic reference, appealed to in standard psychological explanations of non-linguistic behaviour, seems likely to be a precursor to the capacity for linguistic reference. I do not suggest that this observation could lead to 'a non-linguistic characterization of [linguistic] reference' (Davidson 1977: 221). The suggestion is only that linguistic reference builds on non-linguistic reference, and that non-linguistic reference explains how linguistic reference is possible.

2.2 Russellian propositions

Any proposition which we can understand must be composed wholly of constituents with which we are acquainted (Russell 1912: 27).

Although few philosophers nowadays would follow Russell in restricting acquaintance to sense data, the Russellian picture which this quotation encapsulates is still highly influential, even if often subliminally. Propositions are entities with constituents, understanding involves standing in some special relation to these constituents, and a proper question to ask with respect to any word in a sentence is: what constituent (or 'semantic value') does it contribute to the proposition the sentence as a whole expresses? Whereas a Davidsonian answer to the question what proposition is expressed by an utterance of 'Nothing travels faster than light' is simply that nothing travels faster than light, the reflex which I am trying to identify in this section is dissatisfied with such an answer, and will embark without further ado on a quest for a suitable entity—one which will contain light, some relation among velocities, and perhaps other things as well.

The Davidsonian approach has no room for this entity-based conception of our subject matter. One source of the more entity-based perspective is a correspondence theory of truth. For example, Russell (1912) hoped that correspondence would be a kind of isomorphism: elements of the world, particulars and universals, are arranged in a certain way in belief; the belief is true if and only if there is a fact in which these same entities are arranged in the same way, or a matching one. Another source is the conviction that belief and other 'propositional attitudes' are, as the terminology suggests, relations to propositions. On this view, it is natural to think that belief ascriptions, like 'Jack believes that Jill is beautiful' have the overall form of two-place predications, with 'that Jill is beautiful' a singular term for the proposition that Jill is beautiful. If there really are beliefs, there really are such entities as propositions, and the only serious question is what their nature is. (This approach is championed by Schiffer 2003.) Russell's idea seems a promising first attempt to provide an answer to this question.

Russell himself was dissatisfied with his account because the universals have to feature in a different way in the belief from the way in which they need to figure in the world if the belief is to be true. As Russell put it, in the belief the universal is a term, but if the belief is true it is not a mere term but 'really relates' the other terms. Othello believes that Desdemona loves Cassio. Othello thereby gathers together Desdemona, love, and Cassio. Love is just a term, related to the other terms, Othello, Desdemona, and Cassio, by the relation of belief. If the belief is true, love is not merely a term, but really relates Desdemona to Cassio, and even if it is false, what has to be considered is love's failure to relate these terms, so again love is not merely a term.

This is one aspect of Russell's problem of 'the unity of the proposition', and it is a problem to which he never felt he had a good solution. He struggled with it in the 1913 manuscript which he is supposed to have abandoned when Wittgenstein said that his 'theory of judgement' had failed to explain why it is impossible to judge nonsense. Much contemporary work seems simply to ignore the problem, yet the question remains: how can a sequence of entities say something? Why are they not just like any other sequence? The right direction in which to look for an answer, I suggest, is Davidson-style truth-theoretic approaches. Entities play no special role in the story. The analogous problem is the 'unity of the sentence': how is it that combining words in certain ways results in something which says something, and not just a string of words? In Davidson's approach, there is no single answer: at some level, this must be a primitive fact. On the other hand, truth-theoretic methodology both identifies which strings of words say something (the strings for which the truth theory has T-theorems) and details what they say. An adequate answer to the question requires at least this much, yet within the truth-theoretic perspective, the notion of a Russellian proposition drops from sight. If an answer also requires more, the additional material is certainly not to be found in Russellian propositions. Without something like a truth-theoretic approach, a systematic semantics which assigns truth conditions on the basis of composition, we certainly have no handle on the problems Russell himself thought were encountered by Russellian propositions; but once we have such an approach, Russellian propositions have no role to play.[6]

They can also be questioned on more detailed grounds. Do they allow for a significant difference between the contributions of 'Hesperus' and 'Phosphorus'? If not, how can they do justice to the propositional attitudes of speakers? If so, Russellian propositions must contain something other than objects and properties. The additional entities might be modes of presentation of objects, or guises under which Russellian propositions are thought. This already undermines the seductive connection between the constituents of these propositions and understanding: the move recognizes that mere knowledge of the constituents Russell envisaged cannot deliver understanding. The connection is further undermined when a Russellian theorist attempts to do justice to other parts of speech. Russell himself wondered whether he would ever have acquaintance with the referent of 'or'; similar worries affect prepositions (like 'in'), intensifying adjectives (like 'very'), adverbs ('unfortunately'), modal and temporal expressions ('might', tense), and so on. It is not that it is impossible to find entities to correspond to such expressions, as shown by the Montague grammar tradition. The point is that these entities unpick the Russellian connection between acquaintance and the constituents of propositions.

This connection links understanding with a special relation, whose paradigm is perception. The view is most plausible in the case of perceptual demonstratives. Understanding such an expression, it has been plausibly argued, involves perceiving and attending to the referent (cf. Evans 1982; Campbell 2002). Understanding of this kind is not available in the case of non-referring referring expressions, and would be unmotivated for semantically complex ones (since their understanding should flow from understanding their parts). This essentially Russellian conception of understanding as acquaintance with an entity has had a very marked influence on the philosophy of reference, an influence firmly rejected by RWR.

Perception is certainly a special source of knowledge, but on a Russellian view it becomes a source of special knowledge, knowledge of a kind not available in other ways. We have already seen that

---

[6] There are sophisticated theories of propositions to which these observations are irrelevant (e.g. Bealer 1998).

this can be questioned: it is hard to find a point in the history of my encounters with a cheese-stealing mouse at which my knowledge acquired a special character (cf. Chapter 1.3.1). In particular, it is not clear that seeing the mouse made any huge difference. A common view is that perceptual knowledge is distinguished by enabling the knower to act on a object. For example,

If I want to pick up the box that contains the money, for example, I can do it only when I know the demonstrative identity, 'That box is the one with the money' (Campbell 2002: 157).

We can agree that I can know that I am picking up the box with the money only if I can refer to a box and knowingly think, concerning that box, that it contains the money. But perception may play no special role. First imagine that the box is one among others in a sealed and unlit room and that I am operating remotely controlled grabbers, using a radar screen to guide me. I know the box with the money will make a bigger blip, so I guide the grabbers to a box I do not literally see. Or perhaps I do count as seeing the box 'on the radar'. We can extend the example so that perception is definitively excluded. On general grounds I know that there will be just one box with money and that it will be heavier than any of the others. I program a machine to weigh the boxes and remove the heaviest. I knowingly act on the box with the money without having perceived it. I can set a trap for my mouse and so perhaps act on it regardless of whether I have seen it. No one can doubt that much of our action is guided by perception, and that such cases form a basic model; it is harder to argue that action on objects must always be guided by perception, or that perception delivers knowledge of a kind not otherwise available.

Russell's own epistemology was motivated by a consideration that would nowadays have little appeal: he wanted objects of acquaintance to be demon-proof, so as to provide a proper foundation for knowledge. This meant that there could be no illusions of acquaintance, which in turn is why acquaintance had to be restricted to things like sense data, things the demon supposedly could not take away without you noticing. This does make knowledge by acquaintance a special kind of knowledge, but not in a way which would be at all attractive to theorists closer to our own times.

The aim of this section has been mostly to articulate the Russellian conception, and indicate some difficulties with it. I do not pretend to have refuted it; but much of the remainder of the book is designed to show how smoothly things go if it is abandoned.

2.3 Negative free logic (NFL)

Free logical languages admit intelligible referring expressions which lack a referent. They stand in stark opposition to languages which conform to Millian or direct-reference theories of reference, according to which the intelligibility of a referring expression ensures that it has a referent. Theorists have been driven to Millianism through fear of descriptivism; the position to be described here is neither Millian nor descriptivist. Even the most ardent advocates of Millian theories recognize that there is something counterintuitive about not allowing empty names, like 'Vulcan' and 'Santa Claus', to be intelligible. In this section, I assume that we should if possible allow for intelligible non-referring referring expressions; the question is how that is best to be done.

Free logics are so called because they are designed to be free of the existence assumptions made by classical logic.[7] These fall under two main heads: (i) in every classical model, every individual constant is assigned some entity from the domain by the interpretation function; (ii) in the classical definition of validity, only models with non-empty domains are relevant. These features ensure the classical validity of the schemata:

1. $\exists x\ x = a$
2. $\exists x (Fx \vee \neg Fx)$

The validity of a schema is the validity of every instance. (1) says that a valid formula results when 'a' is replaced by any 'individual constant' whatsoever. Within the classical formalism, this leads to no problem, since individual constants are formally defined, and it is stipulated that, for every model, each is assigned an element of the model's domain. When we apply logic to natural language, the natural analogue

---

[7] For a recent expert overview, see Morscher and Simons (2001). For the mediaeval background, see Klima (2001).

of an individual constant is a proper name. We do not want to be committed to the view that anything along the lines of '∃x x = Vulcan' or 'Something is Vulcan' is valid or even true. Applying classical logic to natural language would require a prior segregation of its proper names into those which have bearers and those which do not; only the former should be allowed to replace individual constants in the classical formalism. Effecting this segregation does not seem to be part of the job of a logician (traditionally conceived): logic is supposed to be apriori, and not to involve the kind of astronomical or literary knowledge required to determine into which category a name like 'Vulcan', 'Homer', or 'Patanjali' should be placed. The procedure would also constitute a refusal to allow logic to describe the impact of empty names on the validity of our reasoning.

If there were nothing, (2) intuitively should be false: there would be nothing which was any way at all. A valid formula should intuitively be true in all possibilities, and there being nothing appears to be one such. This has led to consideration of how best to adjust the classical conception of validity (see Bostock 1997).

There is general agreement that providing a formal system suitable for representing a language containing empty referring expressions requires changes to the quantifier rules. One may instantiate only using a non-empty term, and one may generalize only with respect to a non-empty term. One could put this into effect by replacing the classical quantifier rules by the following:

Universal Instantiation: From $\forall xAx$ and $\exists x\ x = t$ infer $A(t/x)$ (where '$A(t/x)$' is the formula which results from 'Ax' by replacing every occurrence of 'x' by 't').

Existential Generalization: From $A(t/x)$ and $\exists x\ x = t$ infer $\exists xAx$.[8]

The classical logician would have to regard the rules as correct (though as containing superfluous material).

Free logicians are united in accepting such quantifier rules, but beyond this agreement there are various divergences, deriving from different motivations and different philosophical opinions. A standard classification distinguishes the following three options with regard to

---

[8] Given NFL's Ockhamist truth conditions ('*Fa*' is true iff '*a*' has a unique referent and it satisfies '*F*', and is false otherwise), a simple sentence will entail its existential generalization(s).

simple sentences[9] containing referring expressions which fail to refer (like 'Vulcan is a planet'):

- *Positive free logic:* some such sentences are true: 'Vulcan is Vulcan' is a likely example, given that this 'follows from the unexceptionable identity principle "$x=x$"' (Lambert 1991: 25).
- *Fregean free logic:* all such sentences, indeed all sentences containing a referring expression which fails to refer, are without truth value. This was Frege's view (1892); a formal implementation is given by Lehman (1994).
- *Negative free logic (NFL):* all such sentences are false. Burge (1974a) has argued that this is the appropriate free logic to use in the framework of a semantic theory for languages which may contain empty referring expressions, and Burge's view is adopted here.

Positive free logic is motivated by a desire to do justice to the dictates of logic. Fregean free logic is motivated by the view that there is something defective about a sentence with a non-referring referring expression, a defect which cannot be eliminated by any kind of embedding.[10] Negative free logic is motivated by two thoughts: (i) a true simple predication refers to something and predicates a property which that object possesses (the idea extends to any n-ary simple sentence); (ii) falsehood is failure of truth. Taking the three options in turn, we will see that NFL is best suited for natural language semantics.

No one should challenge the principle that everything is self-identical, and this can be represented in the familiar classical syntax as '$\forall x\ x=x$'; equally, as the view that '$x=x$' is true of everything. This says that each object is self-identical, and does not entail that Vulcan is Vulcan, for there is no such object as Vulcan. What further claim is made by the 'unexceptionable identity principle "$x=x$"'? Whatever it tells us cannot be about how objects are (for this

---

[9] A simple sentence is one constructed by inserting n referring expressions into an n-place predicate. A simple sentence will not be atomic if the referring expressions are semantically complex.

[10] Frege allowed that embedding a sentence containing an expression which normally has no referent within in oblique context could result in something true or false, for example 'According to Homer's story, Odysseus was put ashore at Ithaca while still asleep.' This requires no qualification of the remark above, for in such contexts, according to Frege, 'Odysseus' does have a referent, namely its customary sense.

information could not include that Vulcan is Vulcan). The only remaining possibility is that it tells us something about expressions, for example, that every sentence composed of two occurrences of the same singular term, separated by the identity sign, is true. This makes it plain that we are not dealing with a genuinely logical principle, but with some metalinguistic opinion about referring expressions.

This opinion is dubious independently of empty names. There are false instances of '$x = x$', and true instances which cannot be known apriori (and so fail a familiar test for counting as logical). The first point can be made by the example of someone who thinks that Aristotle Onassis is a reincarnation of the great philosopher. This silly falsehood might be expressed as 'Aristotle is Aristotle'. The second point is made by Paderewski cases, in which one who, according to the scenario, understands 'Paderewski' and uses it for the same person on both of its occurrences in 'Paderewski is Paderewski', is in no position to know apriori that this is a truth.

Other candidates for true simple sentences containing empty names, and which might support positive free logic, are drawn from myth and fiction, for example 'Pegasus has wings'. Is this really a truth? It entails that something is Pegasus, which is how the myth says things are but is not how things actually are. The myth is mere myth and not true: that is, the sentences used to state the myth are not true. If we are inclined to think that sentences like 'Pegasus has wings' are true, we are either ascribing 'truth in the myth' (that is, fidelity to the myth) or else imagining the sentence implicitly prefixed by something like 'According to the myth...'.

If positive free logic is excluded, the remaining free logical options are Fregean and negative free logics.[11] The Fregean insists that no embedding of a referring expression which, in the embedding, has no referent, can yield a sentence with a truth value; the defect induced by failure of reference is radical indeed. Yet it seems hard to exclude the possibility of an operator, say 'Neg', which can attach to any intelligible sentence S to form a truth just on condition that S is not true (cf. Evans 1982: 24–5). Even if S is without truth value, 'Neg S' is true, and so Frege's vision, according to which

---

[11] This puts us in the company of Aristotle, who wrote: 'neither "Socrates is sick" nor "Socrates is well" will be true if Socrates himself does not exist.' (*Categories* 13b, quoted in Morscher and Simons 2001: 23)

truth valuelessness dominates all embeddings, would falter. This provides a general theoretical difficulty for Fregean free logic (a defeasible one, needless to say).

There are also more detailed difficulties in relating Fregean free logic to our actual practice. We often in serious contexts use sentences containing non-referring referring expressions on the way to discovering or establishing truth. A proof that there is no greatest prime may start with the assumption, for reductio, 'Either the greatest prime is even or it is odd'. The discovery that there was no such planet as Vulcan might have been reached in part on the basis of a calculation according to which a planet which could cause the observed perturbations in Mercury's perihelion would have to be large.[12] This could be expressed as some hypothesis like 'Vulcan is at least 1000 miles in diameter'. Such hypotheses help generate a proof, or lead to the discovery of truth (it was because Vulcan would have to be so large, to do its theoretical work, that the repeated failures to observe it eventually led to the rejection of the hypothesis). The most natural way to treat the arguments is to see the reasoning or the empirical facts as serving to refute the relevant hypothesis, that is, to establish that it is false. The assumption that the greatest prime is either odd or even leads to a contradiction, so it must be rejected. Since the greatest prime is a number if it is anything, and since every number is odd or even, the supposition that there is such a thing as the greatest prime, being one which leads to something which must be rejected, must itself be rejected. The hypothesis that Vulcan is at least 1000 miles in diameter does not fit the observational evidence and so must be rejected. These rejections are most naturally construed as denials, amounting to the claim that what is denied is false. Yet in Fregean free logic, there is nothing to choose between the hypotheses and their negations: both are without truth value. By contrast, NFL delivers the intuitively correct assignments of truth value: 'The greatest prime is odd or even' and 'Vulcan is at least 1000 miles in diameter' are both false; both can properly be denied; both have true negations.

---

[12] I take liberties with the facts. The name 'Vulcan' was introduced not by Le Verrier but by Jacques Babinet, and although Le Verrier believed that there was such a planet as Vulcan and also believed that intra-Mercurial matter might explain the anomalous features of Mercury's orbit, he never thought they could be explained by any single planet. See Roseveare 1982.

Fregean free logic has a special problem with negative existential sentences. Frege himself resolved the problem by a second-level view. If 'exists' is an ordinary first-level predicate, Fregean free logic treats both 'Vulcan exists' and 'Vulcan does not exist' as without truth value, whereas intuitively the first is false and the second true. This intuition is very happily accommodated within NFL, since a simple sentence containing a non-referring referring expression ('Vulcan exists') is false, and its negation ('Vulcan does not exist') is true.

The notion of a simple sentence plays a substantial role, and it may be objected that it cannot bear the necessary weight. 'Vulcan is identical to Vulcan' is a simple sentence, since 'is identical to' is a simple predicate. The sentence is false, according to NFL, through failure of reference, so its negation is true. Intuitively 'Vulcan is distinct from Vulcan' is also a simple sentence, built from a simple predicate. If this is right, then this sentence too is false through failure of reference. Yet, arguably, it is synonymous with the true 'Vulcan is not identical to Vulcan'. Synonymous sentences cannot differ in truth value (with respect to the same situation), so something has gone wrong.[13] Of various responses open to the NFL theorist, I prefer to say that 'is distinct' is indeed a simple predicate and functions as the complement of identity (in any world, the set of pairs in the distinctness relation are all and only the pairs not in the identity relation). This is what gives rise to the view that 'Vulcan is distinct from Vulcan' and 'Vulcan is not identical to Vulcan' are synonymous. In reality, the difference in truth value simply shows that these are not synonymous. Things would be different if there were a predicate 'is not identical to', but in fact the predicate is identity and the negation takes the whole sentence as its scope. In short, what is to count as a simple sentence is to some extent to be moulded by the theory.

These are preliminary remarks, designed to make NFL attractive enough to be worth exploring; it is to be judged in the end by its fruits, some of which are harvested in this book. The language of NFL can be introduced by starting with the familiar syntax of first-order logic with identity, individual constants, but not descriptors or function symbols. A model, M, is the usual sort of thing: a sequence

---

[13] David Wiggins and Mark Heller pressed difficulties of this kind.

$\langle D,i\rangle$, where D is a domain and i is an interpretation function which assigns to n-ary predicates an n-place relation defined over D in the usual way, and to constants assigns either nothing or else an element of D. A unary atomic sentence Fa is true in M ($= \langle D, i\rangle$) iff there is an $x \in D$ such that $i(a) = x$ and $x \in i(F)$; otherwise it is false in M.[14] All other features of truth in a model are as normal. A formula is false in a model iff its negation is true in that model. The sequences of objects from the domain are used in the ordinary way in dealing with open and quantified formulas. Sequences s have to agree with i in their assignment to constants: $\forall x,s,a, (s(a) = x \leftrightarrow i(a) = x)$. As usual, they always assign a member of D to variables.

On this simple version of NFL, there is no room for referring expressions to take significantly different scopes relative to the first-order operators. This is fine when it comes to delivering correct truth conditions for negative existentials, with 'exists' treated as a normal first level predicate. Then 'Vulcan exists' will be formalized as having the structure 'Fa', an intended interpretation will assign D to 'exists' (or a corresponding letter) and nothing to 'Vulcan' (or a corresponding letter). 'Vulcan exists' will be formalized as false and 'Vulcan does not exist' will be formalized as its negation, and so as true.

We could enrich the syntax in a non-standard direction by associating the individual constants with scope. Intuitively, the idea is to make room for a distinction corresponding to the one Russell claimed for 'The present King of France is not bald'. Keeping to simple referring expressions, we could introduce into the formalism a distinction corresponding to that between 'It is not the case that Vulcan is a planet' and 'Vulcan is a non-planet'. Evans envisaged that this could be done by the square bracket notion which Russell and Whitehead used to mark the scope of iota-expressions, and I will use essentially that notation. The initial idea is captured by:

If 'A' is a formula containing 'a', '(a)A' is a formula.

An occurrence of the form '(a)' is redundant if no operator intervenes between it and the occurrence of 'a' which it binds. In particular,

---

[14] It seems natural to express this condition in a free logical metalanguage, within which $i(a) = x$ is false of each thing if i does not assign anything to a. Anyone who dislikes these assumptions could express the condition as: i is defined for a and $i(a) \in i(F)$.

there is no semantic distinction between '(a)Fa' and 'Fa'. This emerges in the basic semantic idea:

(a)A is true in M ($=<D,i>$) iff $\exists x\, x = i(a)$ and A is true in M.

We can contrast the reading on which negation has wide scope with that on which it has narrow scope as follows:

¬ (a)(Fa) (wide scope negation)

(a) ¬ (Fa) (narrow scope negation)

A formula of the first kind is true in M iff (a)(Fa) is false in M (for whatever reason: either there is no x such that $i(a) = x$ or there is such an x but $x \notin i(F)$). A formula of the second kind is true in M iff there is an x such that $i(a) = x$ and $x \notin i(F)$.

In two-place atoms, there are four semantically distinguishable ways to insert negation:

¬ (a)(b)Rab

(a) ¬ (b)Rab

(b) ¬ (a))Rab

(a)(b) ¬ Rab.

This approach makes more distinctions than we are likely to find in a natural language. Indeed, it will be a real question whether or not any such distinctions are required. The questions cannot easily be answered if we do not have the means required to represent a variety of possibilities.

Another enrichment is to include definite descriptions as terms. The general idea is familiar:

If 'Ax' is a formula with 'x' free, '(The x(Ax))' is a term.

Terms now include these expressions, along with variables and individual constants. Scope indication can be effected in at least two ways. (i) We can precisely mirror the method adopted for names. This produces clumsy-looking formulae like:

¬ (The x (x is King of France)) (Bald (The x (x is King of France))).

This formula is true in the actual model. (ii) We can make a definite description look more like a quantifier by just using the variable in what, according to (i), is a second occurrence of the description:

¬ (The x (x is King of France)) (Bald x).

Either way, we can keep to Russellian truth conditions or could introduce more exotic truth conditions if we are moved by the kind of approach initiated by Donnellan (1966). Here I conservatively illustrate the Russellian truth conditions:

For all M (= <D, i>), for all y, (i)('The x (Ax)') = y iff y and y alone among the members of D satisfies 'Ax').

The notion of an atomic formula can be replaced by that of a simple formula:

A simple subject–predicate formula consists of a simple n-ary predicate suitably concatenated with n terms.

Individual constants are terms. The truth-in-a-model condition for atomic formulae is extended to:

An n-ary simple subject–predicate formula $F(t_1, \ldots t_n)$ is true in a model M (= <D, i>) iff there are members $x_1, \ldots x_n$, of D such that $i(t_1) = x_1, \ldots i(t_n) = x_n$ and $<x_1 \ldots x_n> \supset i(F)$; otherwise it is false in M.

When I speak of NFL, this is the formalism I have in mind. Applying it to natural language involves the claim that some or all of its features are reflected in natural language. For example, to 'apply' classical logic in the most straightforward way to the natural language conditional is to claim that it has the truth conditions of a classical '→' formula. Likewise, to apply NFL to natural language referring expressions is to claim that they may be intelligible even if empty, that they must refer if a simple subject–predicate sentence in which they occur is to be true, and that the false intelligible sentences are just the intelligible sentences which are not true.

The main point of free logic is to allow for intelligible empty referring expressions. As we saw in Fregean free logic, this does not as such ensure that there are any true sentences containing such names. NFL requires that negated simple sentences containing an empty name are true. What other forms of truths containing empty names are there? Some answers are obvious, for example material conditionals with a simple sentence containing an empty name as antecedent. I shall in addition assume that in some non-extensional contexts, an embedded empty name is consistent with the truth of the overall sentence, for example 'Le Verrier believed that Vulcan was a planet'. The explanation I would offer is essentially Fregean: in ascribing a belief, one is attempting to express what is believed. This requires that one use intelligible expressions, but the truth of the ascription is entirely independent of the truth of what is ascribed. There are cases in which one would like to be able to give the same kind of explanation, but in which the linguistic details are recalcitrant. Quine mentions 'Homer believed in Pegasus' (Quine 1960: 179) and 'Tom is drawing Pegasus' (Quine 1960: 180). The first may perhaps be analysed so as to reveal that 'Pegasus' does not occupy the position of an argument (so we are not obliged to count this as a simple sentence, and so not obliged to count it as false). The prospects of doing the same for the second sentence are less good. Problems of this kind affect all theories. A simple minded suggestion for dealing with some of these is offered in Chapter 6.3.

The way in which RWR uses NFL to arrive at a semantics of referring expressions is exemplified by this axiom for 'Hesperus':

for all x ('Hesperus' refers to x iff $x =$ Hesperus).

This can be accepted by a semantic theory set within classical logic, where it is equivalent to the more familiar

'Hesperus' refers to Hesperus.

If we apply the familiar axiom to an empty name like 'Vulcan' we get something false, classically and for NFL:

'Vulcan' refers to Vulcan.

The alternative version, though false classically because it entails that something is Vulcan, is true within NFL:

for all x ('Vulcan' refers to x iff $x =$ Vulcan).

'$x =$ Vulcan' is false of each thing, so if the biconditional is true '"Vulcan" refers to x' is also false of each thing; this is the desired result. The NFL restrictions on the quantifier rules prevent the classical inference to there being something identical to Vulcan.

The intelligibility of predicates like '$=$ Hesperus' was recognized by Frege:

In the sentence 'the morning star is Venus', 'is' is obviously not the mere copula; its content is an essential part of the predicate, so that the word 'Venus' does not constitute the whole of the predicate. One might say instead: 'the morning star is no other than Venus'... What is predicated here is not *Venus* but *no other than Venus* (Frege 1892: 184).

74 FRAMEWORK ISSUES

We can see Frege's idea at work in the recommended reference axioms: 'Venus' refers to anything which is no other than Venus. The RWR axioms agree with McDowell that a semantic theory will be modest or austere: it will not in general attempt to analyse the meanings of individual words, a task which could at best have only a limited success. RWR is thus not a descriptivist theory. It is also, obviously, not a Millian one. It occupies relatively unfamiliar middle ground.

I have represented NFL as a minimal departure from classical logic. NFL ideas can alternatively be incorporated into other logics, for example intuitionistic logic, relevance logic, paraconsistent logic. Can the essential ideas of NFL (that there are intelligible referring expressions that have no referents, and that in simple sentences, failure of reference results in falsehood) be motivated independently of their alleged reflecting of the semantic facts of natural language? Can we justify these ideas without special reference to empty referring expressions? Here is a consideration which points (defeasibly, of course) towards an affirmative answer.

We saw that Kripke defined a 'rigid designator' as an expression that designates the same thing with respect to every world. In order to allow for contingent existence, and so for such truths as '$\lozenge \neg \exists x\ x = $ Kripke', he says that an expression may designate, with respect to a world, an entity which does not exist in that world:

a rigid designator [has] the same reference in all possible worlds. I ... don't mean to imply that the thing designated exists in all possible worlds, just that the name refers rigidly to that thing (Kripke 1972/1980: 77–8).

To express the contingency of Kripke's existence, we need 'Kripke does not exist' to be true with respect to some world. On his view, a world w in which Kripke does not exist is still one in which 'Kripke' designates Kripke. Since Kripke is not among the things which exist at w, the sentence 'Kripke does not exist' is true with respect to w. It follows classically that 'Something does not exist' is true with respect to w, which will be somewhat distasteful to non-Meinongians. On the assumption that something exists only if there is something that it is, we also get the truth with respect to w of '$\neg \exists x\ x = $ Kripke', and so, by classical reasoning, of '$\exists y \neg \exists x\ x = y$' (see Wiggins 1995). Most people would think that the last is something that ought to be true with respect to no world: how could there be something which is not identical to anything? No problem of this kind arises within NFL, if only because it does not accept classical existential generalization. As we will see in §2.5 below, NFL can keep to the intuitive idea that an expression designates with respect to a world only things which exist in the world, and can offer a uniform account of world-relativized existential statements. This counts in NFL's favour independently of its endorsement of intelligible empty referring expressions.

2.4 Ontology

Mill said that every name names something, real or imaginary. If we are generous enough in our ontology we can hold that all names have bearers, more generally, that all referring expressions refer. In that case, there is no reference without referents. For non-fictional apparently empty referring expressions like 'Vulcan', a generous ontologist can hold that they refer to things which do not exist. For fictional apparently empty referring expressions like 'Sherlock Holmes', the generous ontologist can hold that they refer to existing abstract entities, fictional characters, or to non-existing merely possible individuals.

As far as I know, such views cannot be refuted (as Russell supposed) by showing that they entail contradictions (see Parsons 1980). They are sometimes motivated by their capacity to provide solutions to the kinds of problems considered here. What I wish to insist upon is that it is quite needless to go beyond ordinary ontology in order to give a satisfactory account of reference, existence, and fiction. At various points in arguments which follow, I will decline to follow a route which requires any expansion of ordinary ontology, whether the postulation of non-existent things, or of existent but abstract fictional characters, or of non-actual things. I shall assume that everything actually exists, where this is understood tenselessly: anything that has existed, does exist, or will exist exists actually;[15] that is, that everything is actual ('actualism'), and everything exists ('anti-Meinongianism'). There are no non-actual possibles, and no actual

---

[15] For a contrary view, see Yourgrau (1987).

non-existents. Moreover, I believe all this has to be so: there could not be objects which are possible but not actual, or actual non-existents. This is quite consistent with the fact that there could have been things there actually are not, and the fact that things which actually exist might not have done so.

On this view, possible worlds are not non-actual entities. Either they are a mere figure of speech, and we need to check that all the modal claims we wish to make can be made using just modal auxiliaries like 'can' and 'might' and modal adverbs like 'necessarily'; or they are actual abstract entities, presumably representations of some kind.

I will not attempt to defend any of these views beyond saying that even those who oppose them (for example Lewis 1986) allow that they are the views of common sense, and believe they need to be rejected because of tricky philosophical problems. This book is intended to show that reference, existence, and fiction are not among the tricky problems which require any changes in common-sense ontology.

2.5 Rigidity and the essence of reference

As we saw in §2.3 above, Kripke's notion of rigidity is sameness of referent with respect to every world. This does not obviously allow for non-referring referring expressions to be rigid, and it allows that a referring expression can refer with respect to a world to something that does not exist in that world. RWR modifies the notion of rigidity to avoid both these features. It is a modification rather than a distortion because the modified notion delivers precisely Kripke's verdict of world-relative truth for every case he discusses.

The intuitive idea of rigidity is that actual reference is projected onto all worlds. A referring expression which is actually empty is rigid by being empty with respect to every world (holding its meaning constant). As Kaplan put it:

a proper name either denotes the same individual with respect to every possible circumstance or else denotes nothing with respect to any possible circumstance (Kaplan 1973: 510).

Assuming that x refers to y with respect to w only if y is in w, we can express this as a unified condition as follows:

(R) for all worlds w, all rigid referring expressions, x, and all objects y, (x actually designates y and y exists in w) iff x designates y with respect to w.[16]

The rigidity of empty and non-empty expressions is unified by this fact: for both kinds of expression, there is no divergence between actual reference and reference with respect to other worlds, except to the extent to which worlds lack the relevant referent.

There are at least two prima facie reasons for thinking that RWR should not nail its flag to (R). The first is that (R) apparently entails that the semantic classification of 'Vulcan' as rigid has the striking metaphysical consequence that there could be no such object as Vulcan. 'Vulcan' is actually empty, so by (R) it is empty with respect to every world. So 'Vulcan exists' is false with respect to every world, and 'Vulcan does not exist' is true with respect to every world. Hence, for all worlds, w, according to w, Vulcan does not exist; which is presumably another way of saying that, necessarily, Vulcan does not exist, which in turn arguably amounts to the claim that Vulcan could not have existed. Would not a prudent semanticist do best to hand this dispute to the metaphysicians, and look for a weaker notion of rigidity?[17]

The second reason relates to counterfactuals. Intuitively, 'If Sherlock Holmes had existed, then more London crimes would have been solved' is true, and 'If Sherlock Holmes had existed, then more London crimes would have occurred' is false. If we adopt (R), it would seem that such counterfactuals will have impossible antecedents, for the kinds of reason just considered in connection with 'Vulcan exists', and this makes it hard for a semantics for counterfactuals to discriminate appropriately, counting the intuitively true ones true and the intuitively false ones false.[18]

There are weaker versions of rigidity which allow actually empty referring expressions to count as rigid, and which do not have these

---

[16] This account needs minor modifications to allow for indexical rigid designators, whose referent is a function of context.
[17] Thanks to Roberta Ballerin for this suggestion, though it is not one she herself accepts.
[18] Thanks to Robert Howell for this point.

consequences, but my preference is to defend (R) in the face of these apparent difficulties. The impossibility of Vulcan's existence should be accepted on independent grounds. Nothing in any reasonable philosophy of language, RWR included, precludes the possibility of things having been such that Le Verrier would have properly taken himself to be vindicated; that is an uncontentious statement of the possibility that must be allowed. The dispute relates to permissible further descriptions of such possibilities. RWR says that these are situations in which there is a heavenly body other than Vulcan which has all the properties Le Verrier attributed to Vulcan; the opposition says that in these situations, Vulcan exists. The opposition must wrongly allow that the following question may intelligibly be asked of the hypothetical situation, and that it has an affirmative answer: 'This heavenly body has properties like those Le Verrier supposed Vulcan to have; but is it really *Vulcan*?' The italicized occurrence of 'Vulcan' needs to be interpreted relative to the actual situation; but, actually, 'Vulcan' has no referent. If the question is intelligible, it asks whether something is identical to nothing, and the answer has to be No. Second, it is clear that many different objects could have met every condition that Le Verrier placed on Vulcan. Vulcan cannot be more than one object, but there would be no principled reason to regard one of these Vulcan-like objects rather than any others as the 'real', possible Vulcan.[19]

As for the problematic counterfactuals, I think we need a semantics for counterfactuals which can make sense of differences of truth value among those with impossible antecedents. 'If that man had been your father, he would have saved you' is arguably an example of a truth (as uttered in suitable circumstances, of course), and 'If 4 had been odd it would have been divisible by 2' an example of a falsehood. If it really proves impossible to do justice to such differences, I would have to fall back on something more pragmatic: the intended truth is that if someone like Sherlock Holmes had existed, then more London crimes would have been solved.

The essence of reference is closely connected with, and ultimately explains, the rigidity of referring expressions in the sense of (R), and

---

[19] This view coincides with Kaplan's (1973: 505–7).

this provides support for the principle. We find this essence in Evans's principle (P):

1. (P) If S is an atomic sentence in which the n-place concept-expression R is combined with singular terms $t_1 \ldots t_n$, then S is true iff <the referent of $t_1 \ldots$ the referent of t_n> satisfies R (Evans 1982: 49).

The restriction to atomic sentences looks forward to a point Evans makes later in the book, namely that definite descriptions are not singular terms (singular referring expressions). The principle ought to be neutral on whether there are any semantically complex 'singular terms' and on whether all referring expressions are singular. If there are complex referring expressions, a sentence constructed out of these in the way Evans envisaged will not be atomic in the classical sense; we can just drop the restriction 'atomic' from (P). The plausibility of (P) extends also to plural referring expressions: no doubt 'Russell and Whitehead wrote *Principia*' is true iff <the referent of 'Russell and Whitehead', the referent of '*Principia*'> satisfies 'wrote'. We could simply replace 'singular term' by 'referring expression'.[20]

Are the definite descriptions lying between '<' and '>' themselves referring expressions, or are they to be understood in Russell's way?[21] This is connected with how we should extract possible worlds truth conditions from (P). Evaluating a sentence to which (P) applies with respect to some non-actual world, w, should we count the referent with respect to w of some referring expression, t, as the referent of t with respect to the actual world? Or is there some distinct way of determining the referent with respect to a non-actual world? If the definite descriptions are referring expressions in the metalanguage, and referring expressions are rigid, the same object is involved however we answer, and this is intuitively the right result. If the definite descriptions are treated in a Russellian way, it would be clarifying to insert 'actual' at some point. The Russellian version of (P), making

---

[20] With this replacement, (P) incorporates the definiens of what was earlier called a 'simple' sentence.

[21] In a related discussion, Evans speaks of using 'a metalinguistic definite description ("the referent of 'the author of *Waverley*' ") as a referring expression' (Evans 1982: 53). He also says: 'all uses of definite descriptions in this book, both formal and informal, are intended to be understood according to the [Russellian quantificationalist] proposal I have tentatively put forward' (Evans 1982: 60).

also the small adjustments recommended in the previous paragraph, would read:

2. If S is a sentence in which an n-place concept-expression R is combined with referring expressions $t_1 \ldots t_n$, then S is true iff there is exactly one referent, x_1, of t_1 with respect to the actual world, ... and there is exactly one referent, x_n of t_n with respect to the actual world and $<x_1, \ldots x_n>$ satisfies R.[22]

These metalanguage Russellized definite descriptions are in effect rigidified.

Evans is not explicit about what the falsity conditions of these simple sentences are. One option, the Strawsonian one, is that they are false iff the referring expressions all have a referent and the relevant sequence does not satisfy the predicate. Alternatively, in line with NFL (and with Ockham), falsehood is failure of truth, and I incorporate this in the final reformulation at (3) below.[23]

If the thesis that all referring expressions are rigid is correct, and if suitable metalanguage definite descriptions are used as referring expressions, we can leave Evans' formulation of (P) almost unchanged: the relevant referent is the referent of t with respect to the actual world; if there is such a thing, it will be the very same object as its referent with respect to w. I will adopt the convention that an underlined definite description is to be treated as a referring expression, in which case (P) has its neatest formulation thus:

3. If S is a sentence in which an n-place concept-expression R is combined with referring expressions $t_1 \ldots t_n$, then S is true iff <the referent of t_1 ... the referent of t_n> satisfies R; and is false iff it is not true.

A sequence satisfies a predicate by the predicate being true of its elements, taken in the corresponding order.

An expression is a referring expression if and only if it satisfies principle (P), optimally formulated as (3). Satisfaction of the principle ensures that any referring expression is modally rigid, and explains the source of the rigidity. It remains to ask why this thesis should be accepted.

---

[22] This formulation does not happily do justice to plural referring expressions. The needed modifications are not major: see Chapter 5.

[23] It is not that anything which is not true is false. This sheet of paper is not true; but nor is it false. The restriction is to intelligible sentences, and it is assumed that the quantification over sentences is restricted to these.

There are *ad hoc* reasons relating to examples, like those offered by Kripke. These have generally been found convincing, so I will be brief. Kripke says that when we come to consider whether under certain circumstances it would have been true that Aristotle did not teach Alexander, we need to consider circumstances containing Aristotle, that is, containing the very man Aristotle who is in fact the referent of 'Aristotle' (Kripke 1972/1980: 62). This seems indubitable, and if it holds in general for this name, as indeed it seems to do, suggests that 'Aristotle' is rigid: when we use the name to speak of Aristotle, we intend to say something whose truth or falsehood, actual or counterfactual, depends on how things are with him. Since there was nothing special about this name it points to the general conclusion that all referring names are rigid.

The essential role of a referring expression is given by the fact that, normally, in using it in a simple sentence a speaker represents himself as aiming to introduce an object (or objects—I will bracket the plural case) for the rest of the sentence to say something about. If a speaker is sincere, this means that in normal circumstances (not storytelling, negative existential sentences, etc.) she should believe that any referring expression she uses has a referent, and should intend that how things are with this object be what matters to truth, actual and counterfactual (and with respect to other times). A semantic theory should represent the meanings of expressions in line with the way speakers standardly and literally use them to represent how things are, and so should represent a (unary) simple sentence as requiring for its truth the introduction of a referent, and for the truth or falsity of the sentence, with respect to any possible situation, to turn on how things are with this referent. This is what is reflected by Evans's principle (P), and this is why referring expressions are modally rigid. This kind of rigidity is expressed by (R).

2.6 Notions resembling rigidity

The notions similar to rigidity to be considered in this section are: singular truth condition, direct reference, object-involving truth condition, and *de re* sense.[24]

[24] Temporal rigidity could be included in this list. It is not exactly analogous to modal rigidity: whereas typically sentences make no reference to the actual world, and so express a content whose

A feature similar to rigidity can be characterized by starting with the notion of a *singular T-theorem*. A T-theorem is a truth-theoretic theorem of the form '*s* is true iff *p*'. A singular T-theorem is a theorem of the form 'there is an *x* such that *x* = *t* and "...*t*..." is true iff...*x*...'. (I assume that the object language term '*t*' also belongs to the metalanguage.[25]) On the assumption that 'Aristotle' is rigid, a T-theory formulated in classical logic will contain the following theorem:

> there is an *x* such that *x* = Aristotle and 'Aristotle taught Alexander' is true iff *x* taught Alexander.

This will be derivable from the standard T-theorem

'Aristotle taught Alexander' is true iff Aristotle taught Alexander

by the classical unrestricted rule of existential generalization along with the theorem 'Aristotle = Aristotle'. By contrast, the following cannot be classically derived:

> there is an *x* such that *x* = the greatest philosopher born in Stagira and 'the greatest philosopher born in Stagira taught Alexander' is true iff *x* taught Alexander.

The reasons are that (*a*) on a classical (Russellian) understanding of definite descriptions as other than terms, there will be no premise for existential generalization, and (*b*) on any reasonable logic there will be no theorem corresponding to 'the greatest philosopher born in Stagira = the greatest philosopher born in Stagira'. The result conforms to customary views, according to which a world in which Aristotle never existed but Plato was the greatest philosopher born in Stagira, and he taught Alexander, verifies 'the greatest philosopher born in Stagira taught Alexander'; but it would not do so if the target sentence was correctly described by the singular T-theorem just displayed.

The significance of the derivability of singular T-theorems in classical semantic theory is open to question. They are not T-theorems (that is, theorems of the overall form '*s* is true iff *p*'), and so do not

---

evaluation may differ from world to world, most of our sentences carry temporal reference, and so express a content whose evaluation does not differ from time to time.

[25] An alternative condition is: ∃*x* '*t*' refers to *x* and '...*t*...' is true iff...*x*.... In truth theories set within classical logic, such sentences are provably equivalent to corresponding singular T-theorems.

feature in the standard directions for using a T-theory ('First find a T-theorem which mentions the target sentence...'). From the viewpoint of RWR, they emerge in classical logical truth theories simply as artefacts of the logic, with no special semantic significance.

In RWR, no theorems award singular truth conditions. The usual motivation is at work: such truth conditions cannot be guaranteed by semantic facts alone, for they incorporate non-semantic facts, facts which are not merely facts about meaning, namely that the target expression has a referent. RWR theorists, like most theorists, will regard some singular truth conditions as true; it is just that they are not theorems of semantic theories for natural languages.

The phrase 'direct reference' is designed to voice a supposed contrast with reference mediated by a qualitative description or general term.[26] This distinction is not the same as that between rigid designation and non-rigid designation.[27] While it may be true that the designation of any non-rigid designator is mediated by a qualitative description or general term, the converse is false. Some definite descriptions are rigid ('the even prime'), but presumably are paradigms of expressions whose reference is mediated by a qualitative description or general term. While other examples of apparently rigid non-directly referring expressions (complex demonstratives and certain pronouns) are more controversial, they should not be excluded by any kind of fiat. It may be that expressions like 'that F' or 'you' are rigid yet have their reference mediated by some qualitative description (being F, being the addressee).

An expression could be called 'object involving' if it meets one or more of these conditions:

(i) Different referent, different meaning: to suppose that the expression refers to a different object is to suppose that it has a different meaning.
(ii) No referent, no meaning: to suppose that it refers to no object is to suppose that it has no meaning.

---

[26] Salmon has defined direct-reference theories purely negatively, as ones 'according to which the semantic content of a name or demonstrative is not given by any definite description' (1998: 278). By this criterion, RWR is a species of direct-reference theory. I use 'direct-reference theory' so that the theory entails the positive thesis that the meaning of any directly referential expression is its referent.

[27] As Recanati notes (1993: 11) some authors have failed to do justice to the distinction between rigidity and direct referentiality.

(iii) Guarantees a referent: an utterance containing an object-involving expression, however embedded, entails widest scope existential quantification into the position occupied by the expression.

Whether an expression is object involving according to conditions (i) and (ii) depends upon how things are with different possible utterances of the given expression, or with different possible circumstances for the actual utterance, differing in what object if any is its referent. If the utterance in the possibility has a different referent from the actual one, or has no referent, and counts as having the same meaning as the actual utterance, the expression is not object involving. In rigidity, the relevant possibilities hold the actual utterance and its content fixed, and relate to different possible circumstances at which this content is evaluated for truth. If there is a possible circumstance at which the truth or falsehood depends upon a different object, the expression is not rigid. This makes being rigid appear a rather different phenomenon from being object involving according to (i) or (ii). Condition (iii) is purely logical and does not require considerations of alternative possible utterances or alternative possible worlds (save through the notion of entailment, or for specifically modal embeddings). Direct referentiality, as understood here, seems different again, involving quite diverse considerations: whether reference is or is not mediated by something qualitative or descriptive. These considerations bring out a gap between rigidity and object involvingness, though there are some connections.

Being rigid probably entails (i). Even a non-referring, rigid referring expression, being essentially non-referring (by (R) above), meets the condition that if it were to refer to anything else, that is to anything at all, it would need to have a different meaning (and so would be awarded a different semantic axiom). Being rigid does not entail either (ii) or (iii), and RWR denies that all referring expressions are object involving in these senses. Condition (ii) is close to a view that Russell held about 'logically proper names', and (iii) has been endorsed by McDowell, even for propositional attitude embeddings.

According to RWR, conditions (ii) and (iii) are met by all referring expressions which have a referent. Enthusiasts for (ii) could not coherently regard this weaker claim as false, though no doubt they would think it does not go far enough, since (ii) rules out the possibility of an intelligible, non-referring referring expression. Condition (iii) gets its bite from the embeddings. Russellian definite descriptions with no referent (or denotation) can occur in truths if (for example) they are in the scope of negation, but they do not sustain the existential inference. They are thus rightly ruled not object involving by condition (iii). Intuitively they also count as not object involving by the other conditions also.

McDowell says that *de re* senses are 'contents [which] depend on the existence of the relevant *res*' (1984: 291), and this definition may be interpreted as taking us no further than (i) which, as we saw, is probably entailed by rigidity. In addition, he authorizes the existential inference required by (iii) even for the case of propositional attitude embeddings. It is reasonable to think he would accept that the condition is met for the other embeddings. In particular, it is met for negation if and only if a Strawsonian truth condition for atomic sentences is correct, as McDowell certainly assumes: a subject–predicate sentence is true iff the subject uniquely refers to something and that thing satisfies the predicate and false iff the subject uniquely refers to something and that thing fails to satisfy the predicate. He also writes as if *de re* senses satisfied condition (ii). So we can take it that they are object involving by all three standards. Given that the official definition of *de re* sense takes us no further than (i), McDowell's commitment to (ii) and (iii) constitute distinct theses, not entailed by *de re* sense as such.

3
Proper names

A VIEW OF VULCAN
Where and How This Phenomenon Can Be Seen.
The Preparations of Scientists to Observe It.
This is the day when the inhabitants of a goodly portion of the American Continent are to be favored with the rare pleasure of an unobstructed view of Vulcan.
(The Daily Globe, Boston, July 29, 1878).

3.1 Prima facie considerations in favour of intelligible empty names

The main aim of this chapter is to show how to do justice to intelligible empty names. I consider some reasons for thinking that there cannot be such things, show these reasons to be less than compelling, and go on to develop a theory according to which there can be intelligible empty names; a prime example of reference without referents (RWR). Any account of names must include, or at a minimum, make room for the idea of a name-using practice. 'Aristotle' is used in more than one practice: in one, it refers to the philosopher, in another to the tycoon. The last three sections of this chapter give an account of the origination and continuance of such practices in a way which is consistent with there being distinct practices involving distinct empty names.

Here are some initial reasons for wishing to allow that there are intelligible empty names. There are what appear to be coherent practices of using names independently of whether they have or are known to have bearers. The primary examples are names which are falsely believed to have bearers. These count as primary examples because they are or were used in a way which their users could not distinguish from the uses of names with bearers. There was a difference, but not one known to the users.

We cannot knowingly provide examples of apparently intelligible empty names which we falsely believe to have bearers. There are four other kinds of example:

1. names involved in existence disputes ('Homer', 'Patanjali');
2. names used by some past or present population in the mistaken belief that they were non-empty ('Vulcan', 'Santa Claus');
3. names of things which no longer exist ('Aristotle');
4. fictional names, names which are in fact empty but which all or most users have never seriously supposed to be otherwise.

Working from the bottom of this list, fictional names (4) are not well adapted to promote RWR. First, there is a question whether, as used within works of fiction, they are really names. A name is typically used to purport to refer, but creators of fiction do not use their name-like expressions to purport to refer: rather they use them in pretending to refer. Second, there is a question whether they are really empty. Perhaps they refer to fictional characters. In Chapter 6.3 below, I propose an account of fictional names which treats them both as really names and as really empty; but that is a controversial view which I will not presuppose here.

Concerning category (3), Aristotle no longer exists, so one may infer that 'Aristotle' is now an empty name: there is now nothing to which it refers. These kinds of cases are again not well suited to play the role of uncontroversial cases of empty names. An opponent (for example Salmon 1998) may hold that non-emptiness is not a matter of having a referent which exists now, but of now having a referent; and an object which no longer exists may now be the referent of an expression. Alternatively, one could hold that Aristotle does exist 'tenselessly', and that this tenseless existence is enough to secure 'Aristotle' a referent.

The second category of example (2) is seen by RWR as actually (or at least possibly) involving a single name-using practice: the discovery that the name was empty effects no change in its meaning. From this natural perspective, the examples serve well. Le Verrier and a handful of others used 'Vulcan' for some months in the belief that it had a bearer.[1] Using it, they expressed beliefs and hypotheses, ones which turned out to be false. We use the name in just the same sense when we say that Vulcan does not exist and never did. These are primary examples, though we are no longer party to the relevant false belief. A hostile critic will see things differently, distinguishing on the one hand our current practice of using, for example, 'Vulcan' in historical reports of astronomical errors and in the denial of Vulcan's existence; and, on the other hand, an earlier social phenomenon in which an expression was used as if it was a name when in reality it was not an intelligible expression. The current practice may be assigned a special status: the usage is an 'inverted commas' one, or one in which we momentarily pretend that the earlier phenomenon was one of using a name, as opposed to one of mistakenly thinking a name was being used, or one in which we do not really use a name but only a disguised definite description. On such opposed views, neither practice is one in which an intelligible empty name has anything like a normal use.

This critic faces difficulties. Names like this were used in serious contexts, as in the quotation from the *Boston Globe* at the head of this chapter. Intuitively, we want to say that the *Globe* got the facts wrong, not that it printed strictly unintelligible sentences. We seem to need to use such names to explain the mental states and behaviour of the benighted in terms of their beliefs: 'The children are excited because they believe that Santa Claus will come down the chimney tonight'; 'Le Verrier was excited when he saw Lescarbault's calculations because he thought they confirmed the existence of Vulcan'. The critic says that there are no such beliefs, for no belief is expressed by a use of an empty expression. Yet some beliefs are needed to fill the explanatory gap. It is hardly plausible to think of these as metalinguistic beliefs ('The children are excited because they believe that "Santa Claus" is non-empty and...'). No doubt there will be explanatory beliefs to be had: a child believes that there is a jolly Lapp who drives a sled all the way from the North Pole and will come down the chimney tonight; Le Verrier believed

---

[1] I take liberties with the real facts about the use of 'Vulcan' in the nineteenth century. For a proper account, see Roseveare 1982.

that there was a planet between Mercury and the sun, and that it was spotted by the admirable Dr Lescarbault. Intuitively, however, the children all have the same belief when they believe that Santa Claus will come down the chimney tonight, even though their parents have given them slightly different versions of the Santa Claus story; and Le Verrier and Lescarbault express the same belief when they believe that Vulcan is large, even though they associate 'Vulcan' with somewhat different other properties. The direction taken by our envisaged critic involves all the difficulties involved in seeing non-empty names as expressing descriptive thoughts: the whole point of a name (we may add: empty or non-empty) is to enable communication among those who do not coincide in the information they associate with the expression. Even if we allow that every persistent thing falls under a sortal which determines its persistence conditions, it does not follow, and is not true, that thinking about the thing requires exercising a concept for that sortal (see Chapter 7.2.2). Likewise in the present case: as we will see, there can be rational disagreement concerning the truth value of sentences of the form '*a* is *F*', even when '*a*' is an empty name and '*F*' a predicate which introduces a sortal.

The dialectic of the previous two paragraphs can be replayed with theoretical terms from science. Like Le Verrier's hypothesis about Vulcan, phlogiston theories, popular in the eighteenth century, were subsequently discredited. 'Phlogiston' was supposed to name a weightless[2] and odourless component of all flammable substances, the component released and destroyed by burning. There is no such thing. If there are no intelligible empty names, there was never a phlogiston theory to be refuted; rather, nonsense had to be exposed as such. Becher and Stahl did not express beliefs when they claimed that combustion could be explained in terms of the release of phlogiston, and Lavoisier did not strictly refute these hypotheses: he merely showed that the words did not express hypotheses. This is not a contradictory portrayal, but it is not a helpful one. It is preferable to be able to compare the old claims with the new, to

---

[2] The theory was subsequently refined to explain why phosphorus gained mass when it burned: its phlogiston, lost during burning, had negative mass. I hope this sentence struck you as intelligible; it should not have done so if there are no intelligible empty names.

describe how burning is better explained in terms of oxidization than in terms of loss of phlogiston. If there are no intelligible empty names, there is no phlogiston theory or claim to be unfavourably compared with Lavoisier's theory.

The first category of example (1) remains telling. If there are no intelligible empty names, someone who knew this would need to reinterpret what struck her as doubts about whether or not Homer exists as doubts about whether 'Homer' is intelligible. This means that she should have doubts about whether there is an intelligible hypothesis concerning Homer's existence to be doubted. Reflection on the apparent first-order dispute about Homer's existence will suggest to those with the supposedly correct philosophical opinion that there may be no intelligible first-order dispute at all: if anything intelligible is going on, victory belongs to those who believe in Homer. True doubters should thus withdraw from the first-order dispute, since to remain within it commits them to the dispute's intelligibility and so to Homer's existence. This is not a contradictory view, but it would be preferable to avoid it.

If there are no intelligible empty names, then it is likely that, concealed among name-using practices, there are social phenomena which are hard to distinguish from name-using practices but which in fact are no such thing. A semantic theorist who believes that there are no intelligible empty names must see it as a mistake to give any kind of semantic account of such expressions. If a genuine doubt arises, as perhaps it does for uses of 'Homer', then she must resolve it before continuing the theorizing. From her perspective, her decision to include or exclude a semantic description is to take sides on a debated matter, and presumably it would be irresponsible to do this without any investigation. Again, this is not a contradictory result, but it is one it would be preferable to avoid.

From the perspective of RWR, a genuine name-using practice may relate to a name with no referent. Providing a semantic account involves either finding a matching name within the theorist's vocabulary, or else acquiring the native speakers' name by direct immersion in their practice. A theorist's views about whether the name is empty or not need have no impact on her semantic theorizing.

3.2 Names name

The view that any intelligible name must have a bearer has a long history. We can find discussions of what appears to be this issue in mediaeval philosophy. These words from Anselm might be regarded as a contribution:

Si vero non significat aliquid, non est nomen (F. S. Schmitt (ed.), *Anselmi Opera Omnia*, I, 248.15.22. Quoted by Henry 1984: 3).

(If it does not signify anything, it is not a name.) The subject of the sentence is the word 'nihil', which would not be counted as a name in post-Frege/Russell philosophy: 'nomen' was used more widely in the mediaeval period than 'name' has been used in recent times, and often means no more than 'noun'. On the other hand, the passage does reveal an enduring tendency, which Anselm uses to set up a paradox: the tendency to equate being meaningful or significant with meaning or signifying something, an equation which seems to exclude meaningful names lacking referents. We find a similar equation using the notion of naming: a name is something which names, that is, which names something, so it is contradictory to suppose that there are names which name nothing. We can find this line of thought in Boethius:

Nomen... significat id cuius nomen est.... nomen alicuius nomen esse necesse erit. (Boethius, *Logical Works*, 301C; 408D; quoted in Henry 1984: 2–3)

(A name signifies that of which it is a name.... It will be necessary for a name to be a name of something.) Here the context makes 'gargulus' the sample 'nomen', so the discussion bears more closely on names as these might be understood by one of our contemporaries.

The view that every name has a referent is tempting because it is close to the truth. Names without referents are the exceptions, and for understandable and systematic reasons. Referring expressions in general are supposed to refer, and names are supposed to name. Typically, they are brought into circulation thanks to mechanisms whose proper function is to initiate practices in which names are used to name things. Typically, they are sustained in circulation by the expectation or presupposition that they name things. Typically, indeed, they do name things. Normally (that is, setting aside fiction and some other special cases) if you are interpreting a sentence containing a name, the right thing to do is to assume that it has a referent (and you should try to identify this referent in arriving at your interpretation). Meaning is closely linked with the norms of interpretation. So it is natural to infer that, since the right interpretive move is to find the referent, intelligibility, that is, the possibility of interpretation, requires that there be a referent to be found. The view is an understandable overshoot from the truth about the typical and proper role of names.

Arguments for the view that every name has a referent include:

5. 'Names name' is necessary and analytic.
6. An expression which does not owe its intelligibility to description can but owe it to an object.
7. The function of a referring expression is to introduce an object.
8. Understanding is object related, and so is impossible without an object.

(5) 'Names name', like 'Police police', can be understood as a true generic sentence (perhaps necessarily and analytically true), or as a false universal one. As a true generic, it says something like: names normally or typically name, or are supposed to name, just as 'tigers have four legs' says something like: tigers normally or typically have four legs, or are supposed to have four legs. Read as universal, the tiger sentence says, falsely, that every tiger has four legs, and the other sentence says, falsely according to RWR, that every name names. 'Names name' gives a true account of how things are when all goes well; like 'tigers have four legs', it does not state a universal truth.

(6) The reason that has been explicitly most influential in leading contemporary philosophers to hold that every name must name something is that they wish to avoid 'descriptivism', a species of view, sometimes attributed to Frege, and to Russell's treatment of 'ordinary' proper names, that the meaning of a proper name is to be given by one or more definite descriptions. I agree that descriptivism as an account of the public meaning of names is incorrect, but I disagree that this constitutes a positive reason for holding that every name names. RWR constitutes an intermediate position according to which names do not have a descriptive meaning but also are not guaranteed to name anything.

According to RWR, semantic theory associates every name, *a*, with a condition, expressible as *being a*. The pattern is:

$\forall x$('Hesperus' refers to x iff $x =$ Hesperus).

(The logical framework is NFL, as discussed in Chapter 2.3 above.) Since all referring expressions, and so all names, are rigid, those which have bearers have them essentially (subject to holding their meaning constant): there is no world with respect to which the name, holding its actual meaning constant, has a different referent. The upshot is that non-empty names, in being associated with a condition, are thereby rigidly associated with a referent. It would seem that nothing required by classical object-involving views has been left out.

(7) The function of a referring expression is indeed (according to RWR) to introduce an object. This is connected with the rigidity of such expressions (see Chapter 2.5). Something belonging to a functional kind may fail to have the function definitive of the kind. A pencil is for writing, a heart for pumping blood. A broken pencil is still a pencil, even though it cannot be used to write; a malformed heart is still a heart, even though it cannot pump blood. A referring expression which fails in its function of introducing an object is still a referring expression.

(8) The idea that understanding names is always object related, and so impossible in the absence of an object, is an influential source of the view that there cannot be intelligible empty names. RWR accepts the view for non-empty names, but not for all names. It counters this rival view in part by urging a different picture of understanding, one based on immersion in a name-using practice (see §§3.5–6 below). The result of this immersion will often, indeed typically, be to establish a knowledge-transmitting link between the referent and the user, but this is not always the result. There are also direct reasons for suspicion of the view that understanding names is always object involving.

The analogues of knowing the referent of a name are knowing which things a predicate applies to and knowing which truth value a sentence possesses. Such knowledge goes beyond, and also falls short of, what understanding requires. A special case would be needed for making the strong requirement for names, treating them differently from other expressions. The customary view is that understanding a sentence involves knowing what it would be for it to be true, and understanding a predicate involves knowing what it would be for something to satisfy it. I do not challenge this view (it requires only explanation and elaboration rather than rejection); extending it to names delivers RWR: understanding a name involves knowing what it would be for something to be its bearer.

Some fear that if names are not in general object involving, our capacity to think 'directly' about the world is compromised. Perhaps the fear is that we would be forced to see names as putting us in contact not with their referents, but instead with some kind of intermediary, a kind of thing which may or may not have a referent. Within RWR, there is nothing which may or may not have a referent. Holding meaning constant, a referring expression which lacks a referent does so essentially; a referring expression which has a referent has it essentially. There are no intermediaries. The object-involving thoughts expressible by non-empty names are as direct as on direct-reference views. For the cases in which direct-reference theories say that understanding is possible only if there is an object, RWR agrees (though it denies that in these cases understanding is possible only because there is an object). The difference between the accounts is that for direct-reference theorists, but not for RWR, it follows from the fact that something is a name that it has a referent, an object to which the understander is linked in understanding the expression. For direct-reference theorists, but not for RWR, the category of referring expressions which have a referent has special semantic significance. By contrast, RWR allows that we can identify an expression as a referring expression, more particularly as a name, by its role in sentences; direct-reference theorists cannot allow this. Unless there are powerful contrary arguments, RWR is to be preferred.[3]

3.3 Evans and Russellian names

Russell himself said, as we have seen:

a name has got to name something or it is not a name (Russell 1918–19: 243).

This says that, necessarily, anything which is a name names something. Evans does not accept this Russellian position, for he thinks that

---

[3] Direct arguments for the view that every name must have a referent have been rare. Possibly the most detailed and careful were offered by Evans (1982). Some of these are briefly discussed below. They are considered in more detail by Sainsbury (2002: 159–80).

in addition to Russellian names, natural language does or may contain descriptive names which may name nothing (Evans 1982: 47–8; however see also 70). Does Evans's view coincide with RWR? In his view, there are the Russellian names which have to have a bearer; these are like the non-empty names in RWR, whose rigidity ensures that some reasonable interpretation of this necessity obtains: they refer to their actual referent with respect to every world in which it exists. In addition, in his view, there are the descriptive names, ones which may lack a bearer. Are not these like the empty names in RWR?

This thought is wrong on two counts. First, RWR has no room for Evans's descriptive names: the non-referring names it recognizes have non-descriptive reference conditions, just as non-empty names do. Second, the thought fails to do justice to a distinction between RWR and Evans's view which can only be expressed in terms of the notion of a semantic category.

Some facts about the use of language divide the expressions it contains into semantic categories; we may call these the natural semantic categories. Expressions in one natural semantic category have a variety of features in common, not shared by expressions outside the category. In a semantic theory, semantic categories will be determined by the kinds of semantic axiom; call these the theoretical semantic categories. A good theory's theoretical categories will match the natural categories of the language for which it is a theory. In RWR, there is a category of referring expressions: these are the expressions accorded axioms which determine a referent upon a condition. (The category may subdivide in various ways, for example, into the semantically simple and semantically complex.) Evans and RWR agree that there are rigidly referring non-empty singular terms: these have a referent and could not but have it (holding their meaning constant). What separates the approaches is whether these expressions merit a distinctive category in semantic theory. Evans says that they do, RWR says that they do not, the closest relevant significant grouping being that of the rigidly referring singular terms, which may include empty singular terms. Evans expresses his opposed view in terms of categories:

a term is a Russellian singular term if and only if it is a member of a category of singular terms such that nothing is said by someone who utters a sentence containing such a term unless the term has a referent... (Evans 1982: 71).

For RWR, there is such a category in some loose sense of 'category': it is the category of non-empty referring expressions. This category is not a theoretical semantic category in RWR, that is, there is no kind of semantic axiom applied to all and only such expressions; so RWR, in contrast to Evans, is committed to the view that there is no such natural semantic category. How should we choose between these views?

Both parties can agree that there are cases in which names, or seeming names, are used and there is no content but only an illusion of content. One who adopted Evans's approach and one who adopted RWR could agree that an example would be someone who wrongly supposed that a dummy name used in a philosophical example or a logic exercise, say 'Jack', was a real name. The question 'Who is Jack?' would have no answer; we could express this by saying that no real question was asked. Disagreement would focus on cases like 'Vulcan', in which there is what seems just like a genuine name-using practice but no referent. RWR can count such cases as ones in which there really is a genuine name, genuine communication, and understanding. Evans could in theory say of particular cases of this kind that they are examples of successful descriptive names rather than failed Russellian names. This would be to treat them as belonging to a natural semantic category, but one disjoint from the category of names. He declines to take that route in general, since he is vividly aware that even in such cases it may be that no information has the kind of privileged position required for the name to count as descriptive. Evans must allow that something could be to all appearances a name-using practice, yet not in fact be such a practice; from the point of view of natural semantic categories, Evans must claim that this is the correct classification and that a genuine name-using practice must involve a referent. This is the main contrast with RWR.

Evans's view might be persuasive if it led to benefits elsewhere. Both he and McDowell believe that their view alone does justice to a correct philosophy of mind. Yet *de re* senses (senses which could not exist if their referents did not) and object-involving thoughts (thoughts which could not exist if certain objects to which they relate did not) are available on RWR, a view which gives a much more natural description of semantic categories.

Another difference between RWR and Evans's position relates to understanding. According to Evans, a full understanding of a proper name enables one to think of the referent (Evans 1982: 400) where this in turn requires the subject to possess 'a capacity to distinguish the object of his judgement from all other things' (1982: 89). He outlines and rejects a rival position, which is in fact the one adopted here:

the suggestion is that... the use of a proper name... [is] an autonomous way of satisfying the requirement that one have discriminating knowledge of the objects of one's thoughts (Evans 1982: 403).

When we come to master the use of a name with a bearer, we thereby come to know (I hold) who or what the bearer is, and more generally we satisfy any reasonable demand for discriminating knowledge of the bearer. This is defended in more detail in §3.6 below.

3.4 Alternatives to RWR

There are three ways to treat the appearance of intelligible empty names as illusory:

(i) The candidate names are intelligible but are not really empty: they refer to fictional characters, or to non-existent things, or to existent but non-actual things.
(ii) The candidate names are not really intelligible.
(iii) The candidate names are indeed intelligible and empty but are not really names.

I will not consider the first approach, on grounds of the ontological conservatism sketched in Chapter 2.4. (Fictional names are discussed in Chapter 6.) The second approach is preferred by direct-reference theorists and by neo-Fregeans like McDowell. I do not aim to refute this approach, but only to show that there is no need for it (even by the standards of its adherents).[4] The third approach is Quine's

---

[4] Most attacks on direct-reference theories are not fully persuasive. They consist either in undermining its motivations, or in pointing out that it has implausible consequences. I agree that the proffered motivations are unsatisfactory (often consisting in nothing more than a recoil from descriptivism) and that the consequences are implausible; but I do not regard either point as constituting a refutation. Bealer (2004) has raised the level of the debate by arguing that direct-reference theories have contradictory consequences.

'elimination of singular terms', which shares two significant features with RWR. First, Quine allows the intelligibility of predicative expressions formed by prefixing an empty name by a sign for identity, for example 'is Vulcan'. Allowing this is crucial to the axioms envisaged by RWR within its free logical setting:

$\forall x$('Vulcan' refers to x iff $x =$ Vulcan).

Secondly, the effect of Quine's elimination is to make the same judgements of truth value as those made by NFL. For Quine, 'Vulcan is more than 1000 miles in diameter' becomes 'Something Vulcanizes and is more than 1000 miles in diameter'. The latter is false, so the former is interpreted as false also, just as in NFL. Quine summarizes his position on this point thus:

Any existence claim that is felt to inhere in the meaning of singular terms is well eliminated (1960: 182).

These similarities aside, there is all the difference in the world between RWR and Quine's elimination. RWR attempts to describe the semantics of natural language as it is. Quine aims to reform natural language to bring it in to line with certain supposed desiderata. The aims are totally orthogonal, and elimination is not a serious candidate for a theory which attempts to describe how singular terms function in unreformed natural language.

If it is accepted that there really are intelligible empty names, there is, other than RWR, only one serious alternative approach: some form of description theory. The world will probably be no better a place for yet another attack on description theories (readers in full agreement may move directly to §3.5 below; Kripke's position was rehearsed in Chapter 1.5). Here I offer two versions of description theories which are rather more explicit than some familiar targets.

One description theory says this:

9a. For all names, n, there is a description, d, such that for all utterers, U, all sentences, s containing n, all occasions, o:

if U produces a declarative utterance of s on o, he is best reported as having said that p, where s' says that p and results from s by replacing every occurrence of n by d.

According to (9a), a speaker who declaratively utters 'London is beautiful' is not best reported as having said that London is beautiful, but rather as having said that, perhaps, the capital of the UK is beautiful. Part of the idea behind (9a) could be put in Russell's words:

the thought in the mind of a person using a proper name correctly can generally only be expressed explicitly if we replace the proper name by a description (Russell 1912: 29).

Russell had a special reason for thinking that if we report one who utters 'London is beautiful' as having said that London is beautiful, our report is not fully 'explicit'. He thought that understanding a name required acquaintance with its bearer, but that no one is acquainted with London (it is not a sense datum). Hence using the word 'London' requires some mental act other than directly 'thinking of' London, for direct access, were it possible, would be acquaintance. Hence an explicit expression of the mental act involves citing the definite description which made the thought possible. On the other hand, Russell explicitly denies the structure of (9a), which makes the relevant description common across speakers and occasions:

the description required to express the thought will vary for different people, or for the same person at different times (Russell 1912: 29).

Russell's position is not obviously false, and is consistent with RWR: it may well be that there is a useful way of describing the mental states of users of names by replacing the names by descriptions. These replacing descriptions have no claim to identify the public meaning of a name. On the contrary, as Russell saw, public meaning needs to bracket the idiosyncratic descriptive associations, which are the proper study of individual psychology but not of semantics. Part of the point of using names is that people can share an understanding of them without sharing much (perhaps any) information concerning their bearers. If description theories are tempting, it may be because the distinction between what is required of semantics and what is required of psychology is not always enforced.

One way to modify (9a) is to revise the envisaged link. Instead of basing it on the demands of speech reports, let us base it on the idea of the knowledge which (perhaps implicitly) guides speakers in their use of names for things. In addition, in order to allow for some individual variation among speakers, let us think of the relevant descriptions in a disjunctive way. An inspiration of this kind comes from Frank Jackson. He considers a familiar kind of criticism of description theories which proceeds by considering sample name–description pairs, and describing possible situations in which the referent of the name diverges from that of the description. He continues:

if speakers can say what refers to what when various possible worlds are described to them, description theorists can identify the property associated in their minds with, for example, the word 'water': it is the disjunction of the properties that guide the speakers in each particular possible world when they say which stuff, if any, in each world counts as water (Jackson 1998: 212).

The argument seems to go like this: we are in fact quite good at saying which object in a described possible world would be the referent of some term we understand. In other words, we are good at picking out the referent of a term by description. These descriptions, Jackson suggests, are what guide our application of the term.

This line of thought faces a familiar dilemma: different speakers will be guided by different properties, so the guiding properties do not constitute a public sense. The disjunction of all the properties has a claim to be public, but it is not what guides. Each horn in turn is grasped by the following two attempts to sharpen Jackson's idea:

9b. For all names, n, there is a set Σ of descriptions, $d_1 \ldots d_n$, such that for all utterers, U, all sentences s containing n, all occasions, o:

if U produces or understands a declarative utterance of s on o, for some member d_i of Σ his knowledge of what n refers to is based on his (explicit or implicit) knowledge that it coincides with the referent of d_i.

9c. For all names, n, there is a set Σ of descriptions, $d_1 \ldots d_n$, such that for all utterers, U, all sentences s containing n, all occasions, o:

if U produces or understands a declarative utterance of s on o, his knowledge of what n refers to is based on his (explicit or implicit) knowledge that it coincides with the referent of the disjunction of the members of Σ.

(9b) makes no claim that the same descriptions or disjunction of descriptions guide each user, so it could not attain anything public enough to constitute a public meaning. (9c) requires all speakers mentally to confront a set of descriptions whose members exhaust the ways of being guided to the referent. It is very implausible that this confrontation could consist in awareness of each member of the disjunction, so one would await some alternative account.

Setting the familiar dilemma aside, it seems that Jackson overestimates the extent to which speakers can, on the basis of qualitative descriptions of possibilities, determine which individuals are in the possibilities. There is some plausibility in his claim as applied to 'water': possibly some of us are (if we are not already in the thrall of externalism) ready to agree that if a world contains a transparent liquid that falls from the sky, etc., then it contains water. There is no plausibility in the claim as applied to ordinary proper names and their bearers. A world containing no prover of the incompleteness of arithmetic may or may not be a world containing Gödel; a world containing such a prover may or may not contain Gödel. Someone other than Gödel might have possessed all the properties commonly attributed to him, and Gödel might have lacked most of the properties commonly attributed to him.

As Schiffer has said (2003: 144), a view like Jackson's presupposes the kind of distinction that Russell made between knowledge by acquaintance and knowledge by description. Jackson must allow that some things, for example the properties which do the guiding and the places a thinker refers to as 'here', can be identified directly, without the need for descriptive guidance. Failing this, nothing could come before the mind except by means of some other things which figured in a guiding description, and we would have begun a regress. Russell had a clear motivation for making an ontological distinction between the things with which we could be acquainted and the things we could know only by description: the former but not the latter are demon-proof. It seems unlikely that anyone nowadays would wish to share this motivation; it is unclear where one is to look for an alternative one.

We should not uncritically accept the claim that descriptions genuinely operative within a thinker's psychology guide the application of names. One may come to think of Jack as Jack by recognizing him as Jack by sight. Following a line of thought in McDowell (1977), while there is some explanation of what is going on that makes no mention of a Jack-thought, it is unlikely that this is a complete explanation, or one normally available (even implicitly) to the thinker. Any description the thinker could attain would be true of many people she can easily distinguish from Jack, so such descriptions are not what guide her to the referent of 'Jack'. The property of looking just like Jack may serve as such a guide on a specific occasion, but is not Jack-free: one must think of Jack to think of this property.

There are many cases in which people think of individual objects without any description denoting these objects being available. Evans mentioned someone who attends to a brick in a wall. It is too far from the edges to be identified as the brick in such-and-such a row, such-and-such a column (the perceiver loses count whenever she tries to attain such a description); and a description on the lines of 'the brick which is causing such-and-such a feature of my current visual experience in such-and-such a non-deviant way' seems altogether too sophisticated to be what guides normal (and especially very young) attenders to bricks (cf Schiffer 2003: 147–8). Even sophisticated philosophers do not know how to fill the blanks marked by 'such-and-such' or 'non-deviant'.

Strictly speaking, Jackson's account, at least as I have presented it, is consistent with RWR, for it says nothing about public meanings, regarded as governed in the first instance by the demands of reporting speech. Version (9c), as opposed to (9b), could readily be extended to make such a claim: the public meaning of a name would be identified with the meaning of the corresponding disjunction Σ. By the standards adopted here, the result would be absurd: one who utters the words 'Gödel was a genius' does not thereby say that the satisfier of Σ was a genius. It might be that people are guided descriptively to the referents of names, yet these descriptive guides do not enter into the semantics of names. There certainly are descriptive facts about how expressions have the referents they have, facts involving baptisms and transmissions (see §3.5 and §3.6 below), but there is no reason to think that these are encoded in an accessible way in the psychology of speakers, and so no reason to think that these play the role of guides.

Description theories are usually attacked along the following lines. For any name–description pair, $<$'a', 'the F'$>$, we can imagine a situation in which competent speakers without irrationality doubt something they express as '*a* is the *F*'. If 'the *F*' was implicated in the semantics of '*a*', understanding the name would involve appreciating that its referent satisfies 'the *F*'. If rational understanders of the name can sensibly doubt what they express by '*a* is the *F*' then they do not know that the truth of this sentence is guaranteed by the semantics. If they do not know this, it is not so, for semantics records just what speakers know in virtue of understanding.

Before checking that the argument is no worse when applied to empty names, it requires nuance. It appears to rely on the following principle:

> If '*a*' and '*b*' have the same sense, then a rational thinker cannot doubt something she could express as '*a* = *b*'.

Do not Paderewski cases show that this principle is false? Supposedly, a competent speaker can without irrationality doubt something she would express as 'Paderewski is Paderewski', even though both occurrences of 'Paderewski' have the same sense. If this is right, the kind of examples the anti-descriptivist argument envisaged do not establish the falsity of description theories of names.

It is one thing to claim that a competent speaker might rationally doubt whether a sentence (say 'Paderewski is Paderewski') is true; another to claim that, concerning what the sentence expresses (in his mouth), such a speaker might rationally doubt it. On one presentation of Paderewski cases, a rational person could both fully understand 'Paderewski' yet fail to appreciate that the two learning experiences were initiations into the same name-using practice. This speaker can rationally doubt whether the sentence 'Paderewski is Paderewski' is true, associating the first occurrence of the name with a musician and the second with a politician. It does not follow that the speaker can doubt what this expresses. Since the speaker has, by hypothesis, achieved a complete understanding of the name, the sentence in his mouth expresses just what it expresses in ours. What it expresses in ours is the most trivial kind of self-identity, something that cannot be rationally doubted. Thus understood, we do not have a case in which what is stated by the relevant kind of identity sentence (one whose referring expressions have the same sense) can rationally be doubted.

Another account of Paderewski cases treats the deluded speaker as using the identity sentence in some non-standard way, on which the two occurrences of the name differ in sense. Then perhaps it could be rational, concerning what the sentence says, for the speaker to doubt it. Then we do not have an example of the kind supposed to undermine the argument against descriptivism: the displayed principle gets no grip.

The standard pattern of anti-descriptivist argument seems to rely on the possibility of new information flowing from the referent, or on the referent being accessed from different perspectives. This might encourage the thought that these arguments do not happily extend to empty names. What is wrong with the description 'the intra-Mercurial planet' as an account of the semantics of 'Vulcan', or 'the sledge-driving Lapp who brings children presents at Christmas' as an account of the semantics of 'Santa Claus'?

As it happened, the original form of the hypothesis about Vulcan (according to which a single planet was responsible for the whole anomaly in Mercury's orbit) was quickly shown to be incorrect. At Le Verrier's request, Galle looked through his superior German optics at the part of the sky where Vulcan should have been and did not see it. But things could have happened otherwise. Suppose that, before this crucial disconfirmation had occurred, some anti-intellectual turbulence hit Europe, so that scientific research was brought to a standstill, and there was a rapid decline into superstition and darkness. Le Verrier's supposed 'discovery of Vulcan' was never tested, but news of it reached the popular press, and Vulcan-stories abounded. Astrologists claimed that those born when Vulcan was in the ascendant would have the ability to resist mercury poisoning, and naturepaths claimed that a pinch of dust from Vulcan, taken with a small glass of Irish bog water, would protect against syphilis. In time, the way the name was introduced was forgotten, and some rational people, fully understanding the name, came to doubt whether Vulcan lay between Mercury and the sun. Even in the case of an empty name, the originally associated description (or, more generally, information) may cease to be associated with the name, without our having good reason to say that a new name has been introduced, or the meaning of the original name perverted. The constancy of meaning is shown by the fact that, as Europe emerged from these imagined new dark ages into a new enlightenment, historians could properly tell the tale as I have told it: Vulcan was originally supposed to be a planet between Mercury and the sun which affected Mercury's orbit in a specific way, but in the dark ages this was forgotten and it was believed to have all kinds of absurd properties. Finally, the new enlightenment would reveal that there was no such planet as Vulcan. The story makes use (not merely mention) of the name 'Vulcan', and makes plain that there is supposed to be a single unequivocal subject.

Arguments of this kind are not, as such, decisive. They at most show that some selected definite description is not associated with the name in the right kind of way. There certainly are definite descriptions which are constant and which do not vary from speaker to speaker. Whether for a non-empty or an empty name, one could use the pattern exemplified by 'the object (if any) to which "Vulcan" refers', or 'the object (if any) upon which the name "Vulcan" was bestowed when the practice of using this name was initiated'. All theorists who agree that there is a non-trivial answer to questions of the form 'to what does NN refer?' will agree that a correct answer can be couched as a definite description. This leaves unsettled the question whether these constant definite descriptions count as 'associated' with the name in the way envisaged by whatever description theory is under discussion.

From the point of view of RWR, what matters is the public meaning of names. This is what the semantic axioms for them are supposed to capture, axioms whose correctness is to be judged by their delivery of correct speech reports. The usual anti-descriptivist considerations can be worked into a dilemma: either the proffered descriptions are inconstant, either across time or across speakers, in which case for that reason alone they do not do justice to the constant and interpersonal public meaning; or they are constant, in which case they will typically be metalinguistic, and will be too sophisticated to be plausible candidates for what a good reporter should use in place of her subject's names. The constant descriptions are not well fitted to meet the test of association, interpreted in terms of how speech is best reported, and the descriptions which do not obviously fail this test of association are not constant. The dilemma is as acute for empty as for non-empty names.

3.5 Baptism

Kripke suggested that the use of a name propagates outwards from an initial 'baptism', in which the name is bestowed on an object. A use of a name counts as referring to an object just if that object was baptised in the baptism from which the current use derives. Many theorists have been attracted by one or another version of this picture. RWR aims to develop Kripke's idea in a direction of which he might well not have approved: the notion of a baptism is extended to include cases in which no object is baptised. These will be the kinds of baptism involved in empty name-using practices. It is also extended to include unwitting baptisms: events which originate a new name-using practice, even though the agent of the event had no such intention.

A baptism has at most one referent. Each name-using practice involves exactly one baptism; baptisms metaphysically individuate practices, and thus fix the referent, if any, of a practice, though when we wish to know to which practice a given use of a name belongs, or what the referent of a practice is, it is rare that we can reach an answer by first identifying the baptism. Normally our evidence is associated information, even though this is evidence only, and does not make a practice the practice it is.

In a religious baptism, a priest openly and publicly bestows a name upon a child identifiable by the congregation. There is an object of the priest's baptismal intentions, and this object is normally the referent of the name introduced in the ceremony. When all goes well, the object-related intention ties world and baptism perfectly. But things are not always perfect.

An object-related intention (I stipulate) is a mental state properly described along these lines: there is an object x such that the subject intends that... x.... On some views, a deeper characterization of such states is that an object is 'directly present' to the subject in a way involving no representation. On other views, it is somewhat misleading to speak of object-related intentions, for a subject's intentions can relate to an object only by representing that object; it would be better to speak of an object-related ascription of intention, characterized as one in which the ascription relates an intention to an object but gives no information about how the subject represents the object.

I have no need to choose between these views. I assume that for an object to meet the relevant condition it must have played a suitable causal role in the origin of the object-related mental state.

A descriptive intention is one describable along the lines: the subject intends that... the F.... Typically, when an object is intentionally acted upon, there are descriptive as well as object-related intentions: the cup is such that I intend to pick it up (object-related) and I intend to pick up the cup (descriptive). However, these kinds of intentions can come apart: it might be that Jack is who I intend to greet, and my wave is also animated by my intention to greet the person who lives next door, yet Jack is not the person who lives next door; in brief, I greet Jack, mistaking him for my next door neighbour.

Suppose the priest is to baptise the twins Jack and Jill. The children's mother, before the ceremony, explains that she will hold Jack on her left and Jill on her right. The priest is long of years and short of memory, and in any case not strong on the left/right distinction. Sprinkling water on Jack's head the priest says 'In the name of the Lord, I baptise thee "Jill" '; sprinkling water on Jill's head he says 'In the name of the Lord, I baptise thee "Jack" '. The priest's intentions here are mixed: he intends to baptise *the boy* 'Jack'; he intends to baptise *the child on the mother's left* 'Jack'; *that girl child*, the one on whom he is now sprinkling water, is such that he intends to baptise *her* 'Jack'. Unbeknownst to him, these intentions cannot all be realized. Very likely it would be taken that, although the ceremony contained a mistake, Jack ended up baptised 'Jack' and Jill 'Jill'. The object-related intentions (Jill was such that the priest intended to baptise her 'Jack') would in this case probably be trumped by descriptive intentions. The explanation may be that the descriptive intentions mattered more to the priest (and to everyone else concerned).[5]

Here is another case in which object-related intentions would not be decisive. You are asked to cut the cord in a dockyard naming ceremony. This will allow a bottle of Krug to smash wastefully against the bows of the newly commissioned yacht. There are two new yachts in the dock, and you assume that you are due to name the red one. You hardly notice the blue one. You cut the cord and say

---

[5] Roberta Ballerin suggests that descriptions might not dominate if the children were of the same gender.

'I name this good ship Spraydotcom and may she bring fair winds and good fortune to all who sail in her.' To your surprise, the bottle of Krug does not smash against the red yacht, but against the blue one you had barely noticed. The red yacht was such that you intended to name it 'Spraydotcom', but there is no doubt that you in fact conferred this name on the blue yacht. The cord (along with your descriptive intention to name whatever yacht the cord is linked to) affords a firmer connection to reality than your red-yacht-related intentions. The explanation may be, once again, that the descriptive intentions mattered more to you (and to everyone else concerned).

Object-related intentions in some cases trump descriptive intentions. The priest may believe he is baptising his illegitimate daughter, and so perform the ceremony with special reverence intending to baptise her 'Jill'. He has an illegitimate daughter, but the child at the font is not her. Concerning the child at the font, he intends to baptise her 'Jill'. This is the upshot of the ceremony, even though it does not satisfy the most salient of the priest's descriptive intentions, to baptise his own daughter. In a sense, the object-related intentions mattered more to the priest: had he become aware of all the facts, he would have acted just as he actually acted in all respects relevant to conferring a name (his emotions might have differed). What matters most is often a merely conventional matter, not involving any deep principles. There may be cases in which it is not clear what to say about who or what, if anything, has been named.

What makes a baptism successful? One kind of success, successful object-introduction, is the baptising of an object in accordance with the baptiser's intentions. Another kind of success, successful practice origination, is the bringing into existence of a name-using practice. The first kind of success may be achieved without the second: an object may be baptised, but this have no impact; the name is never used again (for that object). The second kind of success may be achieved without the first: an empty name-using practice may be originated; this is a name-using practice whose baptism did not involve an object being baptised in accordance with the baptiser's intentions.

Object-introducing success does not require object-related intentions. Mathematical objects like π are examples, if they are both nameable and causally inert. It is said that some children are named before they are conceived. Assuming there is no backwards causation, the relevant intentions cannot be object-related.

Practice-originating success is a matter of what happens later. If a baptism is going to 'catch on', then it already has the practice-originating success property, whether or not anyone is in a position to know this.

Will a baptism which is successfully object-introducing, but in which object-related intentions are absent, or are trumped by descriptive intentions, inevitably introduce a name which is 'descriptive' in the sense of Evans? Such names would be 'one criterion' names, to which some description involved in the baptism is essential. There are at least two kinds of case. In one, nothing satisfies the description; can the name be used nonetheless? In another, something does satisfy the description; can speakers intelligibly use the name to express the belief that the object does not satisfy it, or might not have satisfied it?

For the first case, imagine that George and Mary agree

10. If our first is a girl, we'll call her Jill.

'Our first' is mutually understood to refer to something iff it is a child arising from the fusion of genetic material from the two speakers. Suppose that Mary's first child is a girl arising from an egg fertilized by someone other than George, though all parties believe George and Mary to be the biological parents. Intuitively, this regrettable divergence from the norm makes no difference to whether or not the original agreement, recorded in (10), constituted the introduction of the name 'Jill' for Mary's firstborn. It seems that it may make no difference whether or not the crucial description is satisfied.

Names introduced in the absence of object-related intentions do not behave in the way that Evans stipulated descriptive names behave. Suppose George and Mary succeed in naming Jill before conception by means of an agreement like (10), where Jill does indeed satisfy the description. Aware of Mary's generous heart, George may without irrationality come to worry whether Jill is really his child; that is, he may worry whether she satisfies the description whereby her name was introduced. If she is George and Mary's child, then no doubt she could not have been anyone else's, but that is part of her essence however she is described; the baptismal description has nothing to do with it. Even if 'Sealegs' is bestowed in advance on the first dog to be born on Spraydotcom, his being born thus is not essential to Sealegs, and we can without irrationality doubt whether Sealegs was in fact born on Spraydotcom, or born at sea at all.

There are empty baptisms: a name is introduced in the belief that it names an object when in fact there is no object. (Those who find 'empty baptism' self-contradictory are invited to see 'baptism' as an abbreviation for 'baptism*', a neologism true of baptisms and of attempted baptisms.) Le Verrier introduced 'Vulcan' falsely believing he had discovered a new planet. Perhaps the names of the Greek gods were also introduced with serious intent but false belief. What makes it the case that such names are empty? We have seen that the fact that no object satisfies the description in a descriptive intention is not enough. Here is a hypothesis: a name is empty if the baptiser has no object-related intentions (there is no object x such that the baptiser intends that ...x...) and no object satisfies the descriptive intentions. This delivers the right result for Le Verrier's 'Vulcan' and for normal baptisms of the Greek gods. We may test it against the following tricky case.[6] Astonished by the thunder, Manolis attributes it to a god. As he comes to bestow a name on this god, Manolis sees the hoary figure of Christopheros on the next hillside. Mistaking this figure for the god, the Greek proceeds to introduce the name 'Thor' with both descriptive and object-related intentions. He intends to bestow the name on the divine source of thunder, and Christopheros is the object of the object-related intentions. Did Manolis name Christopheros 'Thor' and falsely believe that he was the divine source of thunder? Or did Manolis name nothing (for there is no divine source of thunder) and mistakenly believe that Christopheros was Thor? There may be no definitive answer, but I incline to the latter view. The explanation may again be that in this case the descriptive intentions mattered more to Manolis.

If this is the right way to describe the case, it is consistent with the hypothesis, but shows that we cannot replace 'if' by 'iff'. To get a criterion we might refine it to:

11. A name is empty iff either the baptiser has no object-related intentions and no object satisfies the descriptive intentions; or

---

[6] Mentioned by Almog (2004: 406); he attributes the example to Michael Thau.

the baptiser does have object-related intentions but regards them as mattering less than the descriptive intentions, and nothing satisfies the description.

The account is oversimplified, for there may be and typically are many descriptive intentions. If the ones which matter most are not satisfied, then typically nothing is baptised. It can be vague which matter most (vague how far down the list of intentions we have to go) and so it can be vague whether an introduced name is empty or not.

Suppose Manolis introduced 'Thor' intending it to name the god of thunder. There is no such god, so it names nothing. Can a rational user of the name who falsely believes that Thor exists question whether Thor produces thunder? If 'Thor' is like other names, the answer should be yes. Names are used to store bundles of information, and any information comprising a smallish proportion of the whole can be subtracted from the bundle. We can imagine the myth developing on the following lines. Thor has a brother who greatly dislikes publicity and so keeps his achievements to himself. One of the things he does is produce thunder, but Thor takes all the credit. So it was understandable that people used to believe (as many still do) that Thor makes thunder, even though he does not.

Inadvertent baptism is common, for example with nicknames: a parent calls a spindly child a beanpole, using the word as a common noun and with no intention to originate a practice, but it sticks as a nickname and for years is used as a proper name of the child.

3.6 Transmission

Proper names help us store, sort and label information. The storing and sorting have a social dimension: memories are pooled over the whole. Proper names can be used to transmit knowledge. Belonging to a practice of using a name NN, and so interpreting uses of the name by others, can help one attain NN-related knowledge. This places a constraint on the transmission relation.

A baptism is an event in which a name is bestowed and which originates a practice (in the limiting case, it is the only use in the practice). Some but not all subsequent events which are uses of a name are related to the baptism, and to each other, by a relation which ensures that they belong to the same practice, the *same-practice* relation. It is natural to think of this relation as generated by narrower ones. We need the idea of initiation into a practice: an earlier use, U, belongs to the practice (initially, by being its baptism) and a later use, the first use by a new user of that name in that practice, belongs to it in virtue of being related to U by the *initiation relation*. We also need the idea of the *continuing-participation* relation: some uses belong to the same practice as an earlier use by the same user. A practice can be thought of as a set of uses with a baptism, B, and containing all the uses initiated by B and by any member of the B-practice, and all the uses standing in the continuing-participation relation to any use in the practice. Intuitively, a baptism introduces a name, and all other uses in the practice are either ones in which a neophyte uses the name for the first time, or ones in which an existing member of the practice engages in a further act of participation. A use, in all these cases, can be either a production of the name or an understanding of a production.

Ideas of this kind derive from Kripke (1972/1980), but the present account involves two differences. First, Kripke does not allow empty baptisms. Yet the referent need play no role in a specification of a name-using practice. The reason is illustrated in the following diagram:

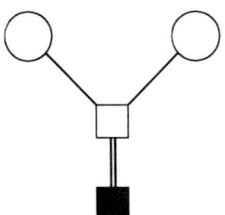

Here the filled square corresponds to the baptised object and the open square to a baptism of it. The open circles represent subsequent uses of the name. The double line from the baptism to the object represents the bestowal relation in that direction; taken in the other direction it is typically some kind of causal relation. The single lines in the upward direction represent the initiation relation: the two circles are uses whereby new users are initiated into the practice thanks to some interaction with the baptism (the square). The diagram shows that the baptised object is causally masked off by the baptism. We need make no mention of it in order to give an account of the propagation of the practice.

A point of difference from Kripke's picture is that nothing has yet been said to connect practice and referent. For all that has been said, a practice might have no referent, more than one, might change referent over time, or might change from empty to non-empty or conversely. For Kripke, by contrast, each practice has just one referent, and this is built into the very idea of a practice. (This is connected with his not allowing empty baptisms.)

The position I propose on behalf of RWR is this: a name-using practice essentially retains its baptism's referent: uses in the practice refer to the unique baptised object, or to nothing if the baptism is empty. This means that the same-practice relation between uses ensures that no uses in a single practice differ in their referent. One consequence is that it is necessary to reject Evans's opinion, supported both by example and by theory, that a name-using practice can undergo a change in referent. This issue will be postponed until we have a clearer idea of the initiation and continuing-participation relations.

3.6.1 Initiation

Typically, a new user enters a practice by resolving to use 'NN' in line with its use in the mouth of another, whose use in fact belongs to the practice. On my first day studying philosophy, I hear the name 'Strawson'. As a diligent student, I resolve to use it in the way it is used by those on whose lips I hear it. I take it that they know of whom they speak in using 'Strawson'; this knowledge is implicitly relative to a name-using practice, for I am aware that the telephone book, even just the Oxford telephone book, would have many listings for 'Strawson'. The existing user, the old hand, must be an unconfused member of the practice. A new user's resolution to use the name 'in the way it is used' by the existing users involves an intention which could be expressed thus:

12. For all x, if the uses of NN I am now encountering refer to x, then I will use NN to refer to x.

Whether or not an event is an initiation into practice P is partly dependent on future properties of the event. Is it the first in a series of causally linked uses in which, for the most part, the user's speaker referent coincides with the semantic referent of P? Or is it the first in a series of causally linked uses in which, for the most part, the user's speaker referent diverges from the semantic referent of P? If the former, it can count as the first participation in P, even if there is a divergence in this case between speaker referent and the semantic referent of P: the divergence will be treated as an error within P, one which is going to be corrected. If the latter, then it is not an event in P, but rather the origination, albeit unwitting, of a new practice. The intention described in (12) must succeed in the long term. If this is right, the following remark by Evans requires qualification:

if a speaker uses a word with the manifest intention to participate in such-and-such a practice, in which the word is used with such-and-such semantic properties, then the word, as used by him, will possess just those semantic properties (Evans 1982: 387).

I am on the ridge in full view of two conspicuous mountains, c and d. A local points to c and tells me that it is called Ammag. I take him to have pointed to d, a mountain just above which hovers the only cloud in the sky. I say 'There's a cloud above Ammag'. I manifestly intend to use 'Ammag' as they used it, and I intend to use 'Ammag' for d. The intentions are not compatible. Does this use count as one within their practice? We need to distinguish at least two cases.

Ammag 1: The old hand says 'No, that's not Ammag. Ammag's the other one (i.e. c)'. I realize my mistake and thereafter, in using 'Ammag', I normally have c-related intentions. The old hand took me to have said something false in my first use, whereas had the referent of 'Ammag' in my mouth been d he should have taken me to have said something true. In this case, my first use is a use within the practice, even though my speaker referent does not coincide with its semantic referent. There are tight limits to this possibility of divergence, as the second case shows.

Ammag 2: Just after my utterance of 'There's a cloud above Ammag', all the original participants in the 'Ammag'-practice are wiped out in an avalanche, but I escape and manage to reach a new village. My use of 'Ammag' for d catches on. I initiate the others into my use, so they and I must be participants in a common practice. We can but say that the semantic referent of the name in this practice is *d*. Had the old hands initiated me into their practice, this is the practice in which all the members of the new village would now participate (for I succeeded in initiating them into my practice), so the semantic referent of the practice would be *c*.

Initiation into a practice is bringing it about that, normally, the neophyte's speaker referent coincides with the practice's semantic referent. In case 1, the local pointing to *c* and telling me that it is called Ammag makes some contribution, albeit incomplete, to creating this disposition; in case 2, it makes no contribution. Although there is some indeterminacy, this makes it permissible, though not compulsory, to regard my first use of 'Ammag' in case 1 as one within the original practice, despite my having the wrong speaker referent, for the disposition is about to be refined. In case 2, there is no possibility for such refinement: the avalanche swept away my only chance for reverting to conformity with their practice, and so my only chance that my would-be initiation should have been really that. In case 2, I unwittingly originated a new 'Ammag'-practice whose semantic referent is *d*.

The content of a new user's intention to conform needs to differ from one name-using practice to another. On my second day studying philosophy I hear what I realize is a distinct use of 'Strawson'. (The previous use was for Peter, today's use is for Galen.) When I use 'Strawson' in this conversation, I need to have intentions with a different content from the ones I had using the same name in yesterday's different conversation. In today's use of the name (in the Galen conversation) I am not trying to achieve what I was trying to achieve by my use of the same name in yesterday's use (in the Peter conversation). If I have really caught on to the practices, yesterday I was aiming to speak of P. Strawson, today of G. Strawson.

There are many problematic cases. For example, what happens if I join a group of speakers who are involved in mutual misunderstanding in their uses of 'Strawson', some being members of the Peter-practice, some of the Galen-practice and some of both?[7] Where there is no firm intuition either way, a proper account should be silent concerning whether or not an initiation has occurred, or should be overtly and unashamedly stipulative. Some such cases show that we

---

[7] Anthony Savile stressed this kind of difficult case, the kind in which a subject is mistaken in believing he is confronted with uses within a single practice.

may well not know what to say about the speaker referent of the new user's uses of the name, so that the condition requiring no divergence between this and the old semantic referent gets us nowhere.

A classic view is that for each name there is some special information which one needs to associate with a name in order to be initiated into its practice. Suppose I encounter some people using the name 'Peter' and join in their conversation. On the present account, all I need for initiation is to acquire the disposition to use the name with a speaker referent that aligns with its semantic referent. Suppose I intend to conform but think Peter is a person when in reality he is a racehorse.[8] Does this not show that I could not have speaker-meant Peter when I used 'Peter'? Is there not a good sense in which I have not understood, and so have not been initiated into the practice? It is true that I did not understand what was going on; I did not understand that Peter was a racehorse. It does not follow, and may not be true (depending on the full details of the story), that I lacked linguistic understanding, that I was not successfully initiated into the 'Peter' practice I encountered. One sign that initiation occurred, even though there was much I did not understand about the situation, is that we can happily use (and not merely mention) the name 'Peter' in saying in what this failure of understanding consists: I did not understand that Peter was a horse. As a result, I formed some false beliefs about a horse, ones I express using 'Peter': for example, I took it for granted that Peter had just two legs.

3.6.2 Continued participation

In a use which continues my practice I have to intend to 'go on as before'. What content can we ascribe to this intention? Is it that I identify in thought a practice of using a name and resolve to continue in that practice? This seems unrealistic. In the case of initiation, it was plausible to suppose that the neophyte could identify a practice by identifying specific uses in specific mouths. These uses could enter into the content of the conformist intention (12): for all x, if the uses of NN I am now encountering refer to x, then I will use NN to refer

---

[8] The specific example is from Jim Hopkins. The objection might crystallize into a sortal-subsumption thesis, rejected in Chapter 7.2.2 and 7.2.3.

to x. It is not plausible to suppose that there is a kind of intentional content that can be ascribed to any subject continuing a practice. It is not obvious that everyone who continues participation has so much as the concept of a name-using practice. Continuing participation does not necessarily involve memory of the events which initiated the participation: for most of the names we use, most of us have forgotten even approximately the circumstances in which we first encountered them. It would also be risky to require memory of any specific event of prior use. I can use a familiar name with no memory of any specific occasion on which I previously used it (for that person or thing). Hence it is difficult to model continued participation on initiation: we can go a long way to explaining the latter, but not the former, in terms of the long-term success of certain kinds of speaker intentions whose content specifies uses. The uses must belong to the practice, but no content explicitly referring to the practice is needed in the intention.

Continuity of participation should deliver continuity of reference. If some object d is systematically and customarily the speaker referent of my uses of a name after a certain time, and before that time some distinct object c was the semantic referent of my uses of that name, the uses need to count as belonging to different practices.

Speakers typically segregate their distinct practices of using a name in terms of different associated information: Aristotle the philosopher, not Aristotle the tycoon; Vulcan the supposed planet, not Vulcan the Greek god. (This may be one source of the idea that such information should feature in the semantics of names.) This suggests a more functional account of continued participation. Because uses are concrete events, they can be ordered by the place and time of their occurrence, and the first use is an initiation, which is explained independently. The second use is 'sensitive to information from' the initiation: some believed information expressed using the name at initiation (e.g. 'That is Ammag', 'Vulcan lies between Mercury and the sun') is associated with the name at the second use. Some information associated with the name at the second use is associated with it at the third. All information can be deleted, but not all at once. In general a later use by a subject continues the subject's participation in a certain practice only if it is sensitive to information from an earlier use in the same practice. Circularity is avoided by the usual recursive structure, and there is no need to attribute to the subject an intentional content which identifies her practice for what it is. This is offered as a necessary condition for continued participation. Is it sufficient? In particular, does it deliver continuity of referent?

Suppose that I am introduced to the name 'Tim' on encountering Tim, but then, unknown to me, Tim leaves for the Orient and I subsequently encounter his twin brother Jim, whom I mistake for Tim. I call Jim Tim, and agglomerate the information I have concerning both of them. Should we say that I have continued to participate in my 'Tim'-using practice? From the functional point of view, the answer should be yes, for I treat all the information as belonging at a single point. In some cases, this may be the right answer, but in others it seems not to be. It seems right if I hardly ever meet Jim, but wrong if he is a frequent companion. How can such a seemingly trivial difference make all the difference? I think we need a condition similar to the one governing initiation into a practice: both for initiations and for continuations, our verdict should not lead to a prolonged and robust divergence between speaker referent and semantic referent (this time within the practice of a single user). If I frequently encounter Jim, he will frequently be the speaker-referent of my thoughts and sayings using 'Tim', for I will frequently allow perception-based Jim-singular intentions to govern my use of the name 'Tim'. If I do not have frequent encounters, I may well not have any thoughts that are incontestably singular concerning Jim. If I frequently encounter him, and I have continued my participation in my original 'Tim'-practice, there will be a persistent divergence between my speaker referent (Jim) and my semantic referent (Tim). Continuation is to be judged in part in the light of how we can best make sense of a speaker, and we do best to achieve, where we can, normal alignment (barring special circumstances) between semantic and speaker referent. We can allow occasional misidentifications, but persistent misidentification under favourable conditions is best redescribed in terms of entry into a new practice in which the apparent misidentifications are revealed as correct identifications. Going back to the very vague intention of 'going on as before' (with its implicit relativization to a practice: going on as before using 'Aristotle' for the philosopher), the intention is successfully realized only if one's speaker referent in later uses normally does not diverge from the semantic referent of one's earlier uses. This explains the intuitions in the Jim and Tim case, and appropriately matches the account of initiation.

3.6.3 *A referent is forever?*

Facts concerning baptism (origination of a practice), initiation into a practice and continued participation in a practice: these between them settle which uses belong to a single practice. We can now consider the earlier question of whether a practice could change its referent, though some of the previous discussion presupposes a negative answer. If this negative answer is the right answer, it is easy to give a sufficient condition for two uses not to differ in referent: they belong to the same practice. I will suggest that this is a convenient result, one which motivates treating practices as having constancy of referent (for all times t, t', and objects x, if a practice has x as its referent at t it has x as its referent at t').

Evans (1979) envisaged a case in which a baby is baptised 'Jack' but through a mix-up on the maternity ward, on the third day after the birth the baby's mother is brought another male child, and this changeling is subsequently called Jack by the person who is taken to be his mother (and who takes him to be her son) and by everyone else in their circle. For a couple of days, there was a practice of using 'Jack' for the biological offspring. According to Evans, the very same name-using practice, persisting thanks to appropriate deferential intentions, subsequently comes to have the changeling as its referent. There are two ways to describe such cases without describing them as ones in which the same practice has changed its referent. We can say that there is no change in referent or practice, so the changeling is miscalled 'Jack', and most instances of the later use of the name result in falsehoods ('Here is Jack', etc). Or we can say that there was an unwitting baptism, an unwitting initiation of a new name-using practice. The first of these alternatives is inapplicable in the kinds of case Evans envisages: if everyone seriously and without irony calls someone Jack, then he is called Jack, that is, his name is Jack. The second alternative seems worth exploring (see Sainsbury 2002: 205-23). It places a constraint on the same-practice relation: there needs to be a feature of the case which generates a new practice. We could not simply say that a use initiates a new practice if the speaker fails in her intention to conform to previous uses, for this would make us classify even a momentary misidentification as a faultless initiation of a new practice. If the changeling had been brought just once to Jack's mother, and thereafter the mistake was corrected and she was always brought her biological child, we ought to say that her 'Jack'-sayings on the day of the changeling referred to the biological child, she expressed many false (or at best accidentally true) beliefs, and that there was no break in the practice. In the one-off case, we can consistently ascribe intentions governing the mother's use of 'Jack' not all of which could succeed: she intended to refer to her son, and to the child before her; concerning her son, she intended to refer to him; concerning the changeling (the child before her), she intended to refer to him. These inconsistencies justify neither the view that a new practice has come into being nor the view that the existing practice has undergone a change of referent. Such views are justified only if there is a long-term switch. In that case, if we hold that the same practice continues with the same referent, we are forced to ascribe a persistent failure of speaker referent to match semantic referent: the mother would predominantly speaker-mean the changeling in using 'Jack'. Something has to change to get these referents to coincide. Evans holds the practice constant and changes its referent, that is, the semantic referent of the uses of 'Jack'. The view I prefer claims that, as well as a new referent, there is also a new practice.

Some cases, and this may be one example, are intuitively neutral between these descriptions: there may be no intuitive reason to prefer Evans's reference-changing account to my practice-changing one. Evans assumes that the mother continues in her original 'Jack'-practice because she intends to 'go on as before' with the name, but since both views agree that in this she failed, the intention gives no reason to think that the practice continued. There are other cases in which the practice-changing account appears mandatory, for example Ammag-2: the old hands who used the name for c are destroyed and the name is conventionally used for d. If the old hands had survived after all, but had had no further contact with me or my new village, we would have to say that there are two practices, one in which 'Ammag' is still used for c and another in which it is used for d, which would mean that my d-related activity on the ridge unwittingly initiated a new practice. I am not aware of any cases in which Evans's account is intuitively preferable. To secure uniformity, we should adopt the practice-changing account for the intuitively neutral cases as well.

There is a theoretical pay-off to this decision. Its upshot is that each practice has at most one referent. This makes name-using practices like uses of names, and so enables us to say more about what makes for different uses of a single (syntactic) name, namely, different practices. 'Aristotle' is used for the philosopher and for the tycoon. On the proposed view, that means there are two name-using practices. It is not that, within a single practice, it might have been that the name was first used for the philosopher and then for the tycoon; that would obliterate the very difference that needs to be accommodated.

An objection might run as follows. There are two possible scenarios which do not differ in their description of the non-semantic facts relating to the third day. One is as already described: the changeling is brought instead of the biological baby, and the mistake is not subsequently corrected. The other is just the same in respect of the third day, but differs in that on the fourth and all subsequent days the mistake is corrected and the mother is connected only with her biological child. In the second scenario we have to say that the mother's uses of 'Jack' have as their semantic referent her own baby. There can be no question either of her having unwittingly originated a new practice or of the name having changed its referent. But the second scenario agrees entirely with the first on the non-semantic facts relating to the third day. Since the semantic supervenes on the non-semantic, and the non-semantic facts in the two cases coincide for the third day, there is no unwitting origination of a new practice in either scenario, nor any change of referent.

The two scenarios *do* differ in the non-semantic facts relating to the third day: on the first scenario, this day is the first in a continuing history of the mother believing of the changeling that it is her biological baby; on the second scenario, this is not so. It is because of what the future holds that the appropriate semantic completion of the first scenario is that there has been an unwitting origination of a new practice.[9] This means that we may not be able to tell that some use is an unwitting initiation merely by observing it (and other contemporaneous facts), just as we may not be able to tell that some pouring of oil into an ear is a murder merely by observing it (and other contemporaneous facts).

3.7 Vagaries in name-using practices

The account of baptism and transmission does not depend upon a name-using practice having a referent. To the extent that the concept of a referent entered into the necessary intentions of users, what was required was no divergence of referent. This condition is typically met when someone is initiated successfully into an empty name-using practice: there is no divergence between the neophyte's intended referent and the semantic referent of the uses by old hands. Just as empty and non-empty names are treated in RWR by the same kinds of semantic axioms, so RWR regards both practices with empty names and practices with non-empty names as name-using practices. In support of this opinion, I conclude this chapter with some examples of cases in which both empty and non-empty name-using practices are subject to similar kinds of vagary and complication.

In cases of fission, a practice splits into two. As I prefer to describe it, a distinct practice with the same name is originated in ways causally connected with the previous practice. We were close to an example when we were on the ridge and imagined that after my flawed initiation into the original 'Ammag'-using practice, I went to a new village and introduced the locals to a use of this name in which its semantic referent is d (case 2). Suppose the old hands were not destroyed but simply withdrew into their usual haunts and made no further contact with me, and never had any contact with the new villagers. There are two 'Ammag' practices, one among the old hands

---

[9] Rigidity does not entail the stability of the referent over time. It relates only to occasions of use, one by one; otherwise demonstratives could not be rigid.

in which its referent is *c* and one among the new villagers in which its referent is *d*. This latter practice arose from the earlier practice, so it can be thought of, metaphorically, as a fission product. The distinctness of the practices springs from the persistent and robust failure of my intention, in using 'Ammag', to refer to whatever the old hands referred to by 'Ammag'. Were people from the new village to encounter one of the old hands, there would be a failure of understanding, which shows the parties do not share a practice.

We can tell structurally similar stories for two empty practices, and for two practices one empty and one not. The old hands on the south side of the mountain use 'Fiamma' for a supposed dragon who lives on the south side of the mountain and eats human babies. I am told this but through mishearing take myself to have been told about a demon who lives in the mouth of the fountain and keeps getting rabies. I leave the village, cross the divide, and spend the rest of my life on the north side of the mountain. I tell everyone there about the rabid demon called 'Fiamma' who lives in the mouth of the fountain. Intuitively, my 'Fiamma' myth differs from the myth on the south side. Unwittingly, I originated a new practice. Did I fail in my intention to refer to whatever the old hands referred to by 'Fiamma'? On the face of it, the answer is no. They referred to nothing and so did I, so there is no divergence of referent. To say that my practice is distinct because it involves different information is to make information figure in individuating empty but not non-empty practices, introducing a multiformity antithetical to RWR. The reason for not regarding my supposed initiation as a real one is simpler: success in initiation is typically thwarted by mishearing. One would say the same for a non-empty name. I hear people using 'Peter' but mishear what they say. They say 'Peter's at his best with plenty of oats' and I hear 'Peter's favourite guest is a keeper of goats'. I am not thereby initiated into the 'Peter' practice.

Fiamma is a myth, but suppose at my purported initiation I take it to be the name of a rock formation on the south of the mountain. Under the right circumstances I might originate a new practice with that formation as its referent. The fission product of an empty practice might be non-empty.

Anthropologists worry about the individuation of myths, legends, and fables. How come we find Atlantis-legends on both sides of the

Atlantic? It might be a coincidence; that is, there might be two distinct name-using practices. Or it might be that there is a single legend which migrated. Even in empty cases, standard considerations of propagation in terms of initiation and continued participation are what matter.

4
Pronouns: anaphora and demonstration

Occurrences of pronouns are dependent for their interpretation on some feature of the context. Demonstrative pronouns like 'that' typically depend upon an act of demonstration, for example, pointing. Indexicals like 'I' depend for their reference upon who utters them. Pronouns like 'he' may stand in place of a proper name or other referring expression, and so depend upon that name or other expression. Pronouns are also used in the expression of generality, and then their interpretation depends upon the word or phrase primarily responsible for that generality ('all', 'some', 'many') and by which they are governed. Finally, they occur in connection with indefinite noun phrases, a fact which may or may not be subsumable under dependence upon quantifiers.

Tradition divides the kinds of dependence into two: dependence on linguistic elements of the context, as when a pronoun stands in for an earlier occurrence of a proper name; and dependence on non-linguistic elements. The depth of this distinction can be questioned, but it is convenient. The first part of this chapter concerns a form of dependence on linguistic elements, anaphoric dependence in the widest sense; the second part concerns a form of dependence on non-linguistic elements.

4.1 Anaphoric dependence

4.1.1 *Some kinds of dependence*

The following sentences exhibit some of the ways in which an occurrence of a pronoun can be anaphorically dependent on other expressions:

1. Pedro is a farmer and **he** grows many potatoes.
2. Every boy loves the woman who begot **him**.
3. Pedro grows many potatoes and takes good care of **them**.
4. A mosquito is buzzing about our room. **It** is keeping me awake.

On the most natural reading of (1),[1] 'he' depends upon 'Pedro'. The dependence is coreference: as a matter of meaning, 'he' refers to whatever 'Pedro' refers to. In (2) and (3), 'him' and 'them' depend on the quantifier phrases 'every boy' and 'many potatoes'. Their dependence is not semantic coreference, since, at least on standard views, the quantifier phrases do not themselves have semantic referents.

There may be readings of (4) on which the 'it' is semantically independent of the material in the first part of the utterance, but in the most natural reading there is dependence. We cannot understand the second part of the utterance unless we have encountered and correctly interpreted the first part. We are tempted to say that in (4) 'it' refers back to the mosquito introduced by the first sentence, though this cannot be quite right, for it also seems that even if the first sentence is true, there is no mosquito which, as a matter of its meaning, it introduces; this is more clearly so if it is false. So it looks as if the dependence of 'it' on the earlier sentence is not coreference.

Classical pictures of variable binding make it impossible for the binding operator to bind an expression lying outside the sentence containing the operator.[2] The model is predicate logic: in a well-formed formula of the form '$\exists x (\ldots x \ldots)$', the scope of the quantifier terminates with the rightmost parenthesis. Accordingly, we could not both represent the first sentence in (4) as a well-formed formula, and also regard the 'it' in the second part as bound by a quantifier (or other variable-binding operator) in the first part. Yet the first part has everything we require of a natural language analogue of a well-formed formula: it is evaluable for absolute truth just as it stands, and does not require the sentence which follows for its full intelligibility and correctness. This is not just an accident of punctuation, for similarly

---

[1] A possible reading sees 'he' as deictic and independent of its linguistic context.

[2] A familiar view is that an expression which functions as a bound variable should be c-commanded by any expression which binds it (cf. Neale 1990: 174). The less demanding and more obvious condition that binding does not cross sentences is enough to establish that the pronouns I will be discussing are not classical bound variables.

dependent subsequent occurrences of 'it' can cross boundaries of speech act and speaker. If one were to try to represent the 'it' of (4) as a bound variable, one would need to determine the scope of the binding quantifier: if scope is marked by parentheses, one would need to know where its rightmost parenthesis falls. Until this has been determined, we cannot represent the 'it' as contained within a sentence which is evaluable for truth. Intuitively, however, the possibility of evaluating each component of (4) for truth is independent of whether the discourse has ended, or whether someone is going to add 'It's not very dangerous'. If the addition is going to be made, then attempts at evaluating (4) for truth are, on the bound variable hypothesis, completely misguided. This is a wholly unintuitive upshot.

In some cases, attempts to see this kind of anaphoric dependence as variable binding get the wrong truth conditions. For example:

5. Just one man drank rum at the party last night. He was very unwell this morning

is not equivalent to

6. Just one man, x, is such that x drank rum at the party last night and x was very unwell this morning (cf. Neale 1990: 170–1).

Given classical views about variable binding, (4) falls outside both previous categories. 'It' is dependent on 'a mosquito', but this dependence is neither the kind of dependence exerted by classical quantifier phrases, nor is it semantic coreference, since 'a mosquito' does not have a semantic referent. Cases with these two features will be the main target of the discussion of the first part of this chapter.

A common response has been to treat indefinite noun phrases, like 'a mosquito', as some kind of referring expression, at least in those uses in which they serve as antecedents to pronouns in the manner of (4), thus enabling these cases to be grouped with (1) as cases of coreference.[3] The approach has to confront the fact that there seem to be anaphor-sustaining uses of indefinites which are consistent with there being more than one satisfier of the noun, and this means that the indefinite itself does not meet the condition for being a singular

---

[3] One example is Chastain (1975).

referring expression that if it refers to x and to y, then $x = y$. Davidson makes the point like this:

> We recognize that there is no singular term referring to a mosquito in 'There is a mosquito in here' when we realize that the truth of this sentence is not impugned if there are two mosquitoes in the room (Davidson 1969: 167).

Davidson's point is not likely to be challenged for cases without anaphoric dependence: most would agree that the claim that a spy is in our midst is not refuted by there being more than one, and that the claim is to be negated by saying that no spy is in our midst, not by saying that there is either none or more than one. The unnegated 'spy' sentence can sustain anaphora (it might be followed by 'He is spilling the beans to the Taliban').

The possibility of anaphora without a referring indefinite is specially vivid in examples like this:

7. A: A mosquito is buzzing around our room.
   B: Yes, I can hear it too.
   A: In fact there are hundreds of them.

A's second remark appears consistent with her first, so we can suppose that both are true. (The relation between A's remarks is like that between 'there is at least one F' and 'there are at least two Fs'.) Yet the first remark, even though verified by more than one insect, was adequate at least to make B's remark intelligible. (It is a more difficult question whether this remark is true or false or neither.)

This discussion suggests that we should not treat indefinites as referring expressions. It may be objected that the most that has been shown is that we should not treat them as definite referring expressions. Indefinites are indefinite, and this is a special mode of referring, to which certain presuppositions of the discussion so far are inappropriate. For example, whereas there must be a definite answer to the question of what a definite referring expression refers to, there need not be, or perhaps even cannot be, such an answer to the question of what an indefinite referring expression refers to: it refers to something, but for each thing in turn it is not the case that it refers to it.

The suggestion might be carried further by citing Hilbert's ϵ-operator as a formal analogue of an indefinite article. The thought is prompted by the historical fact that the semantics of 'ϵ' have been given in terms of a choice operator, which is required to select an object as the interpretation of an ϵ-term, though there is no object it is required to select. The ϵ-operator does not match natural language indefinites in every respect. In Hilbert's system, a free variable may be replaced by an arbitrary ϵ-term (one of the form ϵxA), and this requires that every interpretation, even one which assigns the empty set to A, must assign a value to an ϵ-term. Moreover, Hilbert treats an ϵ-term as genuinely a term, and so fit to stand to one side of the identity sign. Although sentences like 'A sleepy rattler is a dangerous rattler' are acceptable in English, it is doubtful whether 'a sleepy rattler' and 'a dangerous rattler' are genuine indefinites in the context, and doubtful whether the 'is' is the 'is' of identity. By contrast, Hilbert's second axiom schema for ϵ, namely '$\forall x(A \leftrightarrow B) \rightarrow (\epsilon xA = \epsilon xB)$', requires ϵ-terms to be capable of flanking the identity sign. If we really have an identity between terms, it would be hard to explain what semantics would ensure that 'A sleepy rattler is a dangerous rattler' is true: an arbitrarily selected sleepy rattler may be a different rattler from an arbitrarily selected dangerous rattler, even if the class of sleepy rattlers is included in, or even identical to, the class of dangerous rattlers, and neither class is empty.

Leisenring (1969: 34) says: 'Obviously, the η-symbol represents the "indefinite article" in the same way that Russell's ι-symbol represents the "definite article"'. This suggests that it is η we should be considering, rather than ϵ. The former is introduced by the following rule:

If a formula $\exists xA$ is an axiom or is derivable, then ηxA can be introduced as a term, and the formula $A(\eta xA)$ can be taken as an initial formula (Hilbert and Bernays 1939: 10, quoted and translated by Leisenring 1969: 34).

One difference between ϵ and η is that the termhood of ϵxA is unconditional, whereas that of ηxA is conditional upon the satisfiability of A. This makes η a less good candidate for being an analog of the natural language indefinite article, since in English the well-formedness of 'a(n) F' is independent of whether or not there is an F.

The notion of indefinite reference is problematic on account of the way it either loses connection with truth conditions, or else degenerates into familiar existential quantification. Strawsonian and Ockhamist truth conditions agree in making how things are with the referent (if there is one) crucial to truth. In particular, if there is a referent of a term *t* and that object is *F*, then '*t* is *F*' is true. Suppose that in (4), 'A mosquito' is treated as an indefinite referring expression, and its referent is Jerry (let us make an exception to the general rule of not assigning personal proper names to mosquitoes). Perhaps Jerry is not buzzing about our room, though many other mosquitoes are. If how things are with the referent is what matters to truth, the first part of (4) comes out false (for Jerry is not in the room, or at least is not buzzing about the room). Since we can consistently suppose that (4) is in fact true, taking this route severs the connection between reference and truth, and makes it impossible to see why indefinite reference is a species of reference.

In response to the criticism, a theorist of indefinite reference may say that the whole point is that no definite referent matters to truth. Jerry should not enter into the truth conditions. These need to be stated along some such lines as these: 'A(n) *F* is *G*' is true iff there is a referent of 'A(n) *F*' which satisfies *G*. This makes indefinite reference nothing more than familiar existential quantification. There is no distinctive phenomenon of indefinite reference.

I conclude that we should not regard indefinite noun phrases as referring expressions, definite or indefinite, or as having truth conditions upon which there is a (definite or indefinite) object which they introduce into discourse and make available for subsequent back reference. In short, indefinite noun phrases do not have semantic referents. As we shall see in §4.1.3, this is consistent with their being associated on an occasion with a unique object (perhaps as speaker's referent): the implausible claim is that this association is constitutive of their contribution to the truth conditions of sentences in which they occur.

4.1.2 *Dependent unbound pronouns are referring expressions*

I suggest that pronouns like 'it' in (4), those which are in this way anaphorically dependent, are referring expressions. The relevant conception of a referring expression is that sketched at the end of Chapter 1, and exemplified by proper names as treated in Chapter 3: a referring expression is one that 'purports to refer': it needs to succeed if an unembedded occurrence of the expression is to express a truth; it may fail to refer without detriment to intelligibility; a correct semantics will associate it with a reference condition rather than with a referent; a semantic theory for such expressions will be set within free rather than classical logic; truth conditions for sentences of the form '*t* is *F*', where '*t*' is such a pronoun, will be Ockhamist (ones which do not require the existence of a referent for falsehood). These opinions are to be justified by examples. They do justice to, and even throw some light on, the way we intuitively treat the questions of truth, falsehood, and intelligibility which arise in such cases, and are internally coherent.

Wishing to make Jill jealous, Jack says

8. I met a girl last night. She was absolutely gorgeous.

Jill rises to the bait, and starts making enquiries: 'How old is she? What colour hair? Were you alone with her? What's her name?' Jack gives answers, and a painful silence descends. The next morning, noticing Jack's distracted air, Jill asks:

9. Are you thinking about her?

Unreflectively, we are strongly inclined to say that Jill intended to refer to the girl Jack met. We certainly need the utterances which contain the dependent pronouns ('she', 'her') to be intelligible, if we are to explain Jill's state of mind, the motivation for her enquiries, the dynamics of her exchange with Jack, and their emotional situation. However, I have not yet said whether Jack's remark (8) was true or false. Perhaps he was making the whole story up. If he was, there was no referent, but the pronouns were the kind of expression that should have referred. If things had gone as well as could be and Jack had told the truth, they would have succeeded in referring, and this would be so in virtue of something about Jack's initial use of the indefinite 'a girl'. If there is a referent, then Jack's remarks of the form '*t* is *F*' are true iff it (the referent) satisfies '*F*'. If Jack did in fact meet a girl last night, then 'She was absolutely gorgeous' is true iff she satisfies 'was absolutely gorgeous'.[4] If there is no referent, what he says is certainly intelligible, but the data at this point do not give any firm pointer about whether we should say that his remarks are false, or lacking truth value. Either way, some form of reference-conditional semantics is

---

[4] This is a conditional singular truth condition, and reuses the object language devices: the final 'she' (as subject to 'satisfies') is dependent upon the indefinite 'a girl Jack met last night'.

required, along with what that entails in terms of free logic and Ockhamist truth conditions (or at least non-Strawsonian ones).

The views of this subsection and the previous one taken together pose a problem: indefinites are not referring expressions, but pave the way for reference by the pronouns which depend upon them. This dependence is neither semantic coreference nor variable binding. What can it be?

4.1.3 Evans's proposal

There is a kind of solution to the problem that has the following features: it accepts at face value that some dependent pronouns refer, and do so at least partly in virtue of some feature of the governing indefinite; and it accepts that the indefinites themselves do not refer, and do not require a unique satisfier for their truth. There are many ways in which the utterance of a sentence containing an indefinite may be linked with a unique object. Even if the association is required neither for the truth nor for the intelligibility of the utterance itself, it may be required for the truth or for the intelligibility of a subsequent utterance containing a dependent pronoun. According to the solution to be considered in this subsection, from the first part of (4) one can extract a condition, and the referent if any of the dependent pronouns is the satisfier of this condition. Since this condition is typically satisfied, the first part of an utterance like (4) does typically introduce an object for subsequent back-reference. Some versions of the proposal allow that utterances containing indefinite noun phrases can in this way introduce an object even if false and can fail to introduce one even if true.

One well-known account of this kind is by Evans (1977) in his description of E-type pronouns. Evans presents his account in two distinct ways. According to one of these, the suggestion is that a sentence like (4) can be understood as equivalent to:

10. A mosquito is buzzing about our room. The mosquito that is buzzing about our room is keeping me awake.

This guides us to the semantics of anaphora only in the presence of a theory of descriptions (which will need to decide some difficult questions about scope). But the core of Evans's idea can be entirely detached from these controversial issues, and he sometimes presents it in this alternative way:

11. If in an utterance like (4) the first part has a unique verifier, this is the referent of the dependent pronoun in the second part.

Having a unique verifier is not a condition for the truth of the first part of (4), but, on this account, it is a reference condition for dependent pronouns. It is not a condition which must obtain for a dependent pronoun to be intelligible, for intelligibility will be identified with possession of a condition which contributes to the truth condition of the whole sentence, and (11) supplies the pronoun with such a condition in the form of a reference condition, independently of whether the governing indefinite has a unique verifier.

This account has the following welcome features: it does not suppose that the indefinite noun phrases are referring expressions or that simple sentences containing them are true only if uniquely satisfied; it allows that dependent pronouns are referring expressions; it gives the semantics of these referring expressions in terms of reference conditions rather than by assigning referents outright, and so commits to Ockhamist truth conditions and some form of free logic. From my perspective, everything about the structure of the account is as it should be. However, it has been said not to do justice to the semantic details. Considering

Socrates owned a dog and it bit Socrates

(which he numbers as (16)) Evans makes the following admission:

if Socrates owned two dogs, on the proposal which I am defending (16) is not true; the second conjunct would not be true for failure of reference of 'it' (Evans 1977: 127).[5]

By the same token, in the most usual kind of situation in which (4) would be uttered (situations containing more than one mosquito), its second part would fail to be true; and not everything said in (7) could be true. These results are generally regarded as counterintuitive, and have historically formed a frequent basis for rejecting Evans's account.

Rejection on this basis may have been too hasty. Perhaps Evans is right that, strictly and literally, a subsequent utterance using a

---

[5] Evans here speaks as if the 'if' in (11) is to be strengthened to 'iff'.

dependent pronoun is true only if the governing indefinite is uniquely satisfied, and our sense that his position is counterintuitive is based upon a natural attempt to 'accommodate'. In accommodation, an interpreter of something which is strictly and literally false or inappropriate finds an interpretation (not the strict and literal one) upon which the utterance is true or appropriate. Perhaps utterances containing pronouns anaphoric upon indefinites often fail to be strictly and literally true, so we need to seek a non-literal interpretation, for example by envisaging some implicit restriction which does yield a unique satisfier: a particular dog that the person who said that Socrates owned a dog had in mind, or a mosquito which prompted the utterance of (4). It is easy to confuse an accommodated interpretation (which is not properly speaking an interpretation at all) with a proper interpretation; and therefore easy to read utterances which fail to be strictly and literally true as if they were true. Accommodation of this kind is familiar and widespread. The claim that utterances like 'Socrates owned a dog and it bit Socrates' are true relative to a situation in which Socrates owned two dogs may confuse genuine truth with accommodated truth. Arguments against Evans based on such examples would need carefully to separate these features.

There are other examples—correction cases—which in my opinion provide a firmer basis on which to regard Evans's account as inadequate. I distinguish two kinds of case. The first is exemplified by the following perfectly natural dialogue:

12. A: A mosquito is buzzing about our room.
    B: It's not a mosquito. It's just a gnat.

We can imagine B's remark to be true (along with A's being either true or false). If so, the referent of 'It' in B's utterance cannot be a mosquito.[6] In this case B corrects a mistake which A makes, and it might be that Evans's account could be protected by an accommodation story: if there is no relevant mosquito then A's remark is literally false, but B accommodatingly reads it as something like 'A mosquito-like insect is buzzing about our room'. The accommodated

---

[6] Such cases are more problematic for the alternative version of Evans's account, developed by Neale, according to which B's remark is, or is equivalent to, the manifest contradiction 'The mosquito that is buzzing around our room is not a mosquito'. On the present version of Evans's account, the situation is simply one in which B's 'It' has no referent and so his remark is not true; there is no manifest contradiction.

PRONOUNS: ANAPHORA AND DEMONSTRATION 135

reading supplies an appropriate referent (by Evans's standards) for B's 'it'.

A second kind of correction case has features which rule out accommodation. Suppose that Jack's painful conversation with Jill which began with (8) ('I met a girl last night...') has been going on for some time when Jack utters:

13. In fact, I met her before last night, not last night, but couldn't face telling you at the start of this conversation.

Let us assume that Jack did indeed meet the girl he has been talking about before last night and met no one last night. We would like to say that Jill nonetheless was thinking of the right girl all along, and now, if she believes Jack, changes her mind about when Jack met that girl. Yet on Evans's proposal, none of either Jack or Jill's pronouns has a referent at all, and (13) cannot be true. There is no question of accommodation, for the referent (if any) of the pronoun has already been determined before (13) is uttered.[7]

Evans is aware that there are problems in this area, and suggests that his account should be 'liberalized':

In order to effect this liberalization we should allow the reference of the E-type pronoun to be fixed not only by predicative material explicitly in the antecedent clause, but also by material which the speaker supplies on demand. This ruling has the effect of making the truth conditions of such remarks somewhat indeterminate; a determinate proposition will have been put forward only when the demand has been made and the material supplied (Evans 1977: 130).

The demand in question relates to the use of the dependent pronoun, and takes the form: 'Who?' or 'What?'. In the dialogue above (12), B could respond: 'the insect which A was talking about (and which he wrongly thought was a mosquito)'. This is not just a liberalization of the original theory but a new one, and one which gives unlimited licence to speakers' intentions, as if these were in no way governed

---

[7] A third kind of case involves fiction. An example might be

A: A burglar must have made all this mess.
B: He's just a figment of your imagination. You never clear up.

This raises questions about how any negative existential truth is possible, and about the nature of fiction and pretence, which go beyond what can be addressed here. It may turn out that these cases raise no special problem for Evans's account.

by facts of language use. Reverting to Jack's disagreeable remark (8), suppose he did indeed meet just one girl, but that he found her in no way attractive and was simply trying to make Jill jealous. Falling for his trick, Jill might assume that Jack was madly attracted to this girl, and so she might answer an identificatory question concerning her use of 'she' or 'her' in these words: 'Why, the girl Jack is so madly attracted to'. On Evans's liberalized account, taken at face value, this would mean that nothing Jill can say using such a pronoun (unembedded) is true. This is strikingly counterintuitive. In general, one cannot put the referent at the mercy of just any beliefs that speakers or hearers might have.

Evans's account may be inadequate, but I believe that it is not beyond repair. I begin by considering proposals in a similar spirit, but which I argue are also unsatisfactory (§4.1.4). I then consider the proposed repairs (§4.1.5).

4.1.4 *Intention, speaker's referent, and salience*

Another way to link a unique object to an indefinite is through some specific intention on the part of the utterer. Candidate objects range from ones concerning which the utterer of the indefinite has communicative intentions, to ones he merely 'has in mind'. One could classify all these cases as accepting that indefinites have no semantic referent, but claiming that they are fit to be antecedents to anaphoric pronouns only on those occasions on which they are used with a speaker referent.

Anaphoric dependence does not always turn on communicative intentions concerning specific objects. Knowing that you do not know my friend Jill, with whom I am having dinner this evening, I may tell you this:

14. I am having dinner with a friend this evening

without there being anyone I intend you to identify, and so without having communicative intentions towards any object. This is no barrier to subsequent anaphora: 'She is coming down from Manchester'.

The best form of the intentional dependence view is likely to be the weakest, perhaps captured by the idea that the relevant object is the one I have 'in mind' in my utterance. No doubt I do have Jill in mind when I utter (14), which goes some way towards providing an object for subsequent pronouns to refer back to. But (14) is just as true, and need not be misleading, if I am having dinner with my friend Jack as well as Jill and know this, so that there is no one friend I have in mind as dinner companion that evening. This can be fully explicit, as in the following extension of (14):

15. I am having dinner with a friend this evening. She is coming down from Manchester. She's bringing another friend of mine, Jack, to dinner with her.

In such cases, the speaker makes it plain that he has more than one person in mind. There are also cases in which the speaker makes it plain that she has no one in mind. The headmistress thunders:

16. A girl, I don't yet know who, has been smoking in the lavatories. (I smelt it, and found cigarette butts.) When I find out who it was she will be punished severely.

Typically, there is no girl whom the headmistress who utters (16) 'has in mind', and she makes this manifest; yet this undermines neither the intelligibility nor the truth of the last part of her utterance, containing the dependent 'she'. This makes 'having in mind', regarded as a relation between an object and a speaker, a relation which cannot explain all cases. Likewise it means that we cannot save the original idea that indefinites are referring expressions by appealing to speaker referent rather than semantic referent. In the case of (16), such a view would wrongly predict that 'she' has no referent, so that the last utterance is not true, if there is no object which the headmistress had in mind.

There is a weaker, non-extensional, relation (so perhaps not really a relation) which may be intended by the notion of having in mind. We do use the phrase 'have in mind' for cases in which there is no object to which the thinker is related by epistemic or causal relations. For example, the headmistress in this sense has the culprit in mind, even if there is in fact no culprit, and she mistook dead leaves for butts and bonfire smoke for cigarette smoke. This resembles Evans's 'liberalized' account. The idea would be that the referent, if any, of the dependent pronoun, is whatever uniquely satisfies the description the user of the pronoun would give of what she had in mind in using it. As we have seen, this seems to leave too much scope to speaker idiosyncrasies: a speaker might have in mind a description which is intuitively irrelevant to fixing the referent of the pronoun. In a variant of (16), the headmistress may have a quite definite suspicion that Jill is the guilty girl, and this is who she has in mind when she speaks. But if she is wrong, and the culprit is really Samantha, and when the facts are known the headmistress proceeds to punish Samantha, the truth of what she said is entirely unimpugned. Hence even if she has someone in mind in uttering (16), that person may not be the referent of the pronoun.

Can we use the notion of salience to achieve a better account? Indefinites are often used in perceptual contexts, including those in which something is perceived by both speaker and hearer in a situation in which this fact is likely to be common knowledge. As a result of a normal safari utterance of 'Look! There's a black rhino' a unique rhino may get raised to salience, and thus become available for subsequent reference. In David Lewis's words:

> although indefinite descriptions—that is, idioms of existential quantification—are not themselves referring expressions, they may raise the salience of particular individuals in such a way as to pave the way for referring expressions that follow (Lewis 1979: 180).

There is room to doubt whether this holds even for all perceptual cases, and other cases seem to provide clear counterexamples.

Suppose I don't see the rhino which was salient to you. This does not prevent me intelligibly and truly continuing: 'I can't see it'. Intuitively, I refer to something which is not salient to me. Perhaps the relevant theory should require only speaker salience. Then 'it' in my remark ('I can't see it') refers to a presumed unique rhino salient to the speaker. This position has counterintuitive aspects. One is that the exchange goes equally smoothly, and the truth of the second speaker's utterance is unimpugned ('I can't see it'), if two rhinos have an equal degree of salience for the first speaker ('There's a black rhino'). Another is that if there was no black rhino, nor anything else of even roughly the same kind, and you were tricked by the light, the response 'I can't see it' is certainly intelligible, and I have a strong inclination to regard it as true.[8] So we seem to have anaphoric connection in the absence of a salient object.

---

[8] According to NFL, the explanation is that this is the (wide-scope) negation of a sentence ('I can see it') which is false through lack of a referent for one of its referring expressions ('it').

There are clearer counterexamples to the salience view. Called to the scene of a disturbance, a policeman says:

17. Someone with large feet crossed this muddy area. The footsteps end at the wall. He probably jumped over.

No one is salient to speaker or (typically) hearer, but the anaphora is intelligible, and all the utterances may intuitively be true. So salience does not constitute a necessary condition for the intelligibility or truth of unbound pronouns, and could not feature as a necessary condition for the truth conditions of utterances containing them.[9]

Intelligible anaphora without salience also arises in cases in which there is no referent. If Jack was making up the whole story, no one gets raised to salience, but his and Jill's subsequent uses of 'her' are intelligible. The position can be supported by a slightly different kind of case. Consider the narration (we may suppose it to be factual and true):

18. They were lost in the mist. Suddenly Jack grabbed Jill's arm and said 'That looks like a black rhino.' 'Where is it?' Jill replied in alarm.

The story could continue either way (there is, or is not, a black rhino), without detriment to the intelligibility of either of their remarks, though Jill's 'it' is anaphorically dependent on Jack's 'that'. (Cf. Burge 1991, though his example is overtly fictional, which makes it less compelling for present purposes.)

I will show how Evans's account can be modified in a very straightforward way to accommodate the kinds of counterexample we have discussed.

4.1.5 *Evans's account amended*

I suggest that Evans's account gives the default reference conditions for dependent pronouns, but if this condition does not deliver a referent, other conditions are invoked. Once one begins to tinker with Evans's account, one can, if one wishes, accommodate the intuition that a multiply satisfied utterance containing an indefinite may introduce an anaphoric pronoun with a referent. In the original

---

[9] Roberta Ballerin suggests that the tracks render their maker salient. If the supposed tracks were made not by any person but by some freak weather conditions, (19) remains intelligible, and 'he' does not refer to anything (not even to the weather conditions).

mosquito case (4), we imagine that the remark is prompted by some one out of the various mosquitoes, one which played a causal role in producing the utterance, and this intuitively is the mosquito we take to be the referent of the subsequent 'it'. The condition is:

19b. *x*, and *x* alone, both prompted the utterance of 'An *F* is *G*' and satisfies *F*-and-*G*.

The headmistress example (16) shows that we cannot simply eliminate the second conjunct: if no girl, but a whiff of bonfire smoke, had uniquely prompted the remark, the whiff would not be the referent of 'she'.

The required notion of prompt is not easy to articulate, beyond the obvious fact that it is a causal notion. In this example (given by King 1992: 32), we need the prompt to be whoever gave rise to the account, typically by doing some or all of the things related, as opposed to a newspaper report:

20. A Hawaiian surfer was surfing fifteen-foot waves at Pipeline about ten years ago. He took off on a big wave, fell and became trapped in an underwater cave.

Intelligible corrections include that he was not a Hawaiian, or was not a surfer, or was not trapped but only nearly so. If the teller learned the story at second-hand, we do not want his 'source' (in this journalistic sense) to count as the referent. Likewise if the story was pure fabrication: though the fabricator is the source, he or she should not count as the referent.

In the case in which the speaker mistakes a gnat for a mosquito (12), nothing satisfies the *F*-and-*G* condition, but intuitively the 'it' refers to the gnat which prompted the remark. This is because it is easy to make the mistake in question. If B had replied 'It's not a mosquito, it's a penguin' we would need a great deal more scene-setting to achieve an interpretation of the remark upon which it is plausibly true. This suggests that if (19b) does not deliver a referent, we should look to the following:

19c. *x*, and *x* alone, both prompted the utterance of 'An *F* is *G*' and the speaker mistook it for a satisfier of *F*-and-*G*.

This still does not get things right for the case in which, deep into the conversation, Jack retracts some initial information on which occurrences of the pronoun were dependent (13). We need a further condition, to determine a referent if the others fail:

19d. x, and x alone, both prompted the utterance of 'An F is G' and the speaker represented it as a satisfier of F-and-G.

Summarizing, the suggestion is this:

21. For any object x, and any first use of a pronoun anaphorically dependent upon an utterance of the form 'An F is G', the pronoun on that use refers to x iff:

(a) x uniquely satisfies F-and-G, or nothing meets this condition but

(b) x, and x alone, both prompted the utterance of 'An F is G' and satisfies F-and-G, or nothing meets either (a) or (b) but

(c) x, and x alone, both prompted the utterance and the speaker mistook it for a satisfier of F-and-G, or nothing meets either (a) or (b) or (c) but

(d) x, and x alone, both prompted the utterance and the speaker represented it as a satisfier of F-and-G.

Disjunct (a) on its own is Evans's account, and is modified to deal with cases of multiple satisfiers of F-and-G and correction cases. Disjunct (b) (compare (19b)) addresses multiple satisfier cases, (c) gnat-style correction cases like (12) and (d) the Jack-style correction cases like (13) (in which there is no mistake).

I am not aware of counterexamples to this account,[10] but it is somewhat unhappy in various ways. For one thing, although there is some kind of similarity among the conditions (they are either Evans's pure unique F-and-G condition or else some intelligible departure from it), there seems no real unity. The closest to a unifying idea is that the referent of the pronoun (if any) is whatever object the speaker was representing as being uniquely F-and-G; but on a natural understanding of this condition, it is wrong for the headmistress's remark, which may have a referent even if there is no object she represents as being thus; it is also doubtful for gnat-style

---

[10] Ruth Kempson presented interesting cases of stacked indefinites which the account given here does not address: 'A friend—a linguist, a really nice person—is coming to dinner tonight. She will arrive at seven'. Which indefinites determine the referent if any of 'she'? I incline to start with the thought that all are relevant, though there may be interesting cases of differential relevance.

correction cases. The lack of unity means that we have no way of being sure that there are no counterexamples, and so we should advance the account with caution. We might transform it into something more general and more unified: the referent of an anaphoric pronoun, when it is the first in the chain, is to be determined by general holistic applications of the principle of charity (which may use information available only after the time of the utterance); subsequent links in the same chain must agree in referent with the first. This may improve the truthfulness of the principle, since it will now collect anything that is needed for it to deliver the right result; but at the expense of any useful specificity.

Unification in another direction is required, for intuitively, as Evans said, it cannot be that pronouns in the use we have studied are semantically wholly distinct from their use in other cases, for example, those in which they depend upon an indefinite which occurs within the scope of a quantifier. Some such cases may suggest a line of unification. In cases like

22. Everyone who owns a car washes it on Sunday

we may explain the truth conditions in terms of a series of assignments of people to the blank in

23. If... owns a car,... washes it on Sunday.

Relative to any such assignment, 'it' gets as referent, if any, the assigned person's car. Here only condition (a) of (21) would appear to apply. Reference on an assignment can be seen as a variant upon reference on a condition. It is not clear how far this idea (which is present in Evans) can be extended. For example, it may not be able to do justice to the universal force of 'it' in

24. No farmer who owns a donkey beats it,

which is false if any donkey-owning farmer beats any of his donkeys.[11]

One feature of an Evans-style account, one it shares with all those discussed in this section, seems certainly correct, if reference is to play

---

[11] It is not obvious that the 'universal force' needs to be linked directly to the pronoun. What (24) denies is that there is a farmer and a donkey he owns and beats. The universality involved in the denial of an existential may pose no more problems for a theory of singular pronouns than those posed by cases like (23).

PRONOUNS: ANAPHORA AND DEMONSTRATION 143

a role in describing these pronouns: its reference-conditional form, which could be abstracted to the following:

> For any utterance of the form 'A(n) *F* is *G*' which supports subsequent anaphora, there is some feature such that for any object, *x*, a subsequent dependent pronoun refers to *x* iff *x* uniquely possesses that feature.

Having this reference condition ensures the intelligibility of such pronouns; whether they have a referent is another question, determined by whether the associated feature has a unique instance.

4.1.6 *Understanding dependent pronouns*

Can understanding a dependent pronoun (of the kind under discussion) be identified with knowing its reference condition, or with coming to know what its referent (if any) is on the basis of the reference condition together with further contextually supplied information?

There is a structural difficulty in bending an Evans-style account of reference conditions to an account of interpretation or understanding. When the interpreter encounters an anaphoric pronoun, he needs already to possess something which will permit interpretation on the basis of his interpretation of the previous link in the anaphoric chain. If the previous link was itself a pronoun, then its interpretation should simply be carried forward. If it was not a pronoun, then its interpretation should already have equipped the interpreter with a reference condition. The difficulty is that, according to a position like Evans's, one is to interpret an indefinite noun phrase essentially as an existential quantifier. Thus the interpretation of the first part of (4), for example, does not require anything pertaining to uniqueness.

In the process of interpretation, we expect understanders to carry previous interpretations forward; these are available for solving new problems of interpretation. It would be quite another thing to expect understanders to carry forward memories of precise linguistic forms. Yet this is what would be required by an Evans-style account, if it were read as an account of understanding. To use the account, the interpreter who encounters the first occurrence of a pronoun dependent upon an indefinite would need to backtrack and recall not merely the truth-conditional interpretation of the sentence containing the indefinite, but the sentence itself, or at least something isomorphic to it; truth-conditional equivalents of the sentence containing the indefinite may fail to sustain the anaphora. I will first show that we cannot in general expect interpreters to remember previous linguistic forms, as opposed to previous interpretations, and then show that anaphoric reference determination is dependent upon linguistic forms, and not just on interpretations.

Among people who use two languages interchangeably in their conversations, it often happens that one remembers what the other said, but not in which language she said it. Interpretation is remembered, but not linguistic form. In the cases under discussion, the reference conditions for the dependent pronouns do not depend only upon the truth-conditional interpretation of the antecedent indefinite noun phrase. That is the price we pay for not regarding the indefinites as semantically referential. The consequence is that, given only the account so far, there is no guarantee that those who can interpret the antecedent sentences are thereby well placed to interpret the subsequent pronouns.

The difficulty could be modelled like this. In interpreting the first part of, say, (4) ('A mosquito is buzzing about our room') we come to know that what the speaker has said is true iff there is at least one mosquito which is buzzing around our room, and we throw away all other information about the utterance, including the words in which it was couched. We then move on to the second part, and encounter the 'it' ('It is keeping me awake'). On the proposed reference-condition account, the referent of 'it' is fixed by a series of tests which start with the query: is there is a unique satisfier of a certain conjunction of predicates in the first part of the utterance? But we have thrown away the words, and now have only the interpretation, and so we are in no position to ask or answer the question in this form. So far as truth-conditional interpretation goes, the words could as well have been 'Our room is affected by mosquito-induced buzz', which is also true iff there is at least one mosquito which is buzzing around our room. We need to backtrack to make a test relating to the first utterance which goes beyond any information we retain as a result of our interpretation of it. Intuitively, however, interpreting the first part gives us all the information we need in order to go on to interpret the second. This does not show that there is something wrong with the conditions for reference which the account supplied. It shows only that these conditions do not give a full picture of how understanding develops.

Anaphoric dependence is a function not just of possible worlds truth conditions but also of linguistic form. Even though, in the two following sentences, the first parts agree in these truth conditions, only the first of the pair happily supports anaphora:

25. Pedro owns a donkey. Harry vaccinates it.

26. Pedro is a donkey-owner. Harry vaccinates it.

To implement the conventional association between reference and understanding one would need to treat the interpretations of the first parts of these two examples as different, and to be sure to include in the interpretation of the first part of (25) something which enables the second part to be interpreted (without any kind of backtracking). This is not what an Evans-style account offers. The first parts of both are simply interpreted as true iff there is an x such that x is a donkey and Pedro owns x. What is needed in order to interpret the pronoun is something that can be derived from the linguistic form of (25) but not from that of (26). If we cannot expect interpreters to keep track of linguistic forms, as opposed to keeping track of interpretations, we cannot use Evans's account as a complete account of interpretation.

We know from Discourse Representation Theory (Kamp 1981, Kamp and Reyle 1993) and from File Change Semantics (Heim 1982/1988) that it is possible to provide an interpretation of (25) which differs from that of (26). This gives interpreters different interpretations to carry forward: one which in the case of (25) but not in that of (26) will provide what it takes to interpret an anaphoric pronoun. In the next section, I borrow selectively, and without further acknowledgement, from their work. These authors and I have very different goals. The linguistic detail which is their central concern is subsidiary from my point of view. Moreover, they seem not to provide for the possibility that different utterances within a single discourse, which use anaphorically linked pronouns, should have different truth values; as a connected issue, they give no weight to correction cases, which are hard to imagine being accommodated within their accounts. Without supposing that these problems, or others which have been mentioned in the literature, provide knock-down arguments against their positions, I have here taken the opposite line, moved by the general intuition that we are often wrong about specific objects, and so have to delete as well as accumulate information relating to a single object. This dynamic is not easy to register in DRT.

4.1.7 Interpretation and individual concepts

Instead of asking about reference we can ask about how interpreters process the constructions we are discussing. I suggest that interpreting indefinite noun phrases, as they occur in the first part of (4) or (8), requires one to introduce an individual concept. This is then available in interpreting the subsequent pronouns. What is needed for interpretation of the second part is already contained in the interpretation of the first part, without backtracking. The cognitive analogue of 'back-reference' is reuse of an individual concept. The relevant notion of individual concept is that developed in Chapter 7 below. As a preliminary guide, an individual concept can be thought of as a proper name in Mentalese. Like a linguistic proper name, it may lack a referent. Unlike a linguistic proper name, it does not have a public sense or meaning: it is an aspect of individual psychology.

Why should interpreting a merely indefinite noun phrase require the introduction of a corresponding individual concept, a concept fit to be exercised in thinking about a definite individual object? An individual concept is exercised when a person 'thinks about' an object, and cases of such thinking are not confined to those in which there is an object she thinks about. It is a hot day. Imagine that you are drinking a beer. In thinking about the situation by imagining it, there need be no beer to which you are related. What you imagine is in some respects like what you would experience if things were as you imagine them: you are drinking a definite and particular beer, and not some merely existentially quantified beer; the only drinkable beers are definite and particular.

In building a model of an existentially quantified situation, it is natural to think of a witness to the quantification. Consider a team of architects planning a building. 'Let's have a large tree here,' says one, moving a piece of green plastic to a certain position on the model.

We cannot distinguish between what he has thereby asked us to imagine, and what he would have asked us to imagine by saying 'Let's bring it about that *there is* a large tree here.' Berkeley was right to say that we cannot imagine there being a tree which exists unperceived without imagining a tree existing unperceived. More generally, thinking of what it would be for an existential fact to obtain typically involves thinking of an individual as a witness. But thinking of an object involves exercising an individual concept. So interpreting the existential facts which are stated by indefinites typically involves exercising an individual concept. The indefinite shows that there is no definite fact about which object to think of, and hence we are not to draw upon our existing repertoire of thought-about objects. It enjoins us to think of an object even though there is no object of which it enjoins us to think.

As stressed in particular by Heim (though in different terminology), the individual concept introduced in interpreting an indefinite needs to be 'new': by using an indefinite, the speaker marks the fact that she is not requiring her hearer to have a suitable individual concept already in his repertoire. This is why re-using an indefinite suggests (even if it does not entail) that a further object is in question, as in:

27. A mosquito is buzzing about the bedroom. A mosquito is buzzing about the kitchen.

A hearer may in fact have a suitable individual concept in his repertoire. Reconsidering my utterance of (14) ('I am having dinner with a friend this evening') it may be that you already know quite well that the friend in question is Jill.[12] Even so, it would be wrong for you to use some existing individual concept of Jill in interpreting my remark, for doing so was not what my remark required.[13]

Combining the points, the claim is that interpreting an indefinite noun phrase in the kinds of case in question requires that the hearer introduce a new individual concept for a satisfier of the phrase.[14] Of many aspects of this claim requiring refinement, one is the delimitation

---

[12] If I know you know this, my remark is most naturally interpreted as arch.

[13] If the dialogue continues for long, through a number of dependent uses of 'she', it will be natural for you to use in interpretation a concept of Jill you already possess, but you will have gone beyond what has strictly been offered by the speaker.

[14] This would also explain a point made by Evans: 'this' may in some contexts (and in dialects other than Evans's own) be used in place of an indefinite, as in 'Then I met this beautiful girl...' (Evans 1982: 310).

of the kinds of case in question. One should consider excluding some sorts of negated examples ('John doesn't own a donkey') and cases in which the indefiniteness is used for generalization ('A sleepy rattler is a dangerous rattler'); one could raise questions about cases that might be treated as identities ('That's a black rhino') and also about cases in which the noun phrase is playing a predicative role ('John is a lawyer'). It would be satisfying if a syntactic criterion delimited those cases which served as antecedents for anaphoric dependence.

Imagine what Jill should do to interpret the first part of Jack's remark

8. I met a girl last night. She was absolutely gorgeous.

The first part is true iff there is at least one witnessing singular fact, a fact involving an object, the *witness*. If there is a witness, she is a girl Jack met last night. Understanding the remark involves introducing an individual concept fit to enable thought about the witness if there is one. This individual concept prepares Jill to organize further information in an appropriate way, coordinating it with the original representation as if there were a single thing concerning which the information is being collected. If there is no witness, it does not follow that dependent pronouns have no referent (assuming the modified Evans account); and if there is no referent it does not follow that the subsequent dependent pronouns are other than fully intelligible.

The concept introduced for the interpretation of 'a girl' in the first part of (8) is available for the interpretation of 'she' in the second part. A subsequent exercise of an individual concept counts as the exercise of the same individual concept only if appropriately causally related to earlier exercises. The information behaves as if stored in functionally the same 'individual file'. A manifestation of this is that Jill typically exercises the same concept only if she appreciates (no doubt in some implicit way) that, according to Jack, a single witness verifies both parts of his remark.

It would not be enough for Jill's thoughts to remain purely general in form as she interprets Jack's remark. She wants to know more about *this woman*, and so needs an individual concept to organize the information she seeks. The individual concept can be enriched as subsequent information 'about the same girl' becomes available.

All these remarks are neutral about whether this will be an empty or a non-empty individual concept. If there is a girl whom Jack met, then at least after the dialogue has developed over hours or days one cannot doubt that it has a referent and that Jill's remarks refer to that referent.

This account explains why we are tempted to believe that these pronouns refer back to an object introduced by an indefinite noun phrase. The processing truth is that in understanding such pronouns we access and exercise an existing individual concept introduced in the course of understanding the indefinite noun phrase.

An individual concept is robust with respect to the information it contains. Anything, or almost anything, can be deleted without impairing the concept's identity, which is sustained by causal links (mainly memory links). That enables Jill to use the same individual concept, the one she introduced in interpreting the first part of (8), when she digests the information Jack supplies in his correction (13) ('... before last night'). In using her individual concept to represent what Jack has claimed, she will delete information expressible as 'Jack met x last night', for this has been retracted by Jack, and will insert information expressible as 'Jack met x before last night'. (She may or may not believe that things stand as Jack now represents them.) Likewise in other correction cases. Speaker B in (7) ('It's not a mosquito, it's just a gnat') uses an individual concept introduced in the interpretation of 'a mosquito'. As a representation of what the speaker has said, the individual concept contains 'x is a mosquito', but since B does not believe this, and his belief intuitively relates to the very same thing as that which prompted A's remark, he will delete that information in using the individual concept to represent how things stand in the world and add 'x is a gnat'.

In the headmistress case (16), an interpreter will introduce an individual concept in interpreting 'A girl' and this may be available later when the culprit's identity is known and the interpreter attains a belief expressible as 'That's her'. In one kind of case, 'that' will be associated with an individual concept introduced perceptually; 'her' will be associated with a reuse of the individual concept introduced in the interpretation of 'A girl'. This story is thrown into disarray if it turns out that there were many smokers. It seems to me that there are no firm intuitions about the truth value of (16) in this case, and in particular no firm intuition that it is true, or that the headmistress has thereby committed herself to punishing all the smokers.

Possession of an individual concept for an object does not entail anything at all demanding in terms of capacity to distinguish that object from all other things. This does not mean that the notion cannot be put to use to help distinguish cases for which heavier-duty notions of 'identification' have been used. Gareth Evans considers a case in which one of two participants in a conversation says

Do you remember that bird we saw years ago? I wonder whether it was shot (Evans 1982: 308).

Evans says that the hearer does not fully understand the speaker 'until he *remembers* the bird—until the *right* information is retrieved'. Remembering the bird is indeed required, but this is not best understood in terms of the right information, for right information is just any information which in fact relates to the bird, and the question was, in effect, what makes it the case that the hearer accesses information related to the relevant bird. Nothing more is needed than that the hearer can access and bring to bear the individual concept for the bird which he introduced on the earlier occasion, and this is a causal matter. The concept is very unlikely to contain any information which would distinguish the bird from many others.

There is some temptation to suppose that thinking of the right bird is registered by some more internalistic mental property than a causal connection to an earlier state in which the bird was thought of. Despite his general sympathy to externalist positions, Evans succumbs to this temptation; but the very considerations we owe to him suggest that only a suitable causal connection can deliver the correct result. There is no upper bound on the qualitative degradation of information, but its source can still fix reference.

4.1.8 Interpretation and truth conditions

Even if it is agreed that the account of understanding is correct as far as it goes, it may be doubted whether it is complete. If knowledge of reference conditions does not play a role, then there seems no room for knowledge of truth conditions. Yet intuitively knowing what is said by the use of anaphorically dependent pronouns involves knowing what would be so if the utterances in which they are used are true. The present account must somehow address this intuition.

Developing Kripke's distinction between *de re* and *de jure* rigid designation, François Recanati (1993) has suggested that a directly referential expression can be defined as one which is 'semantically marked' as having a singular truth condition, where this is one of the form:

There is something, x, such that the utterance is true iff x is....[15]

This means that an adequate semantics for such an expression should link it with this form of truth condition. Moreover, it would intuitively seem that many uses of pronouns—for example, deictic uses—are directly referential in this sense: uses of these pronouns introduce singular truth conditions. Finally, it would seem that the same goes for some uses of anaphorically dependent pronouns, at least at the later stages of a chain of uses. If Jack was largely telling the truth about his adventures, and replies affirmatively to Jill's enquiry the next morning whether he is thinking of *her* (9), it is natural to suppose that there is an x (the girl he met two nights earlier) such that he has admitted that he is thinking of x.

If all this is correct, it ought to be reflected in a proper account of understanding, for on the present conception of a semantic description or mark, such a thing is constrained by its giving a correct picture of understanding. Yet no such connection with singular truth conditions has been forged by the account of understanding offered here; hence the account is inadequate.

Much of this is to be accepted. There is one major modification: since, according to RWR, understanding does not differentiate between the case in which Jack is telling the truth and the case in which he is not, there cannot be an absolute requirement of knowledge of a singular truth condition, for in the empty case there will be no relevant object. What I believe is involved in understanding is implicit knowledge of relativized truth conditions for uses of utterances containing dependent pronouns: according to Jack, there is an x such that Jack's utterances are true iff x is.... This registers the fact

---

[15] This part of Recanati's account is designed to apply to expression types; it adapts well to the present context in which linked tokens are at issue.

that an understander must appreciate that one who uses such pronouns represents his utterances as having singular truth conditions. It leaves more to be said about understanding, for the occurrence of the relevant variable is embedded not only in a context of quantification, but also within some non-extensional 'according to...' operator. Individual concepts are required in order to explicate knowledge thus represented.

The claim that an understander of ordinary sentences requires implicit grasp of a notion of *according to*... is justified by the fact that in interpretation we must distinguish between how things are and how things are said to be. The latter contains a representation of how things are according to the speaker, and we need to appreciate that this is so, and that things may not be the way they are said to be. Such knowledge requires at least implicit grasp of an *according to* concept. The fact that this concept is so intimately involved in the most ordinary acts of interpretation helps explain why fictional discourse is so easy for us, as consumers and as producers. The crucial, though not the only, component of recognizing discourse as fictional is that we appreciate that the speaker is not even claiming that things are really as they are according to his words.

In sum, the best picture of these kinds of uses of pronouns sees them as referring expressions, expressions which are supposed to have a referent, and which make their contribution to truth conditions in the Ockhamist way, which in turn requires a free logical framework. As Quine has said, the reference of pronouns is fundamental to reference. This foundational quality is manifest in the fact that any proper name, that paradigm of a referring expression, can be introduced by means of a pronoun. For example, the conversation between Jack and Jill could have included the sentence 'She's called Susan'.[16] It is not true in general that when one expression can be used to introduce someone to another, the two coincide in their semantic properties. For example, a rigid proper name can be introduced by means of a non-rigid definite description. However, the two features of the semantics of pronouns which seem to me the most important are ones which could but

---

[16] Should one say: 'She's called "Susan"'? I think not: the 'call' context already ensures that what follows supplies a name rather than a person. No one (as it happens) is called 'Susan', though such a name would help raise its bearer to the top of alphabetized listings, if punctuation marks are ordered before other characters.

transfer: pronouns carry no descriptive information essentially, and are not guaranteed a referent. Even if a pronoun is temporarily associated with some information, this is not transmitted by the mode of introduction: if it were, then what one learned, in learning a name via a pronoun, would depend upon the information currently associated with that pronoun, but in fact the possibility of correct learning is not in that way at the mercy of what elements of the shifting body of information are currently in place. Moreover, as we have seen, an empty pronoun can be used to introduce an empty name; this could be what is happening when Jack says that she's called Susan.

A view of anaphorically dependent pronouns which takes very seriously the fact that their use can be sustained across a number of sentences and speakers, without theoretical upper limit, is open to the charge that the nature of the pronoun undergoes a shift, becoming more like a pronoun with non-linguistic dependency, for example, a demonstratively used pronoun. I think there is some truth in this; but this truth could not be acknowledged by a radical opponent of the kind of view being put forward here, for it allows that a demonstratively used pronoun may lack a referent. Whether or not this is so needs to be addressed directly.

4.2 Non-linguistic dependence

4.2.1 Introduction

An indexical expression is one which depends for its reference upon some features of the context in which it is used, features which may vary from occasion to occasion. Taken literally, this includes more than is generally wanted. For example it includes anaphorically dependent pronouns: in an utterance of the second sentence of (4) ('It is keeping me awake'), the reference of 'it' depends upon the fact that the first sentence was uttered just before and contains the words it does. The definition would also include ordinary proper names: the fact that my utterance of 'Aristotle' refers to the author of the Nicomachean Ethics, as opposed to one of Jackie Kennedy's husbands, may in part depend upon the fact that it was made in the context of the ancient philosophy seminar. More generally, it may well be that all real-life interpretation depends upon potentially variable contextual features which fill in the open texture of linguistic meaning with the details required to fix a truth condition (see Sperber and Wilson 1986/1995).

Even if this is so, the indexical expressions of a language would still stand out as those for which the dependence upon the non-linguistic is conspicuous, systematic, and to some extent encoded in 'linguistic rules', like the supposed rule that, whenever uttered, 'I' refers to the utterer. (As we saw on p. 58 above, this is an idealization.) On this understanding, indexicals include personal and demonstrative pronouns ('you'/'she', 'this'/'that') and adverbs of time and place ('now'/'then', 'here'/'there'). The subset of demonstrative indexicals consists of those whose use is always or typically supposed to be accompanied by an act of demonstration, for example, the use of gesture to indicate the direction in which the intended referent is located. Since words like 'this' and 'that' can be used in other ways—for example, under anaphoric dependence—expressions like 'demonstrative indexical' or 'demonstrative' must be understood as shorthand for something like 'expression used demonstratively'.

The referent of a demonstrative in a specific use is fixed, if fixed at all, by some features of context, the paradigm being an act of demonstration. Generalities about reference fixing belong to what Kaplan (1977) has called the character of the expression. Character is supposed to combine with the specifics of a particular use of a demonstrative to deliver a 'content', the demonstrative's contribution to truth conditions, which, on Kaplan's view, is just its referent. Some such division between general and specific facts seems beyond question, but the following questions have disputed answers:

- How is understanding related to character (the occasion-independent, general facts) and content (the occasion-specific, truth-conditional facts)?
- Should content be identified with the referent?
- Is a use of a demonstrative with no referent intelligible?

4.2.2 Understanding and identification

You do not understand 'that' unless you know some of the general facts about its use, for example, that typically one who uses it demonstratively is aiming to pick out a specific object which she normally represents herself to believe to be accessible to you; that she may provide clues about which object she intends by gesture or by appending nouns or noun phrases, and so on. Suppose, however, that on a particular occasion you do not manage to bring this knowledge to bear in such a way as to identify the referent of a use of 'that'. Should we say that this means that you did not understand? Or should we say that you understand the words, but not what they were used to say (on that occasion)? In short, should we think of understanding in terms of knowledge of character or in terms of knowledge of content? Or both? Or in other terms altogether?

Understanding delivers knowledge: knowledge of what is said (or ordered or asked or whatever). It does not follow that understanding either consists in knowledge or is derived from knowledge. I urge two other routes to an explication of understanding: one is engagement in a practice, as discussed for proper names in Chapter 3; the other is the capacity to report what is said. The former does not get much of a grip on the makeshift and provisional 'practices' of most uses of demonstratives. The latter, however, can give us some guidance. If you understand an utterance like 'That is a fine vase' you know what was thereby said. So you should be able to say what was thereby said. You may not now be able to refer demonstratively to the vase, but that need not prevent you from giving a fully explicit and accurate report: pointing to a piece of tourist trash being sold on the pavement, she said that it was a fine vase. This pattern of reporting, in which the reporter has first to set the scene ('Pointing to a piece of tourist trash') and then use an anaphorically dependent pronoun in the content report ('*it* was a fine vase'), casts light on the understanding of some uses of demonstratives, as I explore more fully below.

To understand a use of a referential expression it is not enough to identify the referent, if any; there are restrictions upon how that identification is effected, restrictions which vary among different categories of referential expression. (It was this variety that gave rise to the title of Evans's *Varieties of Reference*.) In the case of a proper name, the interpreter is supposed to draw upon identificatory information already in his possession and naturally expressed by him using the very name the speaker has used. For example, a hearer might think: in using 'Aristotle', the speaker has referred to Aristotle. In so thinking, the hearer's own use of 'Aristotle', or its mental analogue, is associated with an individual concept under which information is subsumed, and this information is made available through the thought. In the paradigm cases of uses of demonstratives, the speaker should make available a new means of identification, which is to be used in interpretation by being coordinated with a means of identification the hearer already possesses. For example, a horse called Smarty Jones is in plain view to both of us. Not only can I see him, I am aware that you can see him too. Before there is any utterance, each is aware that the other has a means of identifying the horse, by focusing perceptual attention. If you then utter 'That is a winner', pointing at the horse, it is not enough that I believe that you have said something concerning Smarty Jones. Because understanding and interpretation are forms of knowledge, the belief must be formed by a route which is knowledge inducing. When things go as well as possible, rendering the process fully explicit would involve at least the following items of knowledge:

- I know that an act of pointing belonged to the total act of your utterance;
- I know that this pointing was supposed to guide me towards your intended referent of 'that';
- I can see that *that horse* is what you were pointing to, and so is your intended referent.

Here *that horse* represents the hearer's utterance-independent way of identifying Smarty Jones, a visual way; this way needs to be coordinated with a way the speaker has newly made available by the demonstrative gesture. This is summarized in the identity judgement: that horse is what you were pointing to. Things would not have gone as well as possible had I formed the hypothesis, even before we came to the track, that you would say something positive about Smarty Jones, and, when you uttered 'That's a winner', I felt no need to look where you were pointing, but immediately came to the correct judgement that you had said of Smarty Jones that he is a winner. This method is bad if any of the judgements upon which the final, correct judgement is based are untrue or are true but not known. Even if all the constituents are known, things have not gone as well as possible, because in interpreting the utterance you have not followed the route the hearer intended. Even if every component in your route was knowledge on this occasion, applying that method will in general be less reliable than acting more closely in accordance with the utterer's intentions. The relevant requirements cannot be extracted just from the condition that you must *know* what I am referring to. In the less satisfactory case, I might have known in advance to whom you would refer and so, after you have uttered, know to whom you did refer. Moreover, the way the knowledge is to be reached varies for different types of referring expression.

In the case envisaged, the interpreter needed an *independent* way of identifying the referent, one which would have been available to the hearer whether or not she had succeeded in interpreting the utterance. My view of Smarty Jones was available independently of interpreting your utterance; I use it in interpreting your words, as you use a similar view in uttering them. This suggests the hypothesis that this is generally so: when all goes as it should, interpreting a referring expression involves an identity judgement, typically implicit, in which an interpretation-independent way of identifying the referent is coordinated with an interpretation-dependent way. In interpreting, I come to know to whom or what you refer, and this means identifying the object by a means which is independent of your utterance, and judging that that object, thus independently identified, is identical with the object to which you have referred.

4.2.3 *Understanding and theories of meaning*

One test of the adequacy of a semantic theory is that it should state something knowledge of which would suffice for understanding any utterance in the language. Understanding is an ability or skill, and the proposal is to represent it in terms of propositional knowledge which would lead from knowledge of circumstances which form the input to the skill, say the perceptual recognition of an utterance's non-semantic properties, to the knowledge the skill delivers, that is, knowledge of meaning, or understanding. To the extent that there is unclarity about what to count as understanding, there is unclarity about what to count as the goal of semantic theory conceived in this way. How should an adherent of this project think of understanding, so as to maximize the project's value and attainability? There seems to be a dilemma. If understanding is knowledge of character, it does not extend to knowledge of truth conditions, and misses much that is distinctive and important in the exercise of linguistic skills. If understanding is knowledge of content, it seems to involve the exercise of general cognitive abilities, and even if one were optimistic that these could be encoded in statement form, in the way that Davidson envisaged for language, the task would be impossibly large, and the language-specific facts would be lost in a morass of others.

Reference may be determined in ways that need not be appreciated in order for things to go as well as possible in interpretation. This possibility was exploited in the previous section: the referent of an anaphoric pronoun is determined in ways that an interpreter need not appreciate. The general possibility is familiar from theories of proper names. As argued in Chapter 3, the referent of a name is determined by some complex chain of causes running back to an initial baptism. Interpretation can go as well as possible without the interpreter believing this theory, let alone knowing its application to the specific case. I need not know any details of how the chain of causes reaches back from my utterance of 'Aristotle' in the ancient philosophy seminar to the great philosopher. We can know what the referent of an expression on an occasion is without having knowledge of the facts which make this so. There is accordingly room for a 'semantic theory' which is not a theory of understanding: a theory which says in a general way how reference is determined for various categories of expression.

We should therefore expect that in many cases a theory of understanding will take for granted how reference is determined. Tyler Burge has suggested how this might be done in the case of demonstratives. On this picture, understanding is closer to knowledge of character than to knowledge of content; but the suggestion makes room for extracting knowledge of content from knowledge of character together with knowledge of relevant occasion-specific facts. The following subsection adds some detail.

4.2.4 *Conditional truth conditions*

If we take as primitive within the semantic theory what it is for a speaker to refer to an object by using an expression, we can hope to include generalized, conditional truth conditions of the form:

> 28. For all x, if a speaker utters 'That is F' thereby using 'that' to refer to x, the utterance is true iff x satisfies F (see Burge 1974*b*).

This is purely general, in that it refers to no specific entity other than the target expression 'that', but it can combine with occasion-specific information about the make-up of the utterance and what the speaker has referred to so as to deliver a truth condition. If we know the generalization we can apply instantiation to come to know:

> if Jack uttered 'That is a winner' thereby using 'that' to refer to Smarty Jones, the utterance is true iff Smarty Jones satisfies 'is a winner'.

If we know an occasion-specific premise to the effect that John referred to Smarty Jones by uttering 'that' in 'that is a winner', we can apply *modus ponens* to come to know

> John's utterance of 'That is a winner' is true iff Smarty Jones satisfies 'is a winner'

and so to come to know

> 29. John's utterance of 'That is a winner' is true iff Smarty Jones is a winner.

On this approach, just as the generalization does not give one a complete semantic story, so English demonstratives are as such semantically incomplete. They need to be completed by some action on the part of the speaker. Given suitable information about that completion, we can then derive a truth condition. In effect the approach abandons any attempt to give a rule for determining the referent of 'that' as used on a particular occasion in favour of a rule for determining how, given that it has a referent, that fact impinges on truth conditions. In what is abandoned, semantic theory sets on one side an impossible task; in what is undertaken, it goes further than character.

Although the truth of (29) cannot be disputed, semantic theorists aspire to specifications of truth conditions which will reveal the 'meaning' of the utterance in question. This aspiration may be unclear, but one test for its achievement is that the meaning-revealing truth conditions should be useable in a correct and fully explicit report of what the speaker has said. It is not fully correct to report that John said that Smarty Jones is a winner. John said something which committed him to this, but we do not describe his saying as accurately as we could if we use a proper name where he used a demonstrative. This is specially clear for an utterance like 'That is (or is not) Smarty Jones'; it would not be fully correct to report the speaker as having said that Smarty Jones is (or is not) Smarty Jones. We cannot always simply reuse a demonstrative in reporting his speech; for example, this route is unavailable if we are reporting it in a situation in which we are unable to demonstrate Smarty Jones (later that evening in the bar, or years after Smarty Jones's death). These considerations mean that the envisaged application of the strategy of providing conditional truth conditions in the style of (28), though it does not lead to anything false, will not serve standard semantic aspirations. Those aspirations would be met only if consequences like (29) were to contain a truth condition immediately usable to give a full and correct report of speech, but as things stand this is not so.

In interpretation, we want something relatively lasting and context-independent, something that we can recall and reuse and tell others about. This contrasts with the ephemeral and context-dependent nature of many utterances we interpret. The contrast is in practice resolved by abandoning the idea that there is a sentence which will self-standingly and enduringly serve the purposes of interpretation. There is no sentence that we can wheel out on arbitrary occasions which would simply 'give the content' of what John said in uttering 'That is a winner'. Interpretation typically requires that we first set the scene, and only within the scene can we find words adequate to express what was said. In the present case, a possibility is:

30. Pointing at Smarty Jones, John said that he was a winner.

'He' is anaphorically dependent upon 'Smarty Jones': they should have the same referent. This is not a mere 'pronoun of laziness', in the sense of a pronoun which can as well be replaced by the noun upon which it depends, for we have already seen that it is not fully correct to report John as having said that Smarty Jones is a winner. In many cases, of which this is one example, we cannot 'detach' a self-standing content which matches what John said.[17] Interpretation typically requires us to set a scene, upon which the specification of the reported content is essentially dependent. The extra-linguistic dependence characteristic of demonstratives is transformed in interpretation into linguistic dependence, the dependence of an anaphoric pronoun in the content-specifying part of the interpretation upon an expression in the scene-setting part.

[17] Sainsbury (2002: 137–58) calls this the thesis of non-detachability.

There is a close analogy between a report of speech like (30) and what one might hope to derive from a semantic theory. The difference is that (30) contains no reference to the words used, whereas a semantic theory should address them. A semantic theory may model itself on the idea behind (30), using theorems like (28), and preserving the duplex structure of scene setting and content specification, to end up with an 'instance' of (28) along these lines:

31. John's utterance of 'That is a winner', thereby using 'that' to refer to Smarty Jones, is true iff it satisfies 'is a winner'

where 'it' in the content-specifying component is anaphorically dependent on, and corefers with, 'Smarty Jones' in the scene-setting component. I shall say, of both statements like (31) and reports of speech like (30), that they exemplify the 'scene/content' structure.

Pronouns used demonstratively typically have an absolute (not merely conditional) singular truth condition with scene/content structure, one of the form:

32. There is an object, x, such that the utterance is true iff x is thus.[18]

Starting with generalized conditional truth conditions on the lines of (28) we can derive such singular truth conditions from contextually available specific information, using *modus ponens* and standard quantifier rules. A singular truth condition also associates the utterance with a non-self-standing content, for the 'x', or pronoun, depends on a phrase outside the scope of the condition. Even if we suppose that every thought, including whatever thought the speaker had when uttering, say 'That is a winner', must have a complete content involving more than just the object of reference, abstraction from whatever that content might be is of value from the point of view of interpretation. It may be that correct interpretation can go no further, and cannot supply a self-standing singular term fit to occupy the place filled by 'x', for the reasons noted in the previous paragraph. This has two interesting consequences: it provides a gloss on, and an explanation for, the view that demonstratives are 'directly referential'; and it involves a qualification of the view that understanding entails knowledge of truth conditions.

[18] This duplex structure is more frequently employed than discussed. See for example Kripke (1972/1980: 6): 'there is a certain man—the philosopher we call "Aristotle"—such that, as a matter of fact, (1) [Aristotle was fond of dogs] is true if and only if *he* was fond of dogs.'

In a singular truth condition, the referent is specified without any indication of how it was thought of. If a singular truth condition states all that needs to be known for understanding, nothing about how the object was thought of need be known in understanding. This does justice to Kaplan's claim that such expressions are 'directly referential':

> The directly referential term goes *directly* to its referent, directly in the sense that it does not first pass through the proposition. Whatever rules, procedures or mechanisms there are that govern the search for the referent, they are irrelevant to the propositional component, to content (Kaplan 1989: 569).

On the other hand, we saw that when all goes as well as possible, an interpreter's way of identifying the referent is constrained. Hence for the interpreter to know a singular truth condition is not enough for everything to go as well as possible in interpretation. Effectively the same considerations also show that understanding must go beyond knowledge of a truth condition, on a narrow construal of 'truth condition' according to which a truth condition for a sentence or thought s is a complete proposition, whose truth is necessary and sufficient for 'true' to be correctly predicated of s. What I have called a singular truth condition, along with any proposition with scene/content structure, is not a truth condition in this sense. The closest approach to a relevant proposition is incomplete (for example 'x is a winner'). The external quantification in a singular truth condition is a minimal piece of scene setting, playing a similar role to what precedes the comma in 'Seeing a hare, he said that it was a rabbit'. So called *de re* ascriptions are other examples of the duplex scene/content structure, with the scene component containing something like 'Concerning the man in the brown hat'. Anyone who understands an utterance containing an indexical and remembers what they have understood must know something expressible in the scene/content structure, in which the content specification is incomplete, being anaphorically dependent upon material in the scene-setting component. Though the contents in the duplex structures do not strictly give truth conditions, it is convenient to extend the notion of a truth condition beyond its normal use so as to include these incomplete contents.

In a truth condition or speech report with scene/content structure, the content-specifying component attributes a referent to a singular term by means of an anaphorically dependent pronoun, and so without associating the term with anything other than the referent. Yet as we saw earlier there are constraints upon how an interpreter should identify the referent. These constraints must somehow feature in the scene-setting component. How this should be done is addressed in §4.2.7.

4.2.5 Object dependence

Suppose that utterances u_1 and u_2 are associated respectively with the following scene/content truth conditions, where Smarty Jones is distinct from Black Velvet:

33. Smarty Jones is such that u_1 is true iff he is a winner.

34. Black Velvet is such that u_2 is true iff he is a winner.

Intuitively, these are distinct truth conditions, since they involve different objects, despite the fact that the same words follow the 'iff'. The utterances in question are 'object-dependent': what their truth conditions are is dependent upon which object is the referent of some referring expression they contain. Evans gives a similar example to make a similar point: the occupant of a well-oiled bed which is being moved from place to place refers to different places by successive utterances of 'here', so the successive utterances diverge in truth conditions (without any change in the internalistic features of the utterer) (Evans 1982: 201–2).

From the fact that there are object-dependent utterances, we cannot infer that any utterance is 'object involving' in the sense of requiring an object in order to be intelligible. No utterance which contains a referring expression which lacks a referent can have a singular truth condition. The next section considers the impact of this on the intelligibility of utterances containing demonstratives.

4.2.6 Understanding without identification?

Does a hearer understand an utterance involving a pronoun used demonstratively if, although there is a referent, the hearer fails to identify it? In the case of a demonstrative use of 'that' based on perception, the hearer may not be able to see what the speaker demonstrates, and so lacks an independent way of identifying it as the referent. Clearly, things have not gone as well as they could, but the specific question is whether part of the failure is a failure to understand. A preliminary question is what it is for an object to be the referent of the use of a demonstrative.

In the case of proper names, we can distinguish between the public referent of a name as used on an occasion and the referent intended by the speaker on that occasion. Suppose a speaker, seeing Hillary Clinton, mistakes her for Susan Sontag and, pointing to Clinton, sincerely says 'Susan Sontag grew up in Tucson'. It would be wrong to say that the speaker intended to refer to Clinton; but arguably right to say that Clinton is someone to whom the speaker intended to refer. If that is right, the object to which the speaker's referential intentions in fact relate, her speaker referent, may diverge from the public semantic referent of the expression she uses.

In the case of pronouns used demonstratively, it may seem that no such gap could open up, for there are no relevant facts distinct from the speaker's use of the demonstrative pronoun which could ground the notion of a public referent potentially distinct from the speaker's referent. On the other hand, it does not seem right to say that any object to which the speaker intends to refer counts as the referent of the pronoun on that occasion. There seems to be nothing to stop two objects being each such that the speaker intended to refer to it in the use of the pronoun (I assume some sort of confusion on the part of the speaker), but there cannot be two genuine semantic referents of a singular referring expression (relative to a single use). The unsatisfactoriness of identifying the referent with an object intended to be the referent also emerges by example. Suppose the apple on the speaker's left is the one to which she intends to refer in uttering 'that apple looks juicy', but as she speaks she points to an apple on her right. It seems that an interpreter who takes the speaker to have said, concerning the apple on the speaker's right, that it is juicy, cannot be faulted. If so, this means that the public referent of the pronoun is the apple demonstrated, and not the apple intended.

The data in this area are not very firm, but a plausible, and pretty uncontroversial partial principle, would run along these lines:

> if in using a pronoun demonstratively, x is the only object the speaker thereby intended to refer to, and x can also reasonably

be taken as the object of any demonstrative gestures the speaker makes, then x is the referent (i.e. the public semantic referent) of the speaker's act.

When the object of intentions and demonstrative gestures come apart, this condition does not tell us what to say; and perhaps there is nothing very definite to say. For present purposes, it is enough that the question of whether there is a referent is independent of whether the hearer succeeds in identifying one.

A basis for saying that a hearer who does not identify the referent does not understand is that understanding is knowledge of truth conditions (in the liberal sense to include scene/content structures like singular truth conditions). Failure to identify the referent is either having no opinion about the truth conditions or else the wrong opinion (if there is an object one wrongly supposes to be the referent). For the classic direct-reference theorist, either type of failure to know truth conditions is a failure of understanding.

Alternatively, one might say that a hearer who does not identify the referent may still understand, on the grounds that understanding is knowledge of character. Knowledge of character is consistent with either no belief or a false belief about which object is the referent. Classic descriptivist theories would approve of this approach.

Neither of these theory-based answers can be used unless the theories have independent support. Even if some version of the theories do have such support, controversial aspects arise on the very issue in question. For example, the identification of understanding with truth conditions does not apply directly to utterances which lack truth conditions, like questions and commands. The theory has to be modified to allow understanding without truth conditions in such cases; there would be nothing inconsistent with modifying it so that the same is possible in the cases before us. Considering the alternative theoretical approach, knowledge of character is clearly insufficient for participation in real-life interpretation. If understanding is confined to the 'purely linguistic', it may end up as something too anaemic to play an interesting role in an account of communication. The ordinary use of 'misunderstood' and its cognates is too broad to have any theoretical recommendation. For example, we say that a hearer who has not appreciated a conversational implicature has not understood, and even that a hearer who has failed to appreciate some important relevant fact has misunderstood: 'You don't understand: John is a professor, not a student'.

Suppose that one who understands a demonstrative utterance in which reference is made must identify that referent. I aim to show that even if this is correct, it is still plausible that at least some utterances containing demonstratives which fail to refer can be understood. This shows that the main theme of RWR, the possibility of intelligible empty reference, extends to demonstratives.

4.2.7 Understanding empty demonstratives

If we link understanding with the possibility of giving a correct report of what is said, the verdict is that there are cases of demonstrative uses of pronouns which are intelligible though they have no referent. This is because there are scene settings which report a mistake-involving state of the speaker, for example:

35. Wrongly thinking that there was a bull in her field of view, she said that it was not dangerous.

A speaker who meant to refer to a bull but referred to nothing can properly be reported in this way. This gives grounds for saying that there can be intelligible empty uses.[19]

This does not entail that every case in which there is no referent is intelligible. As Evans stresses, there are variations among empty cases. He thinks that most will agree (and I do) that one who points into empty space and says 'That thing is coming towards me' has uttered intelligible words but cannot be understood as having said

---

[19] Are any expressions immune? Can 'I' be used intelligibly yet fail to have a referent? Here is how: a burglar visits a home which he believes to be occupied but which is in fact not. He leaves a message on the answering machine which begins 'I am not at home right now...' intending that callers should treat the 'I' as referring to the occupant. Since there is no occupant, this looks like a case in which an intelligible 'I'-utterance is empty. This kind of deferred or dependent use is also possible for the other indexical expressions. The best candidate for a kind of expression immune to emptiness is tense. Frege said: 'If a time-indication is conveyed by the present tense one must know when the sentence was uttered in order to grasp the sense correctly. Therefore the time of utterance is part of the expression of the thought' (Frege 1918: 358). It also seems that even using the scene/content structure, failing to specify the time of the utterance leads to a less than fully explicit report. 'Speaking at some past time, Jack said that it was raining then' is a less adequate report than one which specifies the time at which Jack spoke.

something. In contrast, he suggests that if the speaker had mistaken a shadow for a woman, a remark containing 'that woman' would express a thought, even though one without an object (Evans 1982: 337 n.). His comment on hallucinatory cases is nuanced:

I do not mean to deny that one can arrive at some kind of understanding of what is going on, if one realizes that the speaker is hallucinating and intends to be speaking of a man he sees. (One could even say: if there were a man he was seeing in having this hallucination, then that man would be the referent of his utterance.) But this kind of understanding does not count as *understanding the remark*: it is not the kind of information-based response the speaker was intending to produce (Evans 1982: 338 n.).

The scene/content style of report allows such cases in a very straightforward way. A hallucination-governed utterance of 'That little green man is bald' can be reported as:

36. Hallucinating a little green man, she said that he was bald.

We can agree with Evans that in empty cases not all of the speaker's intentions will be satisfied. It is not clear that this is best described as failing to understand the remark; that seems to me to be a terminological issue. The availability of scene/content reporting, by contrast, relates to something deep in the very notion of communication.

It is a platitude that in understanding we need to see things from the speaker's point of view. If the speaker makes a demonstrative gesture, we need to work out what object is being demonstrated. We need to make allowances: perhaps we realize that the speaker cannot tell that the demonstrated object is not visible to us because of a difference in our positions. We may need to move or make other adjustments to reach a suitable interpretation. The root of interpretation involves a reconstruction of the speaker's view of things, within which alone are the demands of intelligibility properly set. Normally in a linguistic community speaker and hearer have enough in common in their overall view for the reconstructive effort to seem minimal or even absent. As a fellow academic, you will interpret my words 'I have a paper deadline next week' as saying that I am due to complete an academic paper next week, not that I have a deadline that is on paper only and not set in stone. It is normally so effortless that we do not notice how much reconstruction is involved.

The scene/content reporting structure, and the *de re* attribution which is an example of it, is a manifestation of the general phenomenon to which these platitudes allude. It is often easier to know which objects and properties a speaker is invoking than to know fine details of how they are thinking about them. We are typically on safer ground in saying something like 'Speaking of object *a* and property *F*, the speaker said that the former possessed the latter' than in saying that the speaker said that *a* is *F*. The latter requires that the content the speaker expressed matches the content I associate with '*a* is *F*', whereas the former does not. The former can allow for different viewpoints on a shared world of objects and properties.

The scene/content structure shows how we can approach a good report even when we cannot use demonstratives as the speaker did; demonstration converts to anaphora. This is part of a wider picture in which direct *de dicto* reports are seen as available only as a result of our good fortune in, normally, having closely similar world views. As Quine stressed, homophonic translation may mask our dependence on various assumptions of similarity.

The scene/content structure is tailor-made to accommodate perceived error. Seeing a rabbit, he said that it was a hare. Thinking the male transvestite was a woman, he asked him for a date. Still believing the old phlogiston theory, he surmised that there might be negative quantities of it. In the second example, we can predict that the request was couched using a feminine second-person pronoun (if the speaker used a language with this resource). In the third, we can predict that, if the surmise was voiced, some word like 'phlogiston' was used with no qualification. The structure's capacity to give an intelligible and helpful report of some utterances with non-referring demonstratives, as in (36), is part of this wider picture of what is involved in our understanding of others.

We cannot extend this claim about some utterances to all. Suppose the interrogators have not discovered that their victim is blind, and flash a series of photographs of his possible collaborators on the wall. The victim is asked to say 'That is one!' when the photograph is of a collaborator. Being blind, but wishing to cooperate, the victim shouts 'That is one!' at a point intermediate between pictures being flashed. In this case, there is no way of reporting what he said; so, by the test adopted here, nothing was said. It is not just that the demonstrative has no referent, but also that the speaker was not even intending to use it to refer, and was not even intending that it refer relative to some 'according to' context. One cannot expect utterances produced with incomplete or defective intentions to be capable of being understood; lack of a referent is a symptom but not the essence.

4.3 Main themes reviewed

The concept of a referring expression developed in this chapter is of an expression which is normally supposed to refer, but which may not. It is normally supposed to refer because normally it must refer if what is said is to be true. Understanding such an expression involves using an individual concept, created by a mechanism whose survival is owed to its producing concepts with individual objects as their referent, so cases in which the individual concept lacks a referent are typically cases of malfunction. (There are also cases, in indirect contexts, existential sentences, and fiction, in which lack of a referent does not correspond to any malfunction of any mechanism in the speaker.)

The account allows that referring expressions are rigid designators, and typically express singular thoughts. There are as many singular thoughts on the present view as on a direct-reference view. But on this view, unlike the direct-reference view, a failed singular thought or utterance can be a genuine thought, or an utterance which succeeds in saying something: these have, if not truth conditions, at least conditional truth conditions, and can be reported in the standard scene/content way.

5
Complex referring expressions

The aim of this chapter is to extend the RWR account of reference to complex referring expressions. In §5.1, I discuss cases in which proper names are compounded (as in 'Plato and Aristotle'). I aim to motivate two views which are needed in §5.2: that being semantically simple is not necessary to being a referring expression; and that having a single object as referent is not necessary to being a referring expression. The main business of the chapter lies in §5.2, which argues that some definite descriptions, in some uses, are referring expressions. Although various objections have to be considered, I take it that the upshot of §5.1 removes the need for me to consider the Russellian view that because definite descriptions are semantically complex they cannot be referring expressions. Both plural and singular definite descriptions are under discussion, and I rely on §5.1 to make room for the view that plural definite descriptions refer to many things.

5.1   Compound names

A full account of proper names would address not only their simple use (as in 'Plato is pale') but also their use in compounds, like

1. Plato and Aristotle are philosophers.
2. Plato or Aristotle said that knowledge is recollection.

A familiar idea is that such sentences abbreviate others in which the names have their simple use:

3. Plato is a philosopher, and Aristotle is a philosopher.

4. Plato said that knowledge is recollection, or Aristotle said that knowledge is recollection.

Although the relevant notion of abbreviation is obscure, this is clearly a reasonable option to pursue for such cases, and it may be the best one to pursue for all disjunctive compounds.[1] There are conjunctive compounds for which the option seems less promising:

5. Plato and Aristotle were compatriots.
6. Plato and Aristotle together weighed more than me.

Applying the earlier recipe mechanically produces:

7. Plato was a compatriot, and Aristotle was a compatriot.
8. Plato together weighed more than me, and Aristotle together weighed more than me.

The first of these, (7), is of doubtful intelligibility, and certainly does not have the same truth conditions as (5); the second, (8), is close to intelligible (and would be entirely so were it not for the 'together'), but probably differs in truth value from (6) and certainly differs in truth conditions. More complex paraphrases can be offered, for example:

9. There is a country which is the homeland of Plato and the homeland of Aristotle.
10. If the weight of Plato is added to the weight of Aristotle, the result is greater than my weight.

These may be equivalent to the cases in which 'and' appears to connect names, but they cannot with any plausibility be said to reveal the semantic mechanisms whereby (5) and (6) say what they say. The paraphrases suggest that completely different mechanisms are at work in the two cases. Moreover, there are cases in which paraphrase is hard to find, for example,

11. Plato and Aristotle are together lifting the table.

The problems are acute when compound names (or what appear to be such) occur with predicates which are not distributive, where a predicate, *F*, is distributive if: if some things are *F* each one of them is

---

[1] This is not obviously so. 'Plato or Aristotle could help you' is more like a conjunction of the simple sentences.

F (McKay 2003). Doing proper justice to non-distributive predicates calls for a modification of classical logic. If all the men lifted the piano and Jack is a man, it does not follow that Jack lifted the piano. Yet this is a classical consequence if the first premise is a straightforward universal quantification.[2]

These considerations suggest that we need to regard compound names as a kind of referring expression, thus allowing in general that an expression is not precluded from this status by being semantically complex. The next question is whether we must treat compound names as referring to more than one thing, or whether, rather, we should treat them as referring to a single thing, a set, aggregate or plurality.

Suppose that 'Plato and Aristotle' refers to the set whose members are just Plato and Aristotle. Then, at a first shot, (11) should be true iff that set are together lifting the table. If this is intelligible, it is false, for sets do not lift tables. Pursuing this option would require a thoroughgoing revision of predicates. The first move is to see the plural in the verb not as signalling, as it normally does, some kind of plurality in its subject, but rather as so transforming the verb and its verb phrase that they apply to sets. Perhaps 'are together lifting the table' should, in these special contexts, have as its extension just sets whose members are together lifting the table. Even if one can stomach the rigmarole, the explanatory value is limited, for it is assumed that we know what it is for various members of a set, say Plato and Aristotle, to be together lifting the table. There is nothing objectionable, according to the methodology adopted here, in reusing object language notions in the metalanguage. If this is what one is going to end up doing, one might as well do it at the outset: we should take at face value the plural nature of the verb.

In keeping with this, one could give the following axiom for conjunctively compounded names:

12. If *m* refers to *a* and *n* refers to *b*, then the expression formed by inserting an 'and' between *m* and *n* refers to *a* and *b*.

The variables '*m*' and '*n*' are to range over simple and compound names, so that the clause works recursively, specifying the reference

---

[2] McKay (2003) gives a thorough review of attempts to explain away non-distributivity.

of 'Matthew and Mark and Luke', regarded as abbreviating for example 'Matthew and (Mark and Luke)', and as itself abbreviated by 'Matthew, Mark and Luke'. (Some obvious conventions about bracketing and dropping brackets are taken for granted.) Axiom (12) is firmly non-distributive: it does not follow from the fact that some expression refers to *a* and *b* that it refers to *a* and to *b*. We can first check that this delivers the right truth conditions and then consider some consequences.

The general notion of reference requires that a subject–predicate sentence is true iff what the subject refers to satisfies (the singular case) or satisfy (the plural case) the predicate.[3] 'Plato and Aristotle are together lifting the table' is true iff what 'Plato and Aristotle' refers to, that is, Plato and Aristotle, satisfy 'are together lifting the table'. 'Plato and Aristotle' refers neither to Plato nor to Aristotle. If it did, then 'Plato' would be a correct answer to 'what does "Plato and Aristotle" refer to?' This would mean that, in 'Plato and Aristotle are philosophers', what 'Plato and Aristotle' refers to is Plato, and given the general account of the way reference affects truth conditions, Plato's being a philosopher would be enough for the truth of the sentence. Hence 'Plato and Aristotle' does not refer to Plato; and for similar reasons it does not refer to Aristotle.[4]

A classical singular variable is one fit to occupy the position taken by a singular referring expression, paradigmatically a proper name. The classical explanation of the semantics of such variables starts by thinking of them as temporary names: like names, a valuation assigns to each an entity from the domain. Once we have the notion of a plural referring expression, like conjoined names, we can introduce the idea of a plural variable, one fit to occupy the position taken by a plural referring expression, for example, a conjunction of names. Their semantics is explained classically as their being temporary conjunctions of names: like them, each is assigned entities from the domain. With both these notions in place, one can form the concept

---

[3] This is consistent with both Strawsonian and Ockhamist accounts of truth conditions; at present the argument needs to be as neutral as possible.
[4] If one misses the consistency of ' "Plato and Aristotle" refers to Plato and Aristotle, but not to Plato and not to Aristotle' one will be drawn to an ontology in which there are pluralities. The consistency is like that of 'Plato and Aristotle together weigh 400 lbs; Aristotle doesn't weigh 400 lbs'; or the consistency of: 'Russell didn't write *Principia*. Nor did Whitehead. They did it together.' (Oliver 2000: 371).

of a neutral variable, one fit to be occupied by either a singular or a plural referring expression. Writing such variables as upper-case Greek letters, and using '=' neutrally for identity, whether between singular terms or plural terms, we can state the unified at-most condition on referring expressions, singular and plural:

13. If e refers to Θ and to Π, then $\Theta = \Pi$.

The composition axiom which implicitly defines what it is to be a referring expression was stated just for singular referring expressions in Chapter 2:

14. If S is a sentence in which the n-place concept-expression R is combined with referring expressions $t_1 \ldots t_n$, then S is true iff <the referent of t_1 ... the referent of t_n> satisfies R; and is false iff it is not true.

To make it neutral between singular and plural we can replace each occurrence of 'referent' by 'referent or referents'. A sequent satisfies a predicate by the predicate being true of its elements, taken in the corresponding order. <The referents of 'Plato and Aristotle'> satisfies 'weighed 400 lbs' iff the predicate is true of the referents of 'Plato and Aristotle', that is, of Plato and Aristotle; iff Plato and Aristotle weighed 400 lbs. No third thing, a non-philosopher (a set or a plurality), is required for the truth of such a banal remark.

If compounded names are referring expressions, then (a) being semantically simple is not a requirement for being a referring expression, and (b) referring to at most one single thing is not a requirement on being a referring expression. These theses, together with the RWR idea that a referring expression may fail to refer, help pave the way for a reconsideration of whether definite descriptions are referring expressions.

5.2 Definite descriptions

5.2.1 Introduction

Some definite descriptions are singular, like 'the present King of France' and 'the gold in Zurich', and some are plural, like 'the people in Auckland'. The singular cases, as the examples suggest, may be subdivided according to the nature of the predicate which follows 'the'.

In the usual examples of singular definite descriptions, this is a predicate which 'divides its reference': it is satisfied by individual continuous things. In an example like 'the gold in Zurich' the predicate does not divide its reference but is satisfied, if by anything, by a quantity of a chemical substance. On the face of it, a proper account of 'the' should provide a unified account of its occurrence in all these kinds of cases.

A natural initial thought is that definite descriptions are referring expressions, and an important element in the motivation for the development of free logics was to do justice to this intuitive thought (Lambert 2001: 37). Definite descriptions seem similar to names: they are often or typically used to pick things out, and as focal points for the storage of information. There are domestic examples ('the baby'), etiquette examples ('The Chair will correct me if I am wrong, but...'), near-demonstrative examples ('Now watch: the lioness will let the male feed first'; 'Please pass the screwdriver'), and cases in which a definite description appears to be flanking an expression for identity ('The first man in space was Gagarin'). In these cases, speakers would typically be as willing to use, rather than a definite description, an uncontroversial referring expression like a name or a demonstrative: they may be held back by etiquette ('the Chair'), or by ignorance of a suitable name or there simply not being one ('the lioness'). A definite description is a standard way of introducing a name, and although more complex accounts are possible, the simplest explanation is that the definite description refers to the referent of the name. A definite description can seem more natural than a demonstrative for a familiar object ('the baby': saying 'that baby' might suggest the baby in question was other than one's own; one imagines the participants to have been watching the referent of 'the lioness' for a while). Definite descriptions can answer 'Who?' questions just as names can, and like names they can appear on lists of objects.

According to Russell, these intuitions are mistaken. His theory of descriptions addresses only singular cases in which the predicate divides its reference. It makes two claims which are often run together. One relates to definite descriptions themselves, and says that they are not referring expressions but are quantifier phrases ('in logical form'). The other relates to sentences which contain definite descriptions, and claims that those of the form 'The F is G'

are true iff exactly one thing is F and that thing is G. For Russell, there is an easy route to the first part of the claim: since he believed that a referring expression has to refer, and it is obvious that not all definite descriptions do so, some of them are not referring expressions; and since all should be treated alike ('by parity of form'), none of them are. This immediately makes plausible the view that they are quantifier phrases. Since the RWR notion of a referring expression is of one which can be intelligible even if it does not refer, this reason for excluding definite descriptions from the class of referring expressions is uncompelling. Denying that definite descriptions are quantifier phrases is consistent with accepting Russellian truth conditions for sentences containing definite descriptions.

5.2.2 *Examples of referential axioms*

A candidate referential axiom for definite descriptions is

15. for all x ('the F' refers to x iff x and x alone satisfies F).

In conjunction with uncontentious additional axioms, this will lead to Russellian truth conditions for sentences containing definite descriptions. To simplify, consider this form of composition axiom, confined to monadic predicates, F, and arbitrary singular referring expressions, t:

16. Ft is true iff there is an x such that t refers to x and x satisfies F.

Applying this to a standard example:

'The King of France is bald' is true iff
  there is an x such that 'the King of France' refers to x and x satisfies 'bald', iff
  there is an x such that x and x alone satisfies 'King of France' and x is bald, iff
  there is an x such that x and x alone is King of France and x is bald.

Accepting Russellian truth conditions for sentences containing definite descriptions does not require denying that definite descriptions are referring expressions.

Quite how much 'pragmatic' material features in the reference conditions for definite descriptions is an issue entirely orthogonal to whether or not they are referring expressions. They could be given referential axioms in a way which yields truth conditions very different from Russell's. For example, with some element of caricature, we might suggest something along the following lines as capturing a suggestion of Donnellan's (1966):

17. for all x ('the F' refers to x iff x and x alone is such that:
    the utterer intends his utterance to concern x;
    the utterer intends his audience to realize the utterance concerns x;
    the utterer believes he can realize these intentions by using 'the F').

In the circumstances envisaged by Donnellan, this reference condition would deliver these truth conditions for an utterance by u of 'The man drinking martini is drunk': there is an object such that it and it alone is something u intends his utterance to concern, and intends his audience to realize he intends it to concern and believes he can succeed by these words; and it is drunk. It is obvious that this would not be a good way of reporting what the speaker said. Donnellan never suggested that it would. He has generally been taken to be committed to the view that the person the utterer intended to refer to is such that what the speaker said is true iff that person is drunk.[5] He is certainly not committed to the truth of the biconditional, derived from (17), whose lengthy right-hand side, it would be universally agreed, would not provide a good report of what the speaker said.

Within the RWR account, any referring expression is rigid. This is secured by the composition axiom (a more elaborate version of (16)), not by these kinds of referential axioms themselves. We could move to a more closely homophonic account if referential definite descriptions are allowed in the metalanguage. In place of (15) we would have

18. for all x ('the F' refers to x iff $x=$ the satisfier of 'F').

To derive a homophonic T-theorem we would need supplementary principles:

19. From:
    s is true iff for some x, $x=t$ and x is G

---

[5] Kripke (1977) shows convincingly that Donnellan carefully refrains from making this commitment. But then, as Kripke says, Donnellan's claim that his position is inconsistent with Russell's appears groundless.

infer:

s is true iff *t* is G.

We also need to be able to replace expressions of the form '$x =$ the satisfier of "F"' by corresponding ones '$x =$ the F'. The derivation can be sketched:

'The King of France is bald' is true iff
there is an x such that 'the King of France' refers to x and x satisfies 'bald', iff
there is an x such that $x =$ the satisfier of 'King of France' and x is bald, iff
there is an x such that $x =$ the King of France and x is bald, iff
the King of France is bald.

In a presentation of this kind, the assumptions that metalanguage definite descriptions are referring expressions, and that referring expressions are rigid, tell us that the object language definite descriptions are also rigid even before we examine the composition axiom.

Those who reject the view that referring expressions are rigid may wish to count some or all definite descriptions as non-rigid referring expressions.[6] One could adopt a world-relativized version of (15), for example:

20. for all x, w ('the F' refers-at-w to x iff x and x alone satisfies-at-w 'F').

A parallel version of the composition axiom would be:

21. for all w, 'Gt' is true-at-w iff there is an x such that 't' refers-at-w to x and x satisfies-at-w 'G'.

Rigidity for some uses of 'the', ones we will represent by using bold, could be thought of as something which could be added by a distinctive reference axiom, for example:

22. for all x, w ('**The** F' refers-at-w to x iff x and x alone satisfies-at-$w^\star$ 'F') where '$w^\star$' rigidly designates the actual world.

Some logical matters concerning definite descriptions have long been contentious. Free logic supplies various options (nicely reviewed by Lambert 2001). RWR adopts the version of NFL

---

[6] An example of a free logician who does this is Simons (2001).

argued for by Burge (1974a). The main points are that the following schemas are not valid:

The F is the F.
The F is F.
If for all x (Fx iff Gx) then the F is the G.

In each case the reason is that a simple sentence (one which results from an n-ary predicate by inserting n referring expressions) containing a referring expression with no referent is false. By contrast, the following schemas are valid according to RWR:

If the F exists, the F is the F.
If the F exists, the F is F.
If for all x (Fx iff Gx) and the F exists and the G exists then x is the F iff x is the G.
Fa iff the thing which is a is F.

NFL does not allow that absence of divergence of referent entails the truth of the corresponding identity. This happily avoids commitment to such claims as that the golden mountain is the present King of France.

5.2.3 *Intentions*

What phenomena pertaining to the use of language would justify counting an expression as a referring expression? Why should definite descriptions be thus treated? One piece of evidence relates to users' intentions. While a wide range of expressions may be used with referential intentions, a referring expression is an expression for which such intentions are the standard requirement for an ordinary and non-ironical use. ('Ordinary' excludes use in an existential statement.) Another source of evidence consists in intuitions about the expression's contribution to truth conditions, notably in modal contexts. These should help determine whether the expression is used in the way one would expect of a rigid designator. In this subsection I discuss the kind of intentions with which one would expect definite descriptions to be used if they are referring expressions, and consider evidence that they are sometimes used rigidly; and then (in §5.2.4) I discuss Donnellan's distinction between referential and attributive uses.

There are at least two kinds of referential intentions. One kind is object involving, meeting a condition of the following form: there is an object, x, such that the speaker intends that ... x .... The other kind is not object involving, meeting a condition of the following weaker form: the speaker intends that there be an object x such that ... x ....[7] It will be controversial to say what should fill the blanks. I think that the speaker should intend the truth or otherwise of what he says to turn on how things are with x. When the intentions are object involving, the quantifier which governs this occurrence of 'x' can be placed with widest scope, lying outside the content of the intention; in the non-object-involving case, the quantifier must be placed within the content of the intention. If there are empty referring expressions, we cannot require that something counts as a proper use of a referring expression only if animated by object-involving referential intentions. The relevant question is therefore whether it is plausible to think that the correct requirement on normal uses of definite descriptions is that they be animated by non-object-involving referential intentions. These do not preclude object-involving referential intentions; indeed, object-involving referential intentions normally guarantee the existence of non-object-involving ones, so if examples of these can be found, they normally will serve the purpose.[8]

The kinds of use indicated above seem to meet this condition. Uses of 'the baby' within the family circle are animated by object-involving and by non-object-involving referential intentions. Typically, the baby is such that one family member intends to tell another something about it. There are also non-object-involving referential intentions in the absence of object-involving ones. I know you have a baby, but have never met it, and do not know or cannot remember its name or sex. Politeness requires that when we meet I ask 'How's the baby?' I intend you to have an object-related thought in processing this question. That is, I intend there to

---

[7] Those who hear this as an intention to bring something into existence, and thus as inappropriate, may prefer to regard it as an abbreviation for: the speaker believes that there is an object x such that ... and intends that ... x ....

[8] There is no logical entailment from 'there is an x such that u intends that ... x ...' to 'u intends that there be an x such that ... x ...'. But normally, when something of the first form is true, so is the corresponding thing of the second form.

be an object such that in considering how to answer the question, the only thing that matters to you is how things are with it. But I myself do not have an object-involving thought.

Considerations of this kind might overshoot and suggest at least that someone needs to have an object-related intention, if not the speaker, then the hearer, so that definite descriptions could not intelligibly be empty. All the example shows, however, is that a speaker will normally intend a hearer to acquire an object-related thought; there is no requirement that this intention be fulfilled. The following example brings this out. It is a case of non-object-involving referential intentions in an actually or potentially empty case, and so in a case in which we should not attribute object-involving intentions to any party to a successful communicative act. You have a tennis court and you invite me over to play. We walk to the court together and I see that there is no centre net. I ask, 'Where's the net?' I have non-object-involving referential intentions: I intend that there be an object, namely the net, concerning which you realize that I am asking where it is. For my plan to work, you have to draw upon object-related knowledge: the net needs to be something of which you are aware. (I am hoping that you know, concerning the net, where it is; that is, that you know where the net is.) This is knowledge I must presume you to have in order for my question to be appropriate. By normal standards, I do not have object-involving intentions: I have never played on your court before, and have never had any causal contact, direct or indirect, with the net in question: it is not something I have seen or touched, or seen photographs of, and nor have I been party to any discussion in which it was referred to. It is consistent with my having the described intentions that there is no net and never has been one (the court construction company went bankrupt before completing the job). Whether or not there is a net should intuitively make no difference to whether the semantics of my words called for referential intentions.

Non-object-involving referential intentions can be characterized in a way sometimes thought to mark non-referential uses: we can happily append 'whoever/whichever/whatever it is' to the definite description. In one kind of context in which Jill might utter 'Pass the biggest wrench' she has object-involving referential intentions: some wrench is seen by Jill to be the biggest and known to her to be visibly the biggest for Jack: that is the one she wants him to pass, and she intends that as a result of her words he will come to know this about that wrench. Contrast that with a case in which Jill is confronted with a large nut and does not know whether she has a wrench large enough to deal with it. In asking Jack to pass the biggest wrench, there is no object her referential intention concerns. She wants the biggest wrench, whichever that is. She meets the condition for having a non-object-involving referential intention, for she wants Jack to get into an object-related state of mind towards a wrench, a state of mind that will enable him to act on it (and pass it to her).

An expression standardly and conventionally used on occasion with referential intentions is properly counted as a referring expression (as used on that occasion). The connecting principle is that semantic theory should reflect how the expressions it treats are used. An expression standardly and conventionally used with referential intentions is used with the intention of achieving reference. Semantic theory needs to reflect this fact.

There is another way of testing the classification of an expression as a referring expression. Such expressions are rigid (see Chapter 2.5), so we can see whether intuitions of users of the language about truth conditions and truth values reflect this rigidity. The natural place to look is modal contexts, for example:

23. The teacher of Alexander might not have taught Alexander.

If the definite description 'the teacher of Alexander' is a referring expression, then it is rigid. If it is rigid, then the sentence should strike us as true (in a normal context). It does. So the use of this definite description passes this test for being a referring expression.

Examples like (23) have been put to a very different use. Kripke (1972/1980) cites them in order to show that definite descriptions are non-rigid designators (and so cannot have the same semantics as proper names). The approach might start with a claim of Russell's, in his first formulation of the theory of descriptions (1905), that the following sentence is scope ambiguous:

24. The present King of France is not bald.

Russell claimed that we could hear this as a truth in whose logical form 'not' takes wide scope over the description, or as a falsehood, in which these relative scopes are reversed. There is no doubt that the standard formalizations are scope variants (they differ only in respect of relative scopes). But let us remove our Russellian ear trumpets and listen closely to (24) as a sentence of natural language. I suggest that it cannot in any normal context be heard as false. Here are two pieces of evidence. We can naturally follow (24) with words like 'He doesn't exist'. This is an explanation of (24)'s truth; since he doesn't exist, he isn't anything, not bald, not hairy, etc. The second piece of evidence is that if (24) is ambiguous, one would expect the same to go for 'The King of France does not exist': there ought likewise to be a false reading. There is not. In Russell's formalizations, the existential sentence is awarded a different logical form from (24); but I am speaking of the similarity in the actual ('surface') form of natural language, before it goes through any Russellian analysis or logical form transformation.

RWR need take no stand on this issue. It is mentioned here to suggest that we should not uncritically believe all that we have been told in elementary logic classes about scope ambiguities in natural language. Our main quarry is (23); the verdict on this does matter to RWR, for if these uses of definite descriptions do not manifest rigidity, they cannot be classified as uses of referring expressions. For (23), Kripke holds an analogue of Russell's position regarding (24): there is a true reading, in whose logical form the definite description takes wide scope relative to the modal operator, and a false reading in which these relative scopes are reversed. The standard formalizations are certainly scope variants. But what is the evidence that the English is scope ambiguous? Even when we do our best to make the modal operator have wide scope, as in

25. It might have been the case that the teacher of Alexander did not teach Alexander

we still have something that strikes me as true.[9] There is a natural continuation, offering an explanation of why it is true: he might never have had any pupils at all, or he might have died in infancy. In this respect, the definite description contrasts with what happens if

---

[9] The position of 'not' makes no difference: 'It might not have been the case that the teacher of Alexander taught Alexander' also strikes me as true.

it is replaced by 'whoever taught Alexander'. The analogue of (23) is most readily heard as true:

26. Whoever taught Alexander might not have taught Alexander

but things are different with the analogue of (25):

27. It might have been that whoever taught Alexander did not teach Alexander.

Example (27) is, at a minimum, jarring and should probably count as false. The 'whoever' expression is a standard example of an expression which is not a referring expression. Its markedly different behaviour in modal contexts is consistent with this classification. By the same token, the behaviour of the definite description is consistent with counting it as a referring expression.

The example of (23) was used because of its place in history. We need to make sure that our marks of being a referring expression deliver the same verdict for the same expression (or the same use of a given expression). It is hard to imagine (23) being uttered without a referential intention. In any normal context, the speaker will intend that how things are with the actual teacher of Alexander should be what matters to the truth or falsehood, actual or counterfactual, of what she says, and that her hearer will appreciate this.

Nets are (let's assume) essentially nets, so we cannot expect a true reading of the analogue of (23):

28. The net might not have been a net.

If we take an inessential property we do find unambiguous truth, for example:

29. The net might not have been damaged.

It is in fact damaged, but if Jack had not tripped and stumbled into it, it would not have been damaged. Even if we try to get the modal expression to the far left, it is still hard to hear this as strictly true iff the court might not have had a damaged net.

The case for there being some referring descriptions is strong. These are definite descriptions which are associated with a referential axiom, which are accordingly rigid, which manifest their rigidity in intuitive judgements of truth in modal contexts and which are standardly used with referential intentions. This suggests the (doubtless overbold) hypothesis: definite descriptions in subject position are always used referentially. I would expect most readers to react that this is obviously false. I do not hope to persuade you of its truth, but I will suggest that the most conspicuous and familiar putative counter-examples are far from decisive.

The hypothesis would harmonize comfortably with the view that definite descriptions in non-subject position are not referential, and this is borne out by examples like the following:

30. Napoleon was the greatest French soldier.

As Strawson said, in uttering this sentence 'I should not be using the phrase, "the greatest French soldier", to mention an individual, but to say something about an individual I had already mentioned' (Strawson 1950: 320). In other words, I would not use this definite description with referential intentions. Marching in step, rigidity also fails. The claim that Napoleon might not have been the greatest French soldier is very different from the claim that Napoleon might not have been himself.[10]

Kripke uses an example which nicely illustrates how the very same definite description can occur both as a referring expression and also not as a referring expression within the same sentence, and it is striking that the referential use is in subject position, and the non-referential use in non-subject position.

31. Someone other than the US President in 1970 might have been the US President in 1970 (Kripke 1972/1980: 48).

For this to be true, as Kripke intended, we need to understand the structure thus:

32. The x which was US President in 1970 is such that possibly $\exists y$ $y \neq x$ such that y was the US President in 1970.

The natural truth conditions require the first occurrence of the definite description to be rigid and the second non-rigid. Likewise the first occurrence but not the second would properly be used with referential intentions. In this case there is a syntactic mark: the last occurrence of 'the' could be dropped without any semantic effect.

Another kind of putative example of non-referential use comes from Russell's discussion of knowledge by acquaintance

---

[10] There are also predicative uses of names, as in Frege's famous 'Trieste is no Vienna'.

and knowledge by description. Someone drawing up the rules of a club writes: 'The secretary shall be elected by simple majority vote of the members'. There is no person-related 'identifying information' that the utterer is bringing to bear or trying to invoke; nor is she intending her hearer to bring to bear some identifying information or other. The referent is not a person. It does not follow that we have an example of a non-referential description in subject position, for it might be that the referent is to an abstract object, an office (which a person may or may not fill). Perhaps the drafter does have referential intentions concerning the office of secretary. Similar doubts afflict other familiar examples, like generic cases. 'The whale is a mammal' certainly does not involve reference to a whale, but perhaps it involves reference to a species.

The idea that definite descriptions in subject position are sometimes used to refer to offices could be used to help explain the ambiguity of

33. The mayor was a communist last year.

The explanation would be that the predicate is ambiguous between having an office in its extension or people. If the former, then (33) is true iff the office of mayor was filled last year by a communist. If the latter, then (33) is true iff the current person who holds the office of mayor was a communist last year.[11]

We can demand that a referring expression is normally to be used with referential intentions, but we cannot demand that it is always to be so used. According to RWR, one who knows a referring expression to be empty can use it with propriety, but not with a coherent referential intention. This means that the mere occurrence of cases in which a putative referring definite description is used without a referring intention does not settle that it is not used as a referring expression. For example, when a mathematician starts a proof of the thesis that there is no greatest prime number with, for reductio, 'The greatest prime number is either odd or even', she does not have referential intentions. This does not settle whether the definite description, in that use, is or is not a referring expression.

---

[11] Those who think that there is a further reading can describe it with this apparatus.

Evans gave an example of a non-referential use of a definite description in subject position:

34. The first man in space might have been an American (Evans 1982: 55).

Evans says that there is a reading according to which the relevant possibility is not that Gagarin was an American, but that someone else, an American, was first in space. Indeed, this seems to be the most salient reading. Such examples, though not plentiful, show that the hypothesis that definite descriptions in subject position are always referential requires restriction. A recipe for constructing the kind of counterexample illustrated by (34) is to start with a sentence in which a definite description is used predicatively, in this case 'An American was the first man in space'. If this adequately expresses the relevant contained content (in this case, if it adequately expresses the relevant possibility) then the definite description in its actual position (subject position) is likely to be used non-referentially, or at least has a non-referential reading. Applying the recipe, we would correctly predict that 'The inventor of the zip might not have been Julius' has a true reading. The overbold hypothesis might be saved by restricting the referential definite descriptions to those in subject position but in which the envisaged construction from definite descriptions in predicate position is not available.

Whether or not such a restriction (or some refinement of it) is correct, some kind of dualist treatment of definite descriptions cannot be avoided. In its simplest form, the one invoked by the overbold hypothesis, we would need to treat definite descriptions in subject position as referential and definite descriptions in predicate position as not referential. The best known dualist treatment is Donnellan's, to which I turn in the next section, after a remark locating the relevance of this discussion to RWR.

The thesis that referring expressions can be intelligible even if they lack a referent makes room for, but does not entail, that there are referring definite descriptions. It makes room for it because everyone agrees that a definite description may be intelligible while having no referent: there are ones which have no actual referent, and ones which, while being related to some actual object in a reference-like way, would have meant the same even if that object had not existed. If every referring expression had to have a referent, and had any referent essentially (holding meaning constant), this would mean that few definite descriptions could count as referring expressions. RWR does not entail that any definite description is a referring expression. The optional move from RWR to that conclusion depends on controversial auxiliary hypotheses connecting reference with standard intentions, concerning the proper interpretation of English sentences, and concerning the impact of modal constructions. Though I have sketched this route, I do not pretend to have removed all the obstacles.

5.2.4 *Donnellan and the referential/attributive distinction*

Dualistic treatments of definite descriptions go back to Donnellan (1966). Although the dualistic structure of his position is congenial, the details are not. One difficulty is that what Donnellan calls attributive as opposed to referential uses emerge in my classification as a species of referential uses. Another is that Donnellan makes it a mark of a referential use of 'the *F*' that it may refer to something that is not *F*. Finally, Donnellan's conception of a referential use makes it hard for him to give a plausible account of how the speech of one who uses a definite description referentially should be reported.

Donnellan introduced his distinction between referential and attributive uses of descriptions thus:

> A speaker who uses a definite description attributively in an assertion states something about whoever or whatever is the so-and-so. A speaker who uses a definite description referentially in an assertion, on the other hand, uses the description to enable his audience to pick out whom or what he is talking about and states something about that person or thing (Donnellan 1966: 285).

If 'stating something about whoever or whatever is the so-and-so' is a matter of saying something whose truth or falsehood turns on how things are with x, where x and x alone is so-and-so, and this is what speakers intend, Donnellan's attributive uses get classified with my referential ones.

Donnellan thought that, in referential uses, referential intentions are object involving ('the speaker presupposes of some *particular* someone or something that he or it fits the description' (Donnellan 1966: 288)), whereas I take non-object-involving referential intentions to be critical in this discussion. Apart from conformity to intuitions in such examples as 'Where is the net?' (above), a reason for my approach is that a speaker may not be able to tell whether he has object-involving referential intentions, for whether or not he does depends on how things are in his environment. By contrast, he will normally be able to tell whether or not he has non-object-involving referential intentions. Normally a speaker knows what he is saying and what response he is intending to produce. He can control whether he intends the hearer's interpretation to be object involving, and he can possess this intention even if he is animated merely by non-object-involving referential intentions. The speaker cannot control whether he succeeds in getting the hearer to attain an object-involving interpretation: that depends in part on what is in their environment. This suggests that the significant break is between uses animated by referential intentions of either kind, and uses not so animated.

The overbold hypothesis explains why Donnellan finds it hard to give clear examples of non-referential uses in subject position. He himself notes that predicative uses are often non-referential, and subject position uses referential. Drawing on an example from Linsky (1963: 80), he contrasts the questions 'Is de Gaulle the King of France?' and 'Is the King of France de Gaulle?' The use of the definite description is likely to be animated by referential intentions in the second case but not the first, as the hypothesis predicts.

Demonstrative pronouns are referring expressions not because, for each pronoun, there is a referent invariant across uses, but rather because (a) these pronouns are standardly used with referential intentions and (b) for each occasion of use, there is or is normally supposed to be an object on the state of which the actual and counterfactual truth of what is said depends. This characterization aims at the semantic referent of a use of a demonstrative, which may differ on an occasion from the speaker referent, that is, the object which was the focus of the speaker's referential intentions (for an example see p. 164 above). A difficulty with Donnellan's characterization of the referential use of a definite description is that it seems to speak only to the speaker's referent, and not to the semantic referent. One way in which this contrast could become available is as follows. Suppose we think of the semantic referent of a referential 'the F' in a context as whatever is uniquely F in that context, and the speaker referent as whatever the speaker aimed to refer to in using 'the F' in that context. These could come apart, and Donnellan-style examples would show that they do. However, Donnellan uses the considerations which I take to bear on speaker reference as characteristic of a referential use *tout court*. By contrast, on the position I prefer, there is room here as elsewhere for a distinction between speaker reference and semantic reference.

This situation arises because Donnellan (1966) argued that a criterion for a referential use of a definite description 'the F' is that the speaker could refer to something which is not F. This is better construed as a manifestation of the distinction between speaker reference and semantic reference than of the distinction between referential use and non-referential use.

Donnellan carefully refrains from hinting at what the complete content of the speaker's saying is, when the speaker uses a definite description referentially. We can speak about Jones, using the definite description 'her husband', even though she is a spinster, and in so doing we may say true things of Jones—for example, that he is kind to her. We have just used the scene/content structure to report the speaker, and Donnellan in effect insists that for these cases there is no more complete style of report (Donnellan 1966: 301). We cannot say that the speaker said that her husband is kind to her, using 'her husband' attributively, for this would suggest that this is how the speaker used it, which is not so. We cannot say that the speaker said that her husband is kind to her, using 'her husband' referentially, for 'when a definite description is used referentially there is a presumption that the speaker believes that what he refers to fits the description' (1966: 301), whereas we know that the lady is a spinster. This is a puzzling upshot, for it seems entirely plain that the speaker, in uttering the words 'Her husband is kind to her' did say that her husband is kind to her. We can coherently continue: but she is a spinster, so the speaker made a mistake.

Donnellan reaches this position through not distinguishing speaker referent and semantic referent. A coherent account of the speech act is that it involved a referring definite description which lacked a referent; this makes sense of the speech report and the addendum 'but she's a spinster'. It also involved speaker reference to the woman's lover, thus explaining why the speaker counts as having said truly, of the lover, that he is kind to her.

Despite these disagreements with the details of Donnellan's position, one who uses RWR to develop an account of definite descriptions as semantically referential will accept the dualistic structure of Donnellan's theory. There are at least two kinds of definite descriptions.

5.2.5 *Plural and mass descriptions*

The discussion so far has concerned just singular definite descriptions with predicates which divide their reference. The suggestion has been that, within RWR, one can count some of these as referring expressions. We need to check that this account extends to definite descriptions with other kinds of predicate (plural and mass predicates), for we have found nothing to suggest that different definite articles are required to attach to the different kinds of predicate. We can also consider how a non-dualistic Russellian theory, according to which all definite descriptions are quantifier phrases, can handle these less widely discussed cases.

If some singular definite descriptions are singular referring expressions, then it is likely that some plural definite descriptions are plural referring expressions. To frame an axiom fit for both singular and plural referring expressions, we need to add neutral variables, ones which stand in the kind of position fit to be occupied either by plural or by singular referring expressions. The proposed singular semantic axiom was:

for all x ('the F' refers to x iff $x =$ the satisfier of 'F').

Its singular or plural correlate is

for all Θ ('the F' refers to Θ iff Θ is/are the satisfier/satisfiers of 'F').

Plural instances are:

'the apostles' refers to the apostles iff the apostles are the satisfiers of 'apostles';

'the apostles' refers to Plato and Aristotle iff Plato and Aristotle are the satisfiers of 'apostles'.

Although Matthew and Mark are satisfiers of 'apostles' they are not *the* satisfiers of 'apostles', so their properties alone are not enough to verify a claim about the apostles.

We can understand '*F*' as a position which can be occupied both by reference-dividing predicates and by mass terms. An instance of the latter is

'the gold in Zurich' refers to the gold in Zurich iff the gold in Zurich is the satisfier of 'gold in Zurich'.

The gold in Zurich is worth more than a million dollars, though there are satisfiers of 'gold in Zurich' which are not worth more than a million dollars; for example, the gold in Hans Ernst's wedding ring. The gold in this ring is not identical to the satisfier of 'gold in Zurich', for the latter includes other gold. Although the ring may satisfy 'gold in Zurich' (at any rate, it satisfies 'is made of gold and is in Zurich') it is not *the* satisfier of 'gold in Zurich'.

Extending the referential account from the singular case to plural and mass cases has been painless. If a Russellian account could not be similarly extended, that would count against it. However, a Russellian extension is possible, even though it requires more effort. Because Russell's idea was that the definite description would be 'broken up' in a proper account, and because such expressions 'have no meaning in isolation' (that is, they are not semantic units), the theory, as I understand it, begins with a specification of the logical form of simple description sentences. For the singular case, this is:

The logical form of sentences whose grammatical form is 'The *F* is *G*' is 'there is exactly one *F* and it is *G*'.

This leads to a semantic account of the original sentence via semantics for the logical form.

Extending this to the plural case, we avail ourselves of neutral variables; but we cannot use 'there is exactly one', and it is unclear what should replace it. We cannot simply leave it out, as in the following suggestion:

The logical form of sentences of the grammatical form 'the *F* are *G*' is 'there are things, Θ, such that $F\Theta$; and Θ are *G*'.

This would make Matthew and Mark's happiness sufficient for the truth of 'the apostles are happy'. 'Θ are *G*' is true if Θ things are *G*, so on this proposal 'the apostles are happy' is true if Matthew and Mark are happy apostles. Intuitively, we need some notion corresponding to the uniqueness of the singular case: for *the* apostles to be happy requires all of them to be so. But simply adding this universal quantification will not do the job:

> The logical form of sentences of the grammatical form 'the F are G' is 'there are things, Θ, such that FΘ; and all Θ are G'.

Suppose the department is composed of Ben, Mary, and Joshua. An application of the above is:

> The logical form of 'The members of the department together formed a triangle' is 'there are things, Θ, such that Θ are members of the department and all Θ together formed a triangle'.

Even if Ben, Mary, and Joshua together formed a triangle, Ben and Mary, while members of the department, did not together form a triangle (how could they?), so the proposal would make it too hard for the natural language sentence to be true. The Russellian needs further resources. He could allow the positions occupied by plural variables to be occupied also by expressions like 'all the members of the department taken together'. This is the natural way, but in effect it concedes a treatment of plural descriptions as referring expressions. Alternatively, he can introduce something other than quantifier-variable devices. Richard Sharvy (1980) has suggested a single notion which he claims will do the trick. He calls it *part of*, and we could adapt his suggestion to the approach taken here as follows:

> for plural predicates, F, the logical form of sentences of the grammatical form 'the F are G' is 'there are things, Θ, such that FΘ and any Y that are F are among Θ; and Θ are G'.

Let us call the underlined portion the 'maximality condition'. It implicitly uses Sharvy's *part of* relation (here voiced as 'are among'). Thanks to it, both counterexamples are avoided: Matthew and Mark's happiness is not enough for the apostles to be happy, because Matthew and Mark by themselves do not meet the maximality condition and so will not constitute a verifying value for Θ in 'there are things, Θ'; that the members of the department together formed a triangle does not require Ben and Mary to, for they do not meet the maximality condition. Sharvy's maximality condition can be regarded as an extension of, and so as subsuming, Russell's uniqueness condition. In the singular case, for x to be among y is just for x to be y. So we can write a single logical form proposal to cover singular/plural descriptions. The formulation requires no amendment for mass terms. For example, it delivers:

for mass terms in the singular, F, the logical form of sentences of the grammatical form 'the F is G' is 'there is Θ such that $F\Theta$ and any Y that is F is among Θ; and Θ is G'.

Applied to an earlier example, this tells us, plausibly by Russellian lights, that the logical form of 'The gold in Zurich is worth more than a million dollars' is 'There is gold such that it is in Zurich and any gold in Zurich is among it and it is worth more than a million dollars'.

Both the Russellian and the referential approaches can provide an appropriate generalization. Familiar considerations suggest that referential approaches will in many instances be closer to our actual use of language. In their typical uses in subject position, 'the apostles', 'the Pleiades', 'the water in the lake', 'the gold in Zurich' require referential intentions and are rigid.

6
Existence and fiction

RWR, through its NFL framework, offers a dazzlingly straightforward account of how there can be negative existential truths. Like any simple sentence with a non-referring referring expression, 'Vulcan exists' is false. What is said by 'Vulcan does not exist' is the denial of this falsehood, and so is true. This account is much more simple and straightforward than any rival, and I am not aware of any serious problems with it.

RWR also provides a simple basic account of fiction. Fiction can contain names of real things, like 'London', as well as purely fictional names, like 'Sherlock Holmes'. RWR can count intelligible purely fictional names as intelligible empty names. There will be special things to say about how practice-initiating baptisms occur in the creative process, but these do not call for modification of the general claims about baptisms and transmission made in Chapter 3. RWR entails that all simple sentences containing purely fictional names are false. There is nothing problematic about this, provided one has the usual apparatus required of any account of fiction: a concept of truth in fiction, and an operator along the lines 'according to the story, . . .'. Trouble begins when we consider sentences like 'Tony Blair admires Coriolanus' which state real truths (not mere truths in fiction) and which cannot be regarded as implicitly prefixed by an 'according to the story' operator. I cannot dispel these problems to my entire satisfaction, but I suggest, in §6.4 below, that RWR has as plausible a way of dealing with them as any other account.

§6.1 shows how negative existentials can be used to ground a qualified minimalist view of the scope of negation in natural languages. §6.2 compares the RWR approach with a recent second-level approach

196 EXISTENCE AND FICTION

due to David Wiggins. §6.3 sets out one range of positions an RWR-theorist could adopt about the semantics of fiction. §6.4 compares the RWR approach with one which depends essentially on taking a robust view of the existence of fictional characters.

6.1 Existence and scope

The RWR proposal is that 'Vulcan does not exist' is the negation of 'Vulcan exists'. In that case, one would expect 'Vulcan is not more than 1000 miles in diameter' to be the negation of 'Vulcan is more than 1000 miles in diameter'. Hence it should be true, whereas it might strike someone as false. It might be suspected that names can take semantically significantly different scope with respect to negation. In the formalism of Chapter 2, one might distinguish between

$(a) \neg Fa$

which is true iff 'a' denotes an object which fails to satisfy 'F', and

$\neg(a)Fa$

which is true iff it is not the case that 'a' denotes an object which satisfies 'F', and which is therefore true if 'a' is empty. There is a version of RWR which exploits these scope possibilities to identify scope ambiguities in natural language sentences, but the version adopted here regards 'not' as typically taking wide scope when it occurs in sentences like 'Vulcan does not exist' and 'Vulcan is not more than 1000 miles in diameter'. Some exceptions are mentioned below.

According to Henry (1984: 102), Ockham thought it was worth pointing out a possible scope distinction of this kind:

De virtute sermonis ista est neganda: 'Chimaera est non-homo', quia habet unum exponentem falsam, scilicet istam: 'Chimaera est aliquid'. Similiter, si nullus homo sit albus, haec est neganda de virtute sermonis: 'Homo albus est non-homo', quia ista exponens est falsa: 'Homo albus est aliquid' (II, 2a; ch. 12).[1]

---

[1] 'From the meaning of the words, this is to be denied: "Chimera is a non-man", for it has a false consequence, namely "Chimera is something". Likewise, if no man is white, this is to be denied from the meaning of the words: "The white man is a non-man", for this consequence is false: "The white man is something"' (my translation).

Ockham insists that one or other of a proposition and its genuine negation must be true, genuine negation being expressed in sentences like 'Chimaera non est homo'. By contrast, the 'non-' construction does not form a genuine negation, as we can tell from the fact that 'Chimaera is a non-man' is as much to be denied as is 'Chimaera is a man'. According to Henry, we find the same claim in Abelard's *Dialectica* (Henry 1984: 180).[2]

NFL could allow that English is capable of giving expression to this kind of scope distinction. Just like Ockham, we could treat 'Vulcan is a non-entity' both as false and as containing an occurrence of the very same concept of negation as that which occurs in 'Vulcan does not exist'. This combination of views entails that negation may take different scopes with respect to names. It does not entail that there is any scope ambiguity in English. Consistently with what has been said so far, 'non-' could be the unambiguous expression of narrow scope negation, and 'not' of wide scope negation. I regard this as the default position, though we will see that there are cases for which it needs qualification. It allows us to deny that there are non-entities, which I regard as a point in its favour: every instance of '... is a non-entity' is false, for either the blank is filled by a non-referring referring expression or it is filled by a referring expression which refers to an entity.

If there were scope ambiguity, 'Vulcan does not exist' would have a false reading (one on which the name takes wider scope than negation), but it does not. This is a case in which postulating scope ambiguity would conflict with the semantic data. Other cases are trickier, for example 'Vulcan is not more than 1000 miles in diameter'. On the default position, this counts as the negation of 'Vulcan is more than 1000 miles in diameter' and so as true. Perhaps one could defend this by saying that, since Vulcan does not exist, it is not anything, not more than 1000 miles across, not less than 1000 miles across, not exactly 1000 miles across. On the other hand, the intuitions which animate RWR suggest that every filling of the frame 'Vulcan has a diameter of...' should be false, since the resulting sentences would be attempting to predicate something of Vulcan and there is no such thing. Yet it would seem odd to have different truth values

---

[2] Mediaeval views on scope distinctions for negation are discussed by Klima (2001: 200–1).

for 'Vulcan is not more than 1000 miles across' and 'Vulcan has a diameter of not more than 1000 miles', so perhaps the former should count as false rather than true. And if Le Verrier, having calculated a maximum diameter for Vulcan, utters 'Vulcan is not more than 1000 miles in diameter', it seems wrong to say he has stumbled upon a truth: is not the calculation part of the tissue of error?

In such tricky cases, I think we have to move away from the default position and allow ambiguity. Even setting aside negative existentials, we need to allow that we can form a truth by inserting 'not' into a false simple sentence. If Lescarbault utters 'Vulcan is more than 1000 miles in diameter' and Le Verrier denies this, perhaps in the words 'Vulcan is not more than 1000 miles in diameter', we must regard Le Verrier's denial as true: that is what we, who know the error, might also wish to say. On the other hand, suppose the exchange goes like this:

> *Lescarbault:* Vulcan is partly responsible for the advance in the perihelion of Mercury, is about 900 miles in diameter, or at any rate is not more than 1000 miles in diameter, and has an orbit of 60 days.
>
> *Le Verrier:* I think the orbit must be less than that, but I agree that Vulcan is not more than 1000 miles in diameter.

Here we have to regard this utterance of the very same sentence as false. We parse it not as a negation but as an affirmation, equivalent to the claim that Vulcan is exactly or less than 1000 miles across.

6.2 A second-level approach

Wiggins develops a non-descriptivist second-level view of existential sentences. The non-descriptivism is welcome, and it is interesting to see how close Wiggins comes to providing a motivation for RWR. Indeed, his ideas were used to provide just this in Chapter 2.3.

The main difficulty for second-level views is to find a suitable predicate to attach to an existential quantifier. On the familiar approach, a name is analysed as a description, and this description supplies the predicate to attach to the existential quantifier in the analysis of an existential sentence. This tactic is not available to Wiggins, who is exploring non-descriptivist approaches. He allows that predicates of the form '... = N' (N a name) are perfectly intelligible, and hence allows that '∃x x = N' is perfectly coherent. But since he accepts classical logic and the view that there are no intelligible empty names, he cannot allow that by simply prefixing such a sentence with a sign for negation, or prefixing the result with a sign for possibility, one could express a negative existential truth, or the contingency of existence.

His positive view, in brief, is that a sentence like 'Vulcan does not exist' should be analysed along the following lines:

as regards Vulcan, there isn't really <of> it (Wiggins 1995: 108).

In the first phrase ('as regards Vulcan') we are in 'speculative mode' or 'rehearsing mode': we are entering into the pretence that 'Vulcan' can be used in the way characteristic of names. In the second phrase, the 'really' and '<of>' have special roles to play: they mark a move from speculative mode to 'reality-invoking mode', and they ensure that 'it', rather than being supposed to share its referent with the name upon which it depends, serves merely to introduce that name's sense. I will not be concerned with Wiggins's positive account, but rather with some considerations which Wiggins offers on the way to it.

In discussing the problems of achieving a satisfactory account within the framework of classical logic, Wiggins comes close to providing a motivation for NFL. He points out that

1. ¬∃x x = Caesar

is false but only contingently so, yet it classically entails

2. ∃y¬∃x x = y

which is 'impossible': it says that there is something which is distinct from everything. A possibility cannot entail an impossibility. One might conclude that although (1) *classically* entails (2) it does not really entail it; that is the position of NFL. The dual of the problem is that whereas ∀x∃y(x = y) is necessary, an instance ∃y(Caesar = y) corresponds to something which is intuitively contingent. Once again, the first classically entails the second, but this entailment is not recognized in NFL. Universal instantiation in NFL requires as a further premise the very contingency (∃y(Caesar = y)) which is the classically entailed conclusion.

Wiggins realizes that examples like these may tempt some towards free logic. He tries to scotch the temptation:

when we are *given* the truth of '*Fa*' together with all the presuppositions it brings with it, then we cannot get from *Fa* to a falsehood. If this is all it amounts to, then the principle of existential generalization cannot be invalid (Wiggins 1995: 100).

In the context, this suggests two falsehoods: (a) that NFL will resist the thrust of these remarks; (b) that the remarks are relevant to the logical relation between (1) and (2). Concerning (a), NFL affirms that a simple sentence entails its existential generalizations, so this theory would accept that *if* that were all existential generalization amounts to it 'cannot be invalid'. But classical logic and NFL agree that existential generalization amounts to more than this, since it can take premises other than simple sentences.

In support of (b), the sentence which supposedly entails, by existential generalization, the impossibility, (2), is not a simple sentence: (1) has the overall form of a negation. The NFL view is that although a simple sentence—for example, 'Caesar sings'—entails its existential generalization ('Someone sings'), there is no parallel inference for negations: 'Caesar doesn't sing' does not entail 'Someone does not sing' (in a world in which everyone sings but Caesar does not exist, the premise would be true and the conclusion false). NFL blocks the inference from (1) to (2) without making implausible claims about the truth conditions of simple sentences.

Could Wiggins not reorganize his puzzle so as to have (1) as a simple sentence, one in which non-existence is predicated of Caesar? By NFL principles, this entails that something is non-existent, which is, if not 'impossible', at least inconsistent with the ontological conservativism adopted here. Wiggins's question still has force: how could a contingent falsehood entail something so unacceptable? Suppose we regard the ontological conservatism as necessary: necessarily, there is nothing which is non-existent. Then the analogue of (1) will be a necessary falsehood and not a contingent one. Even if it is contingently false that Caesar does not exist, it would be necessarily false that Caesar is non-existent. Alternatively, if we allow the possibility of non-existent beings, so as to make the analogue of (1) a possible truth, then we should not regard the entailed conclusion as impossible, and there is no problem.

The present version of NFL goes further than Wiggins does, affirming the necessary truth of all instances of a form about which Wiggins wishes to remain agnostic:

3. $Fa \rightarrow \exists xFx$.

When considering the dual case, involving the move from the necessary $\forall x \exists y(x=y)$ to the contingent $\exists y(\text{Caesar}=y)$, Wiggins says something which could have been drawn from an argument for NFL:

> On the supposition of Caesar's existence, we cannot go from a truth to a falsehood in passing from 'everything is φ' to 'Caesar is φ' (Wiggins 1995: 102).

The supposition of Caesar's existence is formalized in the NFL rule for instantiation as a needed extra premise (see above, Chapter 2.3).

In contrast to RWR, Wiggins cannot straightforwardly accept that there is such a predicate as '= Vulcan', since he holds that 'Vulcan' is without sense in a real-world context. He therefore has to suppose that it has a (real) sense within fiction or hypothesis, and that this is somehow brought to bear in negative existentials.

> What the true negative singular existential will force us to recognize is that we need both these modes [speculative and reality-invoking], and that we need the means to negotiate transitions... from the one mode to the other (Wiggins 1995: 106).

> we find ourselves with one foot in Le Verrier's speculation about the perihelion of Mercury and the disturbing influence of Vulcan, this speculation determining the concept of Vulcan, and with the other foot in the real world, saying that in reality nothing answers to that concept (Wiggins 1995: 108).

RWR welcomes the acceptance of the genuine intelligibility of 'Vulcan', in contrast to Evans who regards it as merely 'quasi-intelligible'.[3] But RWR goes further: 'Vulcan' is intelligible *tout court*, and not only in the context of rehearsing Le Verrier's unsatisfactory hypothesis. RWR also welcomes the emphasis on the need to enter into Le Verrier's speculation, even if one's goal is to debunk

---

[3] Concerning a game of make-believe in which use is 'made of empty singular terms in make-believedly referring to things', Evans says that something 'counts as make-believedly understanding such reference'. But he insists that 'there is no real assertion, no real understanding, no real truth' (Evans 1982: 362–3). Contrast Wiggins (1995: 107): 'we can understand as well as you like how it is as if things are...'.

it (this is what metalinguistic accounts overlook). It is consistent with RWR, and independently plausible, that the intentions of speakers who assert negative existentials are best described in the two-foot mode (one foot in the speculation and one foot in the real world). For RWR, however, there is no need to try to represent these points as an 'analysis' of such sentences, or in terms of implicit occurrences of 'really' and '<of>', whose semantics are dubiously coherent (Sainsbury 2002: 159-80).

6.3 A simple RWR account of fiction

Two problems posed by fiction are:
- what account should we give of the meaning of sentences used in fiction?
- what facts determine the truth or falsity of such sentences, and of other sentences in which there occur names from fiction?

Correct answers must be set within the framework of a proper understanding of the nature of fiction, and the intentions and other attitudes that are involved in its production and consumption.

RWR makes room for a very simple answer to the first question. Semantics will recognize no special category of fictional sentences or fictional names. Everything will proceed just as for non-fictional regions of language. In particular:

4. Fictional names belong to the general category of names, and so receive the standard homophonic axioms, for example:
for all x ('Sherlock Holmes' refers to x iff $x =$ Sherlock Holmes).

Since, by the assumption of conservative ontology (Chapter 2.4), nothing really is Sherlock Holmes, 'Sherlock Holmes' is a name which does not really have a referent. (I turn shortly to uses within the fiction; and, in §6.4 below, to the potential value of an ontology which includes fictional objects, thus allowing fictional names to be regarded as non-empty.) In these pronouncements, RWR is the simplest and most straightforward account there is.

Truth, literally understood, is not the aim of fiction, so classifications of typical fictional sentences like 'Holmes was a detective' as not true, or as false, do not undermine the aims of narration. RWR classifies these sentences as false:

5. The truth values of fictional sentences are to be determined in just the same way as the truth values of non-fictional sentences. This makes many or most of them false (as Russell said).

We need to make room for the intuition that

6. Holmes is a detective

contrasts favourably, from some truth-related standpoint, with

7. Holmes is a farmer.

The fiction created by Conan Doyle represents what (6) says as true, and this fiction is in some way inconsistent with the truth of what is said by (7). We sometimes need to evaluate an utterance in terms of its fidelity to a tale: (6) is faithful to the contextually salient tales and (7) is not. This is the basis of the (somewhat uncertain) intuition that (6) is true and (7) is not. We could express the demand of fidelity in terms of 'true in fiction' (with specific fictions entering into the predicate as context dictates) and call (6) true in fiction and (7) false in fiction. One should not rush to conclude that we have a new species of truth. I prefer to use the notion of fidelity and its cognates.

Examples (6) and (7) can also be evaluated as respectively genuinely true and genuinely false, if they are seen as (implicitly) prefixed by an object language operator from the family 'According to fiction'. 'Fiction' in this context can abbreviate 'some fiction or other', or can abbreviate an expression which, in the context, refers to a specific work of fiction (like *The Hound of the Baskervilles*), or a suite of works (like the Holmes stories). Understood in this way, (6) is true, in the only proper use of this adjective, and (7) is false. These judgements are consistent with the RWR claim that, unadorned (implicitly or explicitly), (6) and (7) are both false. There is nothing strange about the view that if we evaluate a fictional sentence from a standpoint wholly outside any fiction, we will not have the resources to distinguish between ones which are faithful to a fiction and ones which are not.

There may not always be a fact of the matter concerning whether truth or fidelity is the crucial issue, as the following example shows. 'No Daddy, you're wrong: Holmes didn't say "Elementary, Dr Watson"; he said "Elementary, my dear Watson". More condescending.'

The rebuke can be regarded as lambasting my purported fidelity, or as saying I had implicitly said something untrue (to wit that, according to the story, Holmes said 'Elementary, Dr Watson'). It is doubtful if there is anything in the example to force us to prefer one description to the other.

On the question of the truth values of straightforward sentences within a fiction, RWR coincides in its verdict with description theories and with some species of views which appeal to fictional characters. Description theorists hold that a fictional name like 'Holmes' is an abbreviation for some definite description on the lines 'the brilliant detective who lived at 221b Baker Street, played the violin, and did such-and-such things'. The view is implausible not because it delivers the verdict that (6) and (7) are alike false (for the definite description has no denotation, there being no 221b in Baker Street) but because it makes knowing what some of the stories attribute to Holmes a necessary condition for understanding the name, whereas there need be no failure to understand the name from the very first page of one's first Holmes story, before one knows his supposed address, before one knows he played the violin, and so on.

Suppose that a fictional character is a really existent but abstract entity; and suppose that names used in fiction refer to such things. Then sentences like (6) and (7) are false, just as RWR says, for abstract entities are neither detectives nor farmers. The only serious alternative to the categorization of such sentences as false comes from those theories which, following Frege, deny that they have a truth value at all. The standard Fregean motivation is that a name used in fiction has no referent, and so deprives any (extensional) sentence in which it occurs of a referent, that is, of a truth value. The implication of such a view is that fictional names require a distinct semantic treatment from non-fictional names. A true semantic theory may make use of a non-fictional name in an extensional semantic axiom, but cannot make such use of a fictional name. For example, on this Fregean view, 'for all x ("Holmes" refers to x iff x iff $x =$ Holmes)' lacks a truth value, and so is not a theorem of a true semantic theory. The further implication is that an interpreter has failed in her work if she fails to distinguish fictional from non-fictional names, for the different kinds of axiom are to represent different kinds of interpretative work. But this is too demanding. Suppose you come across a narrative, but do not know whether it is intended as factual or is intended as fictional. Names are introduced in the usual kind of way: they are simply used for the first time, without apology ('She who raised these questions in Daniel Deronda's mind was occupied in gambling'), or introduced in connection with an indefinite noun phrase ('The Rev. Septimus Harding was, a few years since, a beneficed clergyman residing in the cathedral town of __'). You read on, with understanding but without yet being sure whether you have encountered a novel or an attempt at narration of unvarnished truth, or while forming an incorrect opinion on this point. This seems a coherent description, but does not require that one who understands is thereby capable of distinguishing factual from fictional names. If this is right, semantic theory should make no distinction either, and so should not take the Fregean option of requiring different kinds of semantic axiom for the different kinds of name.

Theories which, like RWR, classify sentences like (6) and (7) as false face three kinds of problem:

8. Negation turns falsehood into truth, so many fictions will contain unexpected truths in the course of a sequence of falsehoods, for example 'Holmes was not deceived by the man's servile manner'.

9. Some relational sentences involving one non-fictional and one fictional name are apparently (strictly and literally) true; for example, 'Tony Blair admires Coriolanus'.

10. Some relational sentences involving more than one fictional name are apparently (strictly and literally) true, for example 'Anna Karenina is more intelligent than Madame Bovary'.

If (6) is false, then if

11. Holmes was not a detective

is its negation, it is factually and literally true. (In this discussion, we must set aside evaluation for fidelity to the Holmes stories; fidelity might wrongly be confused with truth.) One must either take this on the chin, or deny that (11) is the negation of (6). The latter option divides into two: either (11) is unambiguous, and its 'not' has narrow scope relative to the name, so that an utterance of (11) counts as an attempt to predicate of Holmes the property of not being a detective, and so is not true (perhaps false); or (11) is ambiguous, with this as one of its readings, and, as the other, a wide-scope negation on which it is true.

Neither of these options is very promising. If 'not' does or can take narrow scope in (11), we require an explanation of why an utterance of (12) in which Smarty Jones is demonstrated by 'that' would normally count as unambiguously and factually true:

12. That is not Pegasus.

The easy suggestion, made by RWR, is that 'That is Pegasus' is false, thanks to the failure of 'Pegasus' to refer, and (12) is the negation of this falsehood, and so true. Similarly, the other options would need to provide an explanation of standard readings of

13. Sherlock Holmes does not exist.

Obviously (13) is not faithful to the stories, but if we stick to literal truth, and turn our backs against any implicit 'according to the fiction' operator, it seems that (13) is unambiguously true. On the non-RWR options we are considering, and assuming that 'exists' is a predicate like 'is a detective', (13) is either unambiguously false or at least has a false reading.

Once we step out of the world of the stories, it seems clear that Holmes is not a detective: he is not anything at all, since he does not exist. The idea that RWR delivers the wrong verdict of truth value is a hangover from not distinguishing between truth and fidelity, or from holding in place an implicit 'according to the fiction' operator.

Why could we not say that Holmes is not a detective as a way of disabusing someone who has mistaken fiction for fact? Holmes is a detective if he is anything, so if RWR is right we should be able to use his not being a detective to infer that he does not exist. RWR would indeed support the inference, but is not committed to saying that this would be a good way to disabuse the overly credulous. There is a strong and hard to overcome presumption that one who uses a referring expression takes it to refer. The content '... does not exist' reliably overcomes the presumption; '... is not a detective' does not. As would-be disabusers, we would do better to say that Holmes does not exist.

Works of fiction often contain negations of simple sentences. For example

14. Miss Welland made no answer

is naturally understood as the negation of 'Miss Welland made an answer'. Since Miss Welland is a fictional personage, RWR treats (14) as the negation of a falsehood and so as true. This may seem unintuitive: the tale of the age of innocence has falsehood after falsehood and then, strange to say, a truth! This seems odd only if we forget that fiction does not aim at truth. It is not as if the falsehoods are failures, and the occasional truth a surprising success. The aim of the author has nothing to do with truth or falsehood, so it would not be surprising if these properties were distributed in a random way through her sentences.

Relational sentences in the categories picked out by (9) and (10) pose serious problems for RWR, and also, I believe, for all theories. We incline to believe that sentences like

15. Tony Blair admires Coriolanus

should count as literally and factually true, yet according to RWR, if this is a two-place relational sentence as it seems, it is false through failure of reference of its second term. There are *ad hoc* things to say: perhaps what we really mean when we utter a sentence like (15) is that Coriolanus was portrayed in Shakespeare's play as having qualities or doing deeds which Blair finds admirable (and Blair thinks of these things as ones ascribed to Coriolanus in the play). This does not address what semantic mechanisms are at work in (15), and the connection between the false sentence and the truths we may reliably hope to impart by uttering it does not appear to permit generalization to other sentences of the same overt form (see examples (17) and (18) below).

An approach which has more chance of becoming a specifically semantic proposal is that 'admires' does not express a two-place relation, but introduces some propositional attitude. A plausible theory of this kind is not easy to construct for 'admires',[4] but even if it succeeded we would have other similar difficulties. Even keeping to 'admires', most people would wish to allow truths of the form

16. Coriolanus would have admired Tony Blair,

and there are many other verbs to take into account, for example:

17. Tony Blair resembles Coriolanus

18. Tony Blair is more audacious than Coriolanus.

---

[4] Such a theory might be easier to construct for various other examples of this general form, e.g. 'dedicated' as it occurs in 'Tony Blair dedicated his memoirs to Coriolanus'; 'reminded' as it occurs in 'Tony Blair was reminded of Coriolanus when he talked to President Bush'.

In all these cases, the RWR theorist has to say that what we are apt to regard as truths are really falsehoods. Case by case, we can state the genuine truths that the falsehoods are sloppily attempting to communicate:

19. Tony Blair admires some characteristics or actions ascribed to Coriolanus. (15)
20. If someone with features similar to those which Coriolanus is portrayed as possessing had existed nowadays, he would have admired Tony Blair. (16)[5]
21. Tony Blair has features similar to those Coriolanus is represented as possessing. (17)
22. Tony Blair is more audacious than Coriolanus is portrayed as being. (18)

The general idea is that we can get 'Coriolanus' within the scope of 'portrayed', or some similar non-extensional idiom, whereupon RWR can allow that an empty name can feature in a literal and factual truth. What is wrong with these suggestions is that one cannot seriously suppose that (19)–(22) provide 'analyses' of their correlates in the sense of revealing the semantic mechanisms whereby their correlates function; and there is no uniform way of moving from an apparently true sentence containing both a fictional and a non-fictional name which is false according to RWR to a sentence which RWR can allow to be literally and factually true. We have to say that the problematic apparent truths are really falsehoods, though we can normally without much effort find literal truths which the falsehoods can be regarded as failed attempts to state.

Cases in the category of (10) ('Anna Karenina is more intelligent than Madame Bovary') raise somewhat different issues, though the upshot for RWR is again less than ideal. We have apparent truths which are false according to RWR. The relational expressions are firmly extensional. We can say only that the apparent truths are falsehoods, though we would have little trouble in formulating the genuine truths of which the falsehoods are the sloppy expression. For our example, the underlying literal truth is something like: 'The level of intelligence which Tolstoy portrays Anna Karenina as possessing is

---

[5] This counterfactual is constructed so as to have a possible antecedent.

greater than the level of intelligence which Flaubert portrays Madame Bovary as possessing'. The fictional names come within the scope of a non-extensional expression, so their emptiness is no barrier to truth.

6.4 Fictional characters

I admit that RWR's account of the use of names from fiction in serious contexts leaves something to be desired. This section investigates whether we could do better by appealing to fictional characters in the semantics of fiction, and concludes that we could not.

What is a fictional character?[6] Salmon tells us that

> wholly fictional characters like Sherlock Holmes, though real, are not real people. Neither physical objects nor mental objects, instead they are, in this sense, abstract entities (Salmon 1998: 293).

Schiffer glosses fictional characters as

> abstract entities whose existence supervenes on the pretending use of words (Schiffer 2003: 52).

Both authors appear to assume that 'fictional' relates to 'characters' rather as 'happy' relates to 'murderer' (it is a matter of meaning alone that all happy murderers are murderers), and not as 'alleged' relates to 'murderer' (it is not a matter of meaning alone that all alleged murderers are murderers). It is uncontroversial that there are fictional characters, but it is far from uncontroversial that these are a species of entities. Just as 'Jack is an alleged murderer' says that it is alleged that Jack is a murderer, from which it does not follow that there are any murderers, it may be that 'there are fictional characters' is just another way of saying that there are works of fiction in which characters are portrayed, and although this entails that works of fiction really exist, it does not entail that characters really exist.

Modestly understood, to say that there are fictional characters is to say no more than that, in works of fiction, characters are portrayed. Robustly understood, to say that there are fictional characters is to say that there are characters in the real world which are created by

---

[6] A relatively early account of this kind is by Van Inwagen (1977).

creating works of fiction, and are referred to and portrayed in these works. Everyone agrees that there are fictional characters, modestly understood; modest fictional characters, as I shall say. Both Salmon and Schiffer affirm that there are fictional characters robustly understood, that is, that there are robust fictional characters, but since they do not distinguish the robust from the modest interpretation, neither offers explicit arguments in favour of robust fictional characters. For example, Schiffer writes:

it seems clear that it is a conceptual truth that using the name '*n*' in writing a fiction creates the fictional character *n* (Schiffer 2003: 53).

The context makes it plain that he thinks that this delivers the conclusion that there are robust fictional characters. Their robust real-world existence makes them available to be the referents of names from fiction in such literal truths as

23. The fictional spy James Bond is a lot more famous than the fictional detective Adam Dalgleish (Schiffer 2003: 53).

But the argument from the conceptual truth does not deliver the robust conclusion. No doubt it is a conceptual truth that alleging that Jack is a murderer makes it the case that Jack is an alleged murderer, and using the name '*n*' in a work of fiction makes it the case that, according to the fiction, there is such a character as *n*. This takes us only to modest fictional characters. Robust fictional characters require an existential conclusion lying outside the scope of the 'according to the fiction' operator: there is some character in the real world that is created by, or portrayed in, the work of fiction. While this is certainly what Schiffer believes (and Salmon likewise), it does not follow from what he says in the displayed quotation, and it is not clearly a conceptual truth (or indeed a truth at all).

Salmon suggests that the existence of robust fictional characters is a consequence of the existence of robust works of fiction:

The characters of a fiction—the occupants of roles in the fiction—are in some real sense *parts* of the fiction itself (Salmon 1998: 301).

A work of fiction can be thought of as an abstract object, and everyone agrees that there really are such things. If characters are parts of works of fiction, everyone should agree that there really are characters (if Xs are parts of Y, and one agrees that Y exists, one should agree that Xs exist). An uncontroversial thesis is that works of fiction have chapters and paragraphs as parts, thought of not merely as strings of words, but in a more abstract way which allows that the same work, and the same chapter or paragraph, may be available in several languages. These chapters or paragraphs typically portray specific incidents and characters, but this is not to say that the portrayed characters are parts of the work. On the contrary, there is a reason not to say this: in fiction of the ordinary kind, every reasonably large part contributes to the portrayal of an incident or character. To say that the incident or character is part of the work is to confuse what does the portraying (the work and its parts) with what is portrayed (the incidents and characters).

I think there are no grounds of this kind to believe in robust fictional characters. However, if they could play some useful role in semantics, this role would itself give us reason to believe in them. In this supposed role, they are the referents of names with a fictional use but no real use, except that which is involved in talking about the fiction; names like 'Sherlock Holmes'. One kind of account (Salmon 1998; Soames 2002; Schiffer 2003) is uniform: whether in their earliest uses by the creator of the fiction or in subsequent uses by consumers of the fiction, in response or commentary, these names refer to robust fictional characters. Another kind of account is non-uniform, appealing to the robust fictional characters as referents only in some later uses, perhaps only in commentary about the fiction. I shall explicitly consider only the former version, though it will be plain that similar points could also be made against the latter.

No abstract object is a detective, or plays the violin, or flies, so ordinary sentences from fiction (like 'Holmes is a detective', 'Holmes plays the violin', 'Pegasus flies') will receive the same truth value, false, whether on the RWR account or on the account in which these uses are awarded robust fictional characters as referents. As opposed to RWR, an account which exploits robust fictional objects has problems fitting them into a plausible account of novelists' intentions or of the states of mind of readers. There is an argument for saying that fictional characters ought to fit in *de dicto*. In the Holmes stories, the real Baker Street is the referent of the occurrences of 'Baker Street'. It could well be that Doyle knew what he was up to, and so intended to use 'Baker Street' to refer to Baker Street in inventing and describing some of the events which make up the story. If Holmes is an abstract entity, and Doyle knew what he was up to, then he intended to use 'Holmes' to refer to an abstract entity. In pretending that Holmes played the violin, he would (on this account) be pretending that an abstract entity played the violin. Unlike what Doyle actually pretended (that a detective played the violin), this is a perfectly silly pretence, which does not help the story along one whit.

This argument depends on reading the proposed semantics back into *de dicto* authorial intentions, as seemed appropriate for the semantics of 'Baker Street'. Salmon has made the following suggestion, in connection not with authorial intentions but with regard to what readers are supposed to do in order to enter into the narrative:

In reading a piece of fiction, do we pretend that an abstract entity is a prince of Denmark (or a brilliant detective, etc.)? ... Taken *de dicto*, of course not; taken *de re*, exactly. That abstract entities are human beings is not something we pretend, but there are abstract entities that we pretend are human beings (Salmon 1998: 316, n. 45).

It is not clear how we get to engage in *de re* pretence with respect to abstract entities (see Sawyer 2002: 194–5). In any case, we cannot eliminate the *de dicto* intendings and pretendings: Doyle pretended that there was such a person as Holmes, and we as readers need to do the same. This seems quite uncontroversial. Because the context is non-extensional, we cannot infer from this, together with the premise that Holmes is an abstract object, that Doyle pretended there was such a person as an abstract object. But if Salmon's theory were true, an author who was fully aware of it should be happy to accept a description of his pretence as that there is such a person as an abstract object. Salmon should regard himself as pretending precisely this in reading the Holmes stories. Yet this is a barely intelligible pretence, which patently falsifies what is involved in the production and consumption of fiction.

The conclusion of this phase is that RWR should be preferred as an account of the use of fictional names within fiction: it agrees with a theory exploiting robust fictional characters as referents as far as truth values go, but allows for a much more plausible account of pretence and intention. If robust fictional characters are to play a useful role it will be in connection with sentences about the fiction, and especially the kinds of relational sentences which proved troublesome to RWR.

Schiffer evidently thinks this is an area in which robust fictional characters can be useful to semantic theory. In connection with (23) ('The fictional spy James Bond is a lot more famous than the fictional detective Adam Dalgleish'), he remarks that it is true by his lights, a fact which can be explained if

the names 'James Bond' and 'Adam Dalgleish' occur as genuinely referential singular terms whose referents are fictional characters (Schiffer 2003: 53).

Certainly we are tempted to think of (23) as true, and this is a variant of the difficulties for RWR discussed in §6.3 above. We should not object to the thought that one abstract object can be more famous than another, so Schiffer is right to say that in some cases like this (for example, 'James Bond is more famous than Adam Dalgleish'), robust fictional characters can offer a straightforward explanation of our intuition of truth.

The explanatory power is limited. Even Schiffer's own example contains a problem: it would be reasonable to expect that if 'The fictional spy James Bond' has a referent, its referent is a spy, but since no abstract object is a spy this would lead to the conclusion that the subject expression has no referent and so (23) is not true, even granted robust fictional characters. Complexities in the semantics of 'The fictional spy James Bond' might afford Schiffer a possible response for this example,[7] but there are others for which it is clear that robust fictional characters are not going to deliver more intuitive results than RWR. These include some cases we have already considered like (10) ('Anna Karenina is more intelligent than Madame Bovary') and (15) ('Tony Blair admires Coriolanus'). Abstract entities cannot be related to one another by the more-intelligent-than relation, and (10) cannot be made true by Blair's admiration for an abstract object, so the robust fictional object theory coincides with RWR in regarding these sentences as false.

---

[7] It is natural to think of 'fictional' in such contexts as introducing something more operator-like: according to the fiction James Bond was a spy. But I see no natural way of moving from this to a systematic semantics for sentences like (23) in which all occurrences of the names fall within such operators.

The most that the robust fictional object theory can do is award truth to a few of the tricky sentences which are intuitively true (like 'James Bond is more famous than Adam Dalgleish'). Its advantages over RWR in this respect are minimal. Yet I admit that both accounts are less than fully satisfactory. A good starting point in the search for a more refined theory is the 'two-foot' account that Wiggins offered of negative existentials. His idea was that in affirming something like 'Vulcan does not exist' we need to keep one foot in Le Verrier's speculation, in order to set up a proper context for the use of 'Vulcan', and keep one foot grounded in reality, in order to set the perspective within which the affirmation is to be evaluated. In contrast, an utterance overall being or failing to be faithful to a tale, or a sentence prefixed by an 'according to the fiction' operator being overall true or false, does not have the flexibility to do justice to the way that both fact and fiction may be in play within a single utterance, both contributing to the overall import of what is said.

Seeking a clear case in which robust fictional characters could help with semantics, I simplified Schiffer's original example (23) ('The fictional spy James Bond is a lot more famous than the fictional detective Adam Dalgleish') in order to avoid tangling with the question whether 'The fictional spy James Bond' could refer to something that is not a spy (but an abstract object). However, the terminology of (23) is natural and illuminating. The overall effect of 'the fictional spy' is to get us into the relevant fictional mode: as Wiggins might say, it steers one of our feet into the Bond stories. Likewise 'the fictional detective' steers another foot into the Dalgleish stories. Finally, we need a third foot, one for the real world, in order to assess non-fictional facts about the impact which these stories have had on the reading public. We can compare the real world with fiction and we can compare fictions with one another for real-world relations, and there is no obvious upper limit to the complexity of the ways in which reality and fictions can be involved in a single utterance. Yet it is hard to think of any systematic semantic explanation. Suppose we begin with uncontroversial 'according to' operators, one for each occurrence of 'fictional' in (23). According to the Bond stories, Bond is a spy, and according to the Dalgleish stories, Dalgleish is a detective. We want to add 'and the former is more famous than the latter'. Our 'former' and 'latter' are within the scope of the 'according to' operators, but neither story has anything to say about the relative fame of its protagonists. We want to step outside the stories, even though the occurrences of 'fictional' seem to pin us within them.

A complete theory would resolve this difficulty, thereby resolving the difficult question of the division of labour in this area between semantics and pragmatics. Does it seem likely that an RWR theory or a robust fictional character theory will be easier to complete? Or do these considerations point us in the direction of some quite different kind of theory?

I feel able to offer only a modest suggestion in response to these questions: robust fictional characters will not deliver all that a completed account requires. Though understanding (10) ('Anna Karenina is more intelligent than Madame Bovary') requires negotiating more than one fiction and also reality within a single interpretive act, the real-world relation is not one in which abstract entities can stand. One can respond as intended to (10) only by bringing to bear some knowledge of two fictions, one according to which there is such a woman as Anna Karenina and one according to which there is such a woman as Madame Bovary, but the relation of *being more intelligent than* which has somehow to connect the women[8] is not one which can intelligibly hold between robust fictional characters. These cases are typical. So however exactly we explain the way in which our familiarity with works of fiction bears on understanding such tricky sentences, it does not look as if robust fictional characters will help.

In the case of (10), we want there to be levels of intelligence, one assigned by one story to Anna Karenina and the other by another to Madame Bovary, and it is these abstract objects which are then compared by the real-world, greater-than relation. We make the fictions *de re* with respect to intelligence levels. It is unclear that this correctly describes the semantic mechanisms of (10) (what linguistic or contextual element transforms the more-intelligent-than relation, defined over animals, into the greater-than relation, defined over numbers or quantities?), and it is unclear that the account could be adequately generalized to the wide range of sentences in which fact and fiction mix.

---

[8] This plural definite description falls within the scope of 'according to' operators (the details of how this is so belong to the dimly envisaged 'complete account' under discussion), so RWR can count the sentence as true even if there is nothing (in particular no robust fictional characters) to which it refers.

7
Mental reference and individual concepts

Thought precedes language, and can occur in creatures which are not, and never will be, language users. Mental reference precedes linguistic reference, and can occur in creatures which are not, and never will be, language users. Pre-linguistic humans refer to things in thought, and this capacity helps them acquire linguistic skills. For both linguistic and non-linguistic creatures, perception provides non-conceptual, and so non-linguistic, contents which contain referential elements. These elements are produced by processes designed by evolution for this task, and being produced in this way is what makes an element count as referential. There is no guarantee that such elements have referents. A productive mechanism which owes its existence to its having, on occasion, produced referring elements which in fact refer may produce such elements which do not refer: they are 'supposed to', in that the mechanism which produced them exists now only thanks to having in the past produced elements which do refer. This does not guarantee that they do what they are supposed to do.

Some aspects of these hypotheses are the topic of this chapter.[1] I shall suggest that mental reference is structurally similar to linguistic reference. Corresponding to referring expressions are what I call individual concepts. These are not Fregean senses or functions from possible worlds to entities, but elements of individual psychology. They can be elements of genuine thoughts even if they fail to

---

[1] The teleosemantic aspects are indebted to Millikan (1984, 2000).

have a referent. The speculations of this chapter are not entailed by RWR, so those who reject them may still accept RWR. Those who find them appealing, however, will see them as supporting RWR, providing a satisfyingly unified picture of thought and language.

In §7.1, I consider some empirical evidence for the existence of mental reference in pre-linguistic children. §7.2 considers the nature of individual concepts. These correspond to the state of mind of a creature engaged in an act of mental reference. A semantics for individual concepts is developed, one which mirrors the RWR semantics for names, and I show how we can use individual concepts to account for various aspects of mental life, including recognition and misrecognition. Finally, in §7.3, I consider the role of individual concepts, or their non-conceptual counterparts, in an account of the content of perception.

According to the methodology I believe is appropriate in the present case, my task is to fashion a notion and show that it can usefully describe the facts. There is a mixture of apriori and non-apriori considerations. The notion of an individual concept is fashioned *ad libitum*, and I will stipulate, and thus make apriori available, conditionals on the lines: if something is an individual concept then it has such-and-such features. Whether or not there are individual concepts, and if so whether they provide a useful way of describing thought, is not in this way apriori; this question is substantive and is to be addressed only by seeing how adequate the notion of an individual concept is to the description of what actually occurs. For example, one stipulated feature of individual concepts is that some are empty: for some, there is no object to which they refer. This is not a substantive thesis, for it follows from the fashioning of the notion. What is substantive is whether a notion which satisfies this thesis is of theoretical value. This is not something that can readily be detected. A wide range of phenomena need to be considered. Such a notion may be of theoretical value even if another more Russellian notion, of mental representations of a kind which cannot contain empty members, is also of value for some purposes.

7.1 Development and individual concepts

Various aspects of infants' behaviour suggest that they are sensitive to individual objects as such; sensitive, that is, to their individuality.

This sensitivity seems to be an early form of mental reference, or perhaps a cognitive precursor of mental reference. I suggest that it is the developmental basis of the formation of individual concepts and shares significant features with them. Accurately describing the sensitivity sharpens our awareness of what will be involved in the individual concepts whose development it permits. We need to think of human babies as operating with some kind of primitive forerunner of individual concepts.

Infants show familiarity with close adults, typically their mother, from an early age, and they can also track moving objects by turning their eyes and head. This demonstrates a sensitivity to individual objects; but, as I use the phrase, not to individual objects *as such*, that is, it does not as such demonstrate, or even provide strong evidence for, sensitivity to the distinction between one individual and another, or to the principles of cohesion and boundedness which in fact govern these objects. Recognition of mother, or tracking a moving object, could as well be recognition of a reappearing or moving feature, rather than recognition of a continuing individual object. By contrast, in some experimental cases, it is much harder to give an account of the infant's representations except as representations of individual objects as such. If we accept this evidence, it is appropriate to think that it is also at work in infants' recognizing adults and tracking moving objects. The evidence in question comes from infants of approximately four months old, at a stage of development well before language use appears, and even before reaching has become reliably visually guided.

Sensitivity is shown to the continuity of individual objects through occlusion and motion, to their cohesion, and even to some mechanical principles which govern them. The data of which I am aware do not indicate sensitivity to the relation between a material object, its weight, and the force needed to move it. Arguably, this means that we should not think of these representations as representations of material objects as such, as opposed merely to individual ones as such.

The evidence I have in mind is based on the claim that infants at the relevant age (four to five months) look longer at what is unfamiliar or unexpected.

1. *Spatial continuity through occlusion:* The subjects are exposed to a rod-shaped object which is moved to and fro while its central part is occluded by a stationary block. The occluding block is

then removed. Infants in one group see one rod, stationary and unoccluded. Infants in the other group see two short rods, the gap between them having previously been occluded by the block. Infants in the second group on average spend longer looking at the result than did infants in the first group. The interpretation is that an infant in this situation 'expected' a single object, and is 'surprised' when two are revealed (Spelke 1988: 344).

The natural account of what makes it possible for an infant to have such an expectation is that he or she represents an individual object as an individual object (by however non-conceptual a means), and the surprise is to see two objects when one is expected.

2. *Distinguishing one object from two:* Infants are first shown one object and watch it being covered by a screen which is then removed. For one group, screen removal reveals just one object (as there 'should' be); for another group, it reveals two. Infants from the second group look longer than do those from the first, which is interpreted as unfamiliarity with or surprise at what they see. In a related experiment, infants watch two objects being hidden by a screen, and then see one object removed from behind the screen. When the screen is removed, they look longer if two objects are revealed than if there is only one. The two objects are as such familiar, in that they were seen at the start of the experiment; the interpretation is that they are unexpected in this context. This suggests that the infants expected one object (Wynn 1992).

A natural interpretation is that in the first experiment the infants had a representation of a single object, and expected the object to persist through screen removal; they did not expect another distinct object. In the second, they initially represented two individual objects, so having seen one removed they were expecting just the other.

The data are suggestive but not decisive, since in both cases the children's mental states could be described in terms of representations of features. For example, in the first case, it might be that the children track, not an individual object, but a complex feature with two rod-feature subcomponents. Variants of the experiments might diminish the plausibility of such redescriptions. In the first case, the rod ends could be of different colours, or of changing colours, even asynchronously changing colours. In the second case, one could vary the appearance of the objects (sometimes they are similar in colour, size, and shape, sometimes dissimilar, sometimes close, sometimes further apart, sometimes in one plane relative to the infant, sometimes staggered). If these variations left the results unaffected, redescriptions in terms of features would require these to be highly abstract ones, which it would be implausible to attribute to very young children.

3. *Temporal continuity through motion:* Some infants were habituated to an event in which a single object travelling left to right passed behind a screen, passed through a gap between that first screen and a second screen, and then emerged to the right of the second screen. Other infants were habituated to an event in which an object moved behind the first screen, then after a pause an object emerged to the right of the second screen. Those habituated to the one-object situation were 'surprised' to be shown two fully visible objects on removal of the screens. Those habituated to the two-object event were surprised to be shown just a single fully visible object (Spelke 1988; Spelke and van de Walle 1993).

The interpretation is that discontinuous motion led to a perception as of distinct objects, and continuous motion to perception as of a single object. The latter perception involved belief (or some nonconceptual correlate of this state) in the existence of the object unperceived (when hidden by a screen). It is unclear whether a suitable notion of existing but unperceived features could be constructed.

4. *Mechanical principles:* The apparatus consists of a ball, a screen, and a platform. The platform can be concealed by the screen, though when the screen is absent the platform is visibly above the floor. In one experiment, infants were habituated to an object being dropped from a visible position so that it passed behind a screen; the screen was raised to reveal the object on the floor. Then the platform was introduced and two situations compared. In one, the dropped object was shown resting on the platform; in the other, it was shown on the floor (the platform being clearly visible). Although the second case showed a

'familiar' display (as in the habituating scenes, the object was on the floor), it elicited more attention. This is interpreted as it being an unexpected situation, which presupposed that infants had some expectation of the impenetrability of the platform (Spelke and van de Walle 1993: 149).

Conceptually represented, the expectation is something like: one object cannot pass through another. Such a representation is possible only by a creature that can represent an individual object as such.

There is more evidence on similar lines (see Spelke 1988; Spelke and van de Walle 1993, and references therein). It suggests that infants are engaged in some primitive or non-conceptual form of thinking of objects long before they are starting to use language. This does not entail that we ought to draw upon the notion of thinking of objects in explaining what it is to refer to them in language; but it makes this a natural opinion. In particular, it is hard to understand the learning of names for individual objects unless the infant can think of the object before it is named, and can use the thought of the object in the process of acquiring the name. Without evidence of thinking of objects before the acquisition of language, these facts would be neutral between thought enabling language and language enabling thought; but given the evidence the natural interpretation is that thought precedes language.[2]

7.2 The nature of individual concepts

Individual concepts are aspects of individual psychology. They are or are closely related to abilities, they are causally efficacious and may endure through time. Here is a sketch of a typical story of an individual concept from its inception to its demise. You show a child a new toy, holding it out for him to see. As he reaches for it you put it behind your back. The child knows it is behind your back: he saw you put it there. On the present proposal, this knowledge is described

---

[2] A recent experimental contribution to this discussion, favouring the precedence of thought, is by Hespos and Spelke (2004). Hirsch (1997) criticizes some conclusions drawn from research in this area, in particular those appealing to the notion of basic objects or to sortal notions. The conclusions offered here are more general: the data are adduced only to suggest that pre-linguistic infants are able to think of individual objects as such.

as involving an individual concept which has the toy as its referent, a concept formed when the child first saw it in your hand. That individual concept will typically continue to be available to the child for some considerable period of time, and, presuming he identifies the toy in subsequent encounters, will be exercised many times in the future, almost whenever he sees, asks for, hides, considers trading, or in any other way thinks about that toy. The individual concept is used and reused in reidentification and memory. It acts as a receptacle for information, which may be added or deleted in the course of time. As the child grows up the toy may be lost or thrown out. For some time, memory thoughts about it may be available, but perhaps the toy is eventually forgotten: the individual concept falls into disuse, and disappears altogether. This sketch indicates the typical role and life cycle of an individual concept. The remainder of the section adds more detail.

The example is of a singular individual concept, one fit to have a single object as referent. There are also plural individual concepts, as might be expressed by 'the family', 'us', or 'the planets of the Sun', some of which have several objects as their referents. The present discussion is confined to singular individual concepts.

7.2.1   *Concepts and information: addition and subtraction*

Individual concepts subsume information. That is their role: to enable their possessor to organize information into object-sized packages (cf. Evans 1982: 126–7). Information is predicative; we can represent it by open sentences ('is red', 'is over there'), without presupposing that its representation in creatures who assemble and exploit it is always linguistic. In the normal case, a subject subsumes some information under an individual concept by entertaining a thought, concerning the referent of the concept, if any, and concerning the properties specified by the information, if any, that the former possesses the latter. (The *de re* formulation is to make some move towards not incorrectly describing the thought as one in which the thinker makes reference to the concept, e.g. that *the bearer of the concept is thus*.) A typical way to entertain a thought is as a belief: then the subject believes, concerning the referent of the individual concept and the properties specified in the subsumed information, that the former possesses the latter. There are other modes of thought in which the subject represents the object (the referent of the individual concept) as having certain properties (those specified by the information) without believing this. For example, a subject may be required to represent things as being a way in which he knows they are not in order to understand what someone has said. On one approach, a subject who knows that Jack has been said to be happy thereby subsumes 'is happy' under an individual concept for Jack; this representation may or may not be believed.[3]

A crucial feature of an individual concept is that it extends in time and so serves as a stable point around which information is added or subtracted. The accumulation of information is fairly straightforward: the child learns more about his toy through playing with it, and this information is added to that subsumed under the original individual concept. As memory fails, it may also be unwittingly subtracted. Witting subtraction occurs when there is discovery of error or a change of mind.[4]

Nothing in the nature of an individual concept requires there to be information which is essential to its identity. There are two aspects to the intuitive basis for this claim, one relating to the representation of thinkable, though perhaps impossible, states of affairs involving objects; the other relating to the updating of believed information. Information which we regard as essential to the referent of an individual concept we may not regard as essential to the individual concept. This would be manifest if, for example, while believing firmly that each human being is necessarily human, we entertain a thought concerning some object x we know to be human that it is not human. We use an individual concept for x, bracketing the associated information 'is human' to attain the thought, concerning x, that she is not human. (We may need to attain such thoughts in trying to answer Plantinga's question 'Could Socrates have been an alligator?' (Plantinga 1974: 65).) This is very different from subsuming both 'is human' and 'is not human' under the same individual concept.

---

[3] In the case of illusions which are recognized as such (e.g. Müller-Lyer cases), the content is just as in a veridical case, and so is, for example, the content *one line is longer than the other*, which is not believed, rather than the content *one line looks longer than the other*, which is believed.

[4] Cf. 'one can discover oneself to be radically mistaken about the object of one's thought' (Evans 1982: 179).

We can use an individual concept in thought while bracketing information, even if we believe the information to be essential to the referent. Turning to the other aspect, in updating our beliefs there is no limit, or almost no limit, to the extent to which we may come to regard information we once believed to hold of an object to be misinformation concerning that very object. At first, we think the animal we saw was a rabbit, but later we come to realize that it was a hare. At first, we subsume 'is a rabbit' in belief mode under the individual concept we introduce for something we see, but later we delete this information and subsume 'is a hare'. Nothing in the nature of an individual concept places a determinate limit to these revisions, and no information is sacrosanct. It may be that necessarily each individual concept is associated with some information; but no individual concept as such requires there to be some information which is necessarily associated with it. This corresponds to the fact that we may succeed in thinking about something even though we are misinformed about it, and even if the information we most trust, or learned first, is in fact incorrect. It mirrors for individual concepts what Kripke said about proper names: no information is privileged beyond possibility of retraction. The individual concept I normally use to think about my mother will typically contain the information 'is my mother' (or 'bore me'), but I may coherently come to believe of the referent of this concept, and using this concept, that she did not bear me: the thought is not a manifest contradiction, as it would be if some individual concept had to subsume both 'is my mother' and 'is not my mother'. Linguistically clothed, the thought might be: *she* is not my mother.

7.2.2 *Information and sortals*

When all goes well, subsumed information is typically persistent, and changes are merely additive; this may have encouraged the view that at least the most general information—for example, information which defines persistence conditions—is persistent. Even if what changes are possible for an object is fixed by a 'sortal' (cf. Wiggins 1980: 7), this does not entail that in thinking of an object I think of it as a possessor of a sortal that in fact characterizes it.[5] I may see and

---

[5] There are properties that cannot be lacked (like being human, for humans), properties which cannot be lost (like being old), properties required for coming to be (like being conceived, for humans). These are different categories of property, as the examples show. I assume that a sortal property cannot be lacked.

think of what is in fact a cat, but wrongly believe it to be an automaton, and so fail to associate it with the persistence conditions it in fact possesses (those of a kind which only living creatures possess). I may see and think of a shadow, and at first take it to be a cliff; correcting my mistake is a matter of coming to realize that *it* is not a cliff, yet presumably cliffs and shadows share no common sortal. It may be that in singling out an object I must have an answer to the question 'What kind of object is it?'; this does not entail that my answer is correct. Intuitively there seem to be both actual and easily imaginable cases in which my giving an incorrect answer (it is an automaton, it is a cliff) does not undermine my having singled out an object for which that answer is indeed incorrect.

In *Sameness and Substance* (1980), Wiggins introduces and defends a purely metaphysical principle:

D(ii): $(x)(\exists g)(t)[(x \text{ exists at } t) \supset (g(x) \text{ at } t)]$ (Wiggins 1980: 59).

Later he couples this with a view about how we think of objects:

Suppose that every natural thing x satisfies throughout its actual existence some sortal concept that those who single x out have to treat as invariant (cf. D(ii)) ... (Wiggins 1980: 117).

The present account of individual concepts is consistent with D(ii), but not with the just quoted supposition of the requirement of invariance in thought. Since Wiggins makes it clear that he accepts the supposition, there is a head-on conflict of view. It is less clear how Wiggins seeks to move from the uncontentious (in the present context) D(ii) to the contentious supposition that, in effect, thinkers know a relevant instance of D(ii) whenever they think of anything. The closest I can find is not an argument, but just a claim, and indeed one qualified by 'seems':

if it is true that any description that the thing is envisaged as satisfying must, *qua* seriously envisaged of it, respect the identity-link holding between the entity of the envisaging and the actual entity with respect to which the envisaging takes place, then it seems the description must not be *incompatible* with absolutely every description actually individuating the entity in question as 'this f' or 'that g' or whatever (Wiggins 1980: 115).

If this means that it seems that one cannot think of something as a satisfier of descriptions inconsistent with the actual sortal under which it falls, I am happy to pit my clear examples against this putative principle.

7.2.3 Individual concepts and discriminating knowledge

Evans would appear also to depart from Wiggins's position. He writes:

> it does not appear to be true that demonstrative identification must be accompanied by a *sortal* which sets the boundaries of the thing in space and time (Evans 1982: 178).

Evans suggests a different kind of counterexample: we may single out something that does not fall under any sortal, like 'an area of someone's arm' or a shape in the sand. If this is right, we have an independent reason for thinking that one can think of things which we subsume under no sortal; hence we should not suppose that sortal information is essential to individual concepts.

On the other hand, Evans argues at length for what he calls Russell's Principle, that 'a subject cannot make a judgement about something unless he knows which object his judgement is about', and suggests that 'knowing which' must be understood as '*discriminating knowledge*: the subject must have the capacity to distinguish the object of his judgement from all other things' (Evans 1982: 89). It seems clear that one could think of one twin, say Jim, while not being able to distinguish him from the other. So long as one encounters just Jim, it seems that there can be no question that one may have thoughts about him (we need not consider more difficult cases in which one encounters both twins without realizing that they are two); and this is inconsistent with Evans's demand for discriminating knowledge, which accordingly should be rejected.

Evans's claim that thinking of an object requires possessing discriminating knowledge of the object would appear to derive from a residual verificationist strand in his thinking. Speaking of a case in which someone has seen two indistinguishable steel balls, but has lost the memory of one of them, Evans writes:

> There is no question of his recognizing the ball; and there is nothing else he can do which will show that his thought is really about one of the two balls (about *that* ball), rather than about the other (Evans 1982: 115).

Presumably we are meant to make a verificationist move: from the fact that there is nothing which will show that his thought is about one of the balls rather than another we infer that the thought is not about one of the balls rather than the other (even if the thought causally originates in one ball rather than the other). In a related discussion of the principles involved, he writes:

> The concept [of knowing what it is for it to be true that p] is one of a capacity, and the proof of its being possessed at a given time must surely reside in facts about what the subject can or cannot do at that time (Evans 1982: 116).

If the subject of the thought experiment involving the steel balls could think of the ball of which he retains a memory, there would be something he could do which would set him apart from one who could not (namely, think of that ball). The requirement that the subject be able to *show* that he can do this comes from nowhere, unless from a residual verificationism, and leads Evans to expect that the ability to think of the one ball can be reduced to some more easily manifest ability. Evans makes it plain that he expects the second quotation to give support to Russell's Principle. His opponents will not take it for granted that the possession of every capacity goes along with a proof that the capacity is possessed, nor will they suppose that exercising the capacity, for example in saying that p, requires that the subject be able to do something else, in addition to exercising the capacity.

In the present terminology, Evans would require that exercising an individual concept involves discriminating knowledge of its referent, and involves being capable of behaviour which would show that one can think of the object. Even if this does not entail that, for each individual concept, there is some information which is essential to it, it does entail that for each individual concept, at every point in its history, enough information is associated with it to enable its possessor to discriminate its referent from all other things, where this discrimination must consist in something other than merely being able to think of the referent rather than of any other object.[6] We have seen

---

[6] A full account of his view would involve discussing his demanding notion of a fundamental Idea: 'One has *a fundamental Idea* of an object if one thinks of it as the possessor of the fundamental ground of difference which it in fact possesses', where a fundamental ground of difference answers the question 'What differentiates that object from others?' (Evans 1982: 107).

that this view is inadequately motivated, and we do better to take a less demanding view of individual concepts.

For individual concepts, as with other things, we may be able to find persistent information or properties if we think of these in a specially thin or haecceistic way. A material thing, x, retains the thin property of being identical to x through its existence. Likewise, if an individual concept, C, has a referent, x, there is identity information that cannot coherently be rejected throughout the lifetime of the concept, namely that C is C; this is one way for the subject to represent x-related information. The information that I claim is inessential is substantive or qualitative, and this is how, in what follows, I will understand 'information'. The notion of an individual concept for which it may happen that no information is persistent moves away from an information-based model of reference, a natural move when one considers the kind of mental reference involved in perceptual tracking. No doubt perception opens a channel whereby information can flow from object to subject; no doubt the source of the information is important in many respects; but there is no guarantee that the information is accurate. The fact that the notion of an individual concept cannot be reduced to that of the information it contains is what makes individual concepts useful in an account of thought.

If one considers very high level information, for example 'is a number' or 'is a shape' or 'is a material object', it may be that one cannot describe a case in which such information concerning some given object is coherently retracted. Perhaps one cannot make sense of someone for whom an individual concept subsumes 'is a number' coherently coming to reject this information and replacing it by 'is a shape'. I do not wish to preclude that such things may be so, but they are not to be considered as emerging from any general requirement about what it is to think of an object, or from the nature of individual concepts. Such cases of persistent information are more likely to be discovered as we move away from perceptual cases. That I think of what is in fact a cat as an automaton or a shadow can be made so by a causal connection, and made manifest by such activities as perceptual tracking. For more abstract objects, like numbers, nothing can make it so that I am thinking of one number rather than another, unless some associated information; such information may supply plausible candidates for being persistent. This requirement emerges not from the nature of thinking of an object, but from the nature of the object thought of.

Two pieces of information are subsumed by the same individual concept only if the subject is committed, within the same mode of subsumption, to there being something satisfying both. If the mode of subsumption is belief, and the pieces of information are *is F* and *is G*, the subject is committed to there being something which is both *F* and *G*. If the mode of subsumption is imagination, the subject is committed to the imagined situation containing something which is both *F* and *G*. Likewise for other modes.

Direct-reference theorists of language hold that some expressions relate 'directly' to their referents, in such a way that two expressions with the same referent need to be semantically described in just the same way, and make the same contribution to truth conditions. An analogue at the level of thought for this approach is that it is objects, not individual concepts, that are used by a subject to organize information: the mind relates 'directly' to the objects, and there is no question of it relating in some different way to one and the same object. On such a view, one could give no adequate account of recognition, identification, and misidentification, as the next subsection shows.

7.2.4 *Concepts and recognition*

One classic kind of recognition involves an identity judgement, the kind one might express as 'That is Jill'. Corresponding to 'that' is a new individual concept, to 'Jill' an old one. Once the identification has been made, the new concept may fade away, and the old one alone be used in the future. Information is used to ground such a judgement of identity: no doubt the information subsumed by the new concept must have some degree of match with the information subsumed by the old, but there is no easy way to be precise about what the match involves. There are at least two cases in which mismatch is no barrier: (i) When an object changes in a systematic way, as when a moving object changes position or a ripening fruit changes colour, an old individual concept may subsume information which is now out of date, and in this sense does not match the information subsumed by the new concept.[7] (ii) One may simultaneously recognize an object and appreciate that a belief about it needs to be changed. One may recognize Jack at the opera and at the same time appreciate that the information 'never goes to the opera' needs to be modified, even if it is subsumed under the very concept one uses in recognizing Jack as Jack.

Finding an object familiar is not the same as recognizing it, though there may be borderline cases between these categories. Equally, simply recalling an object in thought is not the same as recognizing it. I may think about my cat in its absence, thinking about the same object again but not *recognizing* it. It might even be that I recall my cat because I see it but without recognizing it: an unrecognizable feline corpse might make me think with misplaced relief of my cat.

While most would agree that in some cases recognition involves a judgement of identity, in which two individual concepts are coordinated and their subsumed information thereby merged, it is a more difficult question whether this is an essential feature of recognition. In completely automatic cases, as when we recognize family members, perhaps one could as well say that an existing individual concept is simply brought to bear: there is no need to posit a fresh individual concept. On the other hand, there is some temptation to say that an event of recognition is always decomposable into two components which are not essentially related. In perceptual recognition, for example, there is the perception of the object, an event which could have occurred even if recognition had not, and then there is the bringing to bear of the old individual concept which is used in recognizing the perceived object. In cases of forgetfulness, perception can occur without recognition. The bringing to bear of an existing individual concept is naturally thought of as taking the form of an identity judgement: one who recognizes her father perceptually is able to think 'That is my father', using the mental correlate of a perceptually grounded demonstrative, and linking it with the concept of recognition, *my father*. On the alternative view, one can recognize one's father simply by bringing a suitable old individual concept to bear upon a currently perceived object. On this view, something other than identity will be needed to link the bringing

---

[7] This assumes that information is not specific about time. Being specific about time is more demanding than being specific about tense, for the subsumption by one individual concept of 'was red' and by another of 'was green' is not a barrier to identification.

to bear of the old individual concept with the perceptual activity: perception in some way guides the application, and makes it non-accidentally correct. There may be some way other than through an identity judgement to explain the connection, but I do not know what it is.

A familiar object sometimes comes before the mind as if it were unfamiliar: it is not recognized. In such cases, a new individual concept is introduced, even though the thinker already possessed an individual concept with that referent. The lack of an even implicit identity judgement means that information from the past is not brought to bear on the currently perceived object.

An unfamiliar object sometimes comes before the mind as if it were familiar: it is misrecognized. In such cases, a false identification is believed. Information from the past is brought to bear, but if any of it applies to the currently perceived object, that is just an accident.

There are borderline cases. For example, there may be vagueness about whether or not the sense that an object is familiar is tied closely enough to an existing individual concept for the case to count as one of recognition.

One form of remembering an object is recognizing it. Another is simply recalling it in thought. The latter shows how we can begin to say what it is for an individual concept to endure: it is for it to be available to memory, where this requires a causal connection between an earlier exercise and a later one. The right sort of causal connection is what makes the second exercise an exercise of the same individual concept. The connection ensures that at least some of the information subsumed under the concept is preserved in adjacent exercises of it, though more remote pairs of exercises of it may have no subsumed information in common. As with houses and dogs, change has to have some gradualness to it if identity is to be preserved, though this is consistent with something undergoing a total change of its qualitative and non-temporally indexed features.

A cognitively interesting difference is between those thought episodes in which some remembered object-specific information seems to the thinker to be applicable to the present object of thought and those in which this is not so. The bringing forward of such information in memory is distinctive of the reuse of an existing individual concept.

The uses to which the notion of an individual concept have been put in this subsection show that one should not think of individual concepts as waiting in a mental toolbox, from which one selects an appropriate element as occasion demands. This picture would simply push back the original problem of how to give an illuminating account of what is involved in such feats as identifying and recognizing, except that now the question would be how we identify and recognize individual concepts.

7.2.5 Principles governing the reference of individual concepts

Most individual concepts have referents, which raises the question of what facts make one object rather than another the referent of a given individual concept. Before addressing this question, I will suggest various principles governing mental reference, which a correct answer should respect.

(i) *Referents may be shared.* As we have already seen in the discussion of recognition and identification, two individual concepts may have the same referent. This gives rise to quasi-Fregean possibilities (the sameness of reference may not be appreciated even by a rational thinker), despite the fact that we have made no mention of senses, the same-sense relation, or contents. The position here advanced for concepts is analogous to the claim that the fact that the expressions 'Hesperus' and 'Phosphorus' are different can be the basis of a sufficient explanation of the Fregean data about language.

(ii) *A referent is forever.* Once an individual concept has acquired a referent, it retains that referent throughout its existence. This makes individual concepts similar to names in a given use, to name-using practices, and to chains of anaphoric dependence. One reason for not allowing an individual concept to change its referent is that the referent fixes a condition for the coherence of information within an individual concept: if 'is F' belongs in belief mode to a given individual concept, then 'is not F' should not. The constraints on updating would not obtain if an individual concept might shift its referent. I recognize an object, and see that it is F, but also appreciate that an old individual concept for that object which features in my recognition subsumes in belief mode the information *is not F*. On the present proposal, consistency requires some adjustment.

If an individual concept could change its referent, there might be no need for adjustment; then the notion of an individual concept would have no role to play in describing recognition or identification. One form of misidentification is a false identity judgement, say, 'That is Jack' (where the referent of 'That' differs from the referent of 'Jack'). We need the individual concept associated with 'Jack' to retain its referent if the thought in question is to be, as it should be, false.

Suppose that the initial referent of an individual concept, C, is Jim but that after a while Jim leaves the subject's environment and the subject subsequently encounters Jim's twin Tim, and does not notice the substitution. At first, judgements using C to register the presence of a person are false, for they refer to Jim, who is not to be seen. After some years, there may be some inclination to say that it is not that C is misapplied to Tim when its referent is Jim, but that it is correctly applied to Tim: it has shifted its referent. It seems unreasonable to say that the subject judges falsely in using C to judge that the person now before him is the one he met yesterday, when it was Tim on both occasions. We have some inclination to say that the individual concept is C throughout, because of the continuity among its exercises; but we have a stronger inclination to say that it has a different referent, because that seems to lead to the intuitively correct account of the truth value of the subject's judgments. The example parallels something Evans envisages for proper names: we have the same name-using practice, judged by tests of continuity, but a different referent, judged by tests about plausible ascriptions of truth value (Evans 1982: 388–9 and above p. 118–20).

There are three possible descriptions of such cases: (a) an individual concept changes referent; (b) the concept remains the same, and so does its referent; (c) a new individual concept emerges, with a referent different from the original one. The last two options are consistent with a referent being forever; I believe that each problematic case is best described in terms of one or other of these. In the case just described, how would the subject herself describe what has happened? One possibility, once she knows the whole truth, is that she allows she has wrongly thought of Tim as Jim all this time. This judgement recognizes the constancy of both individual concept and referent. She may affirm that while she rightly judged that the person now before her is the one she saw yesterday, she wrongly judged it to have been Jim both times. In that case, (*b*) seems the best description. Now suppose that instead of a smooth transition, in which Tim steps into Jim's shoes, there is a gap. Jim goes out of her life. Later Tim enters it. She does take him for Jim, but she has little information from Jim to bring forward. When all the facts are known, she might say something like: I never really knew Jim. I did mistake Tim for Jim but this was never important: I simply treated Tim for who he was. In that case, (*c*) seems the best description.

A principled reason for avoiding (*a*) is that we cannot normally allow the referent to be fixed by application. The referent is used to determine correctness of application. If application is allowed to determine what the referent is, as envisaged two paragraphs back, we risk erasing the distinction between truth and systematic and widespread error. If we do not make the referent/application distinction, perhaps subsuming both under what object an individual concept is *used for*, we cannot even state the issue.

(iii) *There is at most one referent (barring confusions)*. The point of a (singular) individual concept is that it enables its possessor to use it to think of just one object, and collect information in a manner appropriate to attachment to just a single object. The principle is: if an individual concept has both x and y as referent, then $x = y$.[8] The point of an individual concept would not be served if this principle were violated. The constraints on informational consistency would be unmotivated, and the concepts could not play the envisaged role in recognition, memory and misidentification.

Sometimes more than one object is, confusedly, and normally with inevitable error, the referent of a single individual concept. Tim and Jim are twins but I do not realize this and confuse the two. It is distinctive of an individual concept that any pieces of information subsumed under a single individual concept are thereby represented as satisfied by one object. If I met Jim but not Tim on Monday and met Tim but not Jim on Tuesday and use only one individual concept to represent these facts, my mental states incorrectly represent there being a single person whom I met on both days.

Confused cases are not the norm and I doubt if there is a single right way to describe them. Their abnormality follows from the fact

---

[8] Plural individual concepts meet an analogous condition: if such a concept refers to the things X and to the things Y, the things X are the same things as the things Y.

that the role of subsuming information under a single individual concept is to represent it as belonging to a single object.

7.2.6 Individual concepts without a referent

The RWR thesis that a referring expression may fail to refer has its analogue for thought. As such, this is not controversial: everyone believes that a thinker can exercise in thought a concept (e.g. *the present King of France*) to which nothing answers. In § 7.2.9, I argue, with Russell, that these complex concepts do not count as individual concepts. The controversial aspect of the present subsection is the claim that simple individual concepts can lack a referent.

Many aspects of our mental life require the admission of empty individual concepts. It is a familiar claim that there are two states of the world which could verify a sentence like

5. John wants a girl to marry him.

One is that John has a purely general desire to terminate his bachelorhood, and the other is that someone is the object of John's matrimonial desires. It is less often remarked that there is a third possible way for (5) to be true.[9] It might be that John falsely believes that William has a delectable sister, Martha, and this is who he wants to marry. But William is an only child, and John's dreams about Martha have been pure fantasy (it is not that there is some girl whom he wants to marry and who he falsely believes is William's sister). John's desires have something in common with the internal configuration they would have if they had an object, despite having no object. He is clearly in a state which differs both from that of one who merely wants relief from bachelorhood, and from that of one for whom there really is an object of matrimonial desire. I shall say that in both of the two not purely general cases, but not in the purely general one, John exercises an individual concept, a concept which in one case is empty and in the other is not.

Whenever it is possible for a thinker to be mistaken about what there is, it is possible for him to have an attitude of a kind appropriate to relating to some specific object without in fact doing so; when this

---

[9] The example and the point are from Grice (1969: 144–5).

happens, the thinker exercises an empty individual concept.[10] The scope for empty individual concepts is therefore large, and the history of science is replete with examples (Le Verrier's individual concept of Vulcan is the one most often cited by philosophers). They are also exercised in the production and consumption of fiction.

In non-empty cases, an individual concept can in part be individuated by its referent: since that remains constant, we can allow the information to change. A tempting view is that, since this source of constancy is lacking for empty individual concepts, they must be individuated in terms of constant subsumed information. However, the possibility of deleting associated information holds as much for empty individual concepts as for non-empty ones. Suppose that it was because John greatly admired William and believed him to have a sister that he set his heart on marrying her. The fantasy developed in a rather pathological way over the weeks. John came to persuade himself that the woman was not really William's sister or indeed anyone else's sister, but that she was an only child who had been raised in William's family; and then even that she was not raised in William's family although William had pretended this was so. It is plausible to hold that the same individual concept is being exercised throughout, and that according to John's fantasy there was always just one woman about whose properties he changed his mind. What makes the various thought episodes ones involving the same individual concept is to be settled in terms of functional and causal roles: for example, John must appreciate that he has changed his mind as opposed to merely changing his fantasy. Even the information *being the woman John wants to marry* may not be constant throughout the fantasy for in subsequent elaborations he may dump her, and maliciously fantasize about how she takes this rejection. Looking at the information subsumed in belief mode of the individual concept he introduced in forming his matrimonial desires, it at one point includes 'is a girl I want to marry', 'is William's sister', 'was raised in William's house', but all these pieces of information are deleted. As in earlier cases, a qualification about time is required: 'is at t a girl I want (timeless) to marry' may, for suitable t, be constant even if corresponding information for some

---

[10] One of Grice's interesting suggestions is that a referential use of an expression is to be defined in terms of the exercise of an individual concept. If this concept is empty, a referential use will correspond to no object. This opens up the possibility of an empty name being introduced by a referentially used definite description (Grice 1969: 143).

time $t'\neq t$ is not constant. But perhaps even the seemingly constant information can be deleted, as John reflects that he never really wanted to *marry* her but only to date her.

I envisage three lines of objection to this position: in empty cases, no genuine concept is formed; such cases need to be assimilated to pretence or fiction; and even in such cases the individual concepts are not empty since there are non-existent objects for them to refer to. The first objection is in line with a view which Evans and McDowell and others have taken about proper names: empty ones are without meaning, and a person seriously using one can neither think nor express a thought thereby. Applied in the most straightforward way, it simply obliterates John's fantasy: what appears to be a rich and complex structure of thought must be held to be not genuine thought at all. While general considerations might force one to this view, it would clearly be preferable to avoid it. In Chapter 1 I suggested that McDowell gives no reason at all to accept the corresponding position for language. In his presentation, only an uncritical acceptance of classical logic suggests any connection between the claim that a semantics for names should be of the modest homophonic variety and the doctrine that there are no intelligible empty names. Evans does provide reasons for his position, but I have argued that they are unconvincing (see Chapter 3 above and Sainsbury 2002: 181–91). The second objection, understood in the most straightforward way, seems to require the intelligibility of empty concepts or empty singular terms, if these can be intelligibly used in pretence or fiction. The third objection I reject on the basis of the ontological scruples confessed in Chapter 2.4 above.

The Meinongian position brings to light an obligation which the present position needs to discharge: to say what it is for an *empty* individual concept to be usable to 'think about an object'. How could Le Verrier have used an individual concept to think about Vulcan if there is no such object? On the face of it, *thinking about* is a relation, and 'x thinks about y' entails that y exists. The obvious conclusion is that we speak incorrectly when we say that Le Verrier thought about Vulcan; more generally, it cannot be strictly correct to say that every individual concept is usable to think about an object. However, Le Verrier did try to think about Vulcan (compare: good Christians try to behave so as to gain admittance to Heaven). Once we have a suitable embedding, for example an intensional context, we can use empty names or concepts in the expression of thoughts we believe to be true, without commitment to the existence of a corresponding referent (see Chapter 2.3 above).

Strictly speaking, there is no state of thinking about *something which does not exist*. We use this loose description when the thinker is trying but failing to think about something, which typically means (setting aside pretence, fiction, etc.) that she is in a state which she cannot discriminate from one in which she is actually thinking about something.

7.2.7 The value of individual concepts and of the mechanisms which produce them

The point of having individual concepts is to enable their possessor to think about, and collect information about, individual objects. It is valuable for a creature to be able to organize information in object-related packages, associating one object with one package of information, another with another, adding to and subtracting from these packages in the light of new experiences. This capacity is mediated, on the present hypothesis, by individual concepts. This is why mechanisms which produce individual concepts have survived. Few mechanisms function perfectly, so it would not be surprising if those for producing individual concepts were sometimes to fail, and so produce an individual concept with no referent.

This teleological perspective explains the sense in which individual concepts *should* have a referent: they are produced by mechanisms which have survived because they are good at producing non-empty individual concepts. It also explains why an empty individual concept counts as an individual concept: it is for the same reason as that for which a malformed heart, supposed to pump blood but incapable of doing it, is nonetheless a heart.

Empty individual concepts can also be commandeered in the service of fiction or other kinds of pretence. In these cases, there is nothing corresponding to malformation. Rather, the normal function of the mechanisms is suspended. Deleterious results do not ensue since typically no information is associated in belief mode with these empty concepts.

7.2.8 The determination of reference

Setting aside cases of confusion, some feature of the formation of an individual concept determines its referent, if it has one, or else determines that it has no referent. The referent-determining feature is not always supplied by the information subsumed in belief mode by the individual concept, for an individual concept whose referent is a certain object may be formed under the influence of misinformation concerning that object. Seeing a hare, I take it for a rabbit, and subsume, in belief mode, 'is a rabbit' under the individual concept introduced for what I saw. If the referent of the individual concept were determined by the subsumed information, this concept would have no referent (or would refer to something other than what I was using it to think about).

In this kind of perceptual case, the reference-determining feature is: being the object which controls the thinking, the perceived and attended to object.[11] In the case of unwitting hallucination, an individual concept is fixed as empty by this condition, since no object controls the thinking. Empty individual concepts are all alike in being empty, but there is no danger that they all collapse into a single concept, since the identity of an individual concept is determined by the mental history of a subject. All that would be impossible would be the introduction of distinct empty individual concepts in a single mental act. Otherwise, distinctness of act provides distinctness of individual concept.

Although it is obvious that the reference-determining feature is not always supplied by the subsumed information, it is not obvious that it is never so supplied. Time and again, my cheese disappears overnight, and I posit a common cause for the disappearances, and so take myself to be able to think about *whatever is causing my cheese to disappear*. The referent of such an individual concept (if that is what it is) must possess the property of causing my cheese to disappear. If there were no single thing responsible for the disappearances, there would be no referent. In effect, this raises the question whether there are descriptive ways of thinking of objects. In § 7.2.9 below I suggest that there are not; or at least, following Russell, that these descriptive concepts do not really count as concepts 'of' an object at all, and so do not count as individual concepts. If I am wrong about this, then I exclude them by stipulation from the class of individual concepts.

[11] Compare 'Conscious attention to the object has in effect to provide an address for the thing, so that the right information-processing procedures can operate for verification or action' (Campbell 2002: 243–4).

If the referent-fixing conditions determine that an individual concept has no referent, this fact too is constant, enabling one to describe a thinker as wrongly believing in some object and endlessly changing her mind about how things are with *it*. Even in fantasy, we need an analogue of a change of mind about an object: the creator of the fantasy may start out by describing an object which is *F*, but later say that this was a mistake and that very object is not *F*. That there is no referent is determined at the outset, but, as with non-empty individual concepts, the subsumed information may be deleted.

7.2.9 *Acquaintance versus description as ways of thinking of objects*

Russell argued that there are two very different ways in which an object may, in some loose sense, come before the mind: by acquaintance and by description. In acquaintance, the mind is genuinely related to an object, but if we think of something by description, what is really happening is that we are rehearsing a proposition, rather than standing in some cognitive relation to the object. We know a sense datum by acquaintance: it comes before the mind directly. We know the winning candidate 'by description': we know that there will be just one winner, but we do not know who it will be. *That there will be just one winner* is the proposition to which our 'knowledge by description' of *the winning candidate* reduces.

Russell's categories of acquaintance and description correspond at the level of thought to the direct-reference theories and descriptivist theories at the level of names. Intermediate positions in the philosophy of language have not received much attention; similarly, Russell's dichotomy is still influential among theorists of thought: either one thinks about an object 'directly', by acquaintance, or else by description; there is no third possibility.

The category of mental states in which an individual concept is used to think of an object is not either of Russell's categories. It is not the category of acquaintance, since it includes thoughts containing individual concepts which lack a referent. It is not the category of descriptive thoughts, for at a minimum this would require individual concepts to subsume some privileged and essential information, which we saw was inconsistent with their role. Defending the present taxonomy requires showing what is wrong with Russell's.

As Russell insisted, thinking of an object by description (in his sense) is not really thinking of an object at all, but is rather having a purely general thought, one to the effect that there is a unique so-and-so. The best candidate for a thought which counts as both descriptive and genuinely singular—as genuinely thought about an object—would be one in which the mental state was analogous to a referentially used definite description. What we find in this case is that the descriptive content is not essential, and hence the mental state can be described as the exercise of an individual concept. Suppose someone thinks about Plato using a content verbalizable as 'the teacher of Aristotle'; we imagine a mental analogue of the definite description to be used referentially in her thought. Initially she thinks something expressible as 'The teacher of Aristotle was probably only a few years older than Aristotle himself'. This can serve as the head of a chain of subsequent thoughts. She may go on to wonder whether he was proud of his pupil, and how hard he tried to defend his own views in the course of their discussions. She speculates that these discussions might more closely have resembled discussions between colleagues than the delivery of instruction by teacher to pupil, and so might consider the possibility that he does not properly count as the *teacher* of Aristotle, but merely as someone whose discussions Aristotle found helpful. If this story is coherent, a single concept for Plato is repeatedly exercised, and the information expressible as 'x taught Aristotle', which the concept initially subsumes, is deleted. This marks the fact that the concept is functioning in the way I have characterized an individual concept, and not in some distinctively descriptive way, a way in which this information would be essential. The phenomenon is quite widespread. Standard examples of referential uses of definite descriptions are domestic, like 'the cat', 'my car' (supposing this to be equivalent to something like 'the car I own'), and in such cases it is even more striking that this kind of deletion of information is coherent, even though the information should be essential if a special kind of descriptive concept were involved. The cat might turn out to be a demon in feline shape, and my car not mine at all through some legal fault in the transfer of ownership. The thoughts that *the cat is a demon (not a cat)* and that *I do not own my car* are coherent. The explanation of their coherence is that they are thought through individual concepts, which subsume substantive information only inessentially.

There is a category of thoughts in which individual concepts are successfully used to think about objects; but this does not correspond at all closely to the category of thoughts involving Russellian acquaintance. Members of the category will include the sequence of thoughts I have about the mouse which eats my cheese at night, starting with the purely theoretical thoughts about it, and continuing through to the thoughts I have when I finally catch sight of it. Russell's supposition that perception makes possible some entirely new kind of thought seems without foundation, and none is provided within the framework offered by the notion of an individual concept.

7.3 Perceptual content

7.3.1 The issue

Perceptual states are commonly said to possess content.[12] In this section, I accept this, and ask what kind of content it is. I am drawn to the notion that some or perhaps all perceptual content is of a distinctive kind, rather like pictorial content and not like propositional content. Here, I bracket that opinion, and assume with the current majority that perceptual content is propositional in form, or at least is adequately describable in terms of propositions. To illustrate the distinction: propositional content makes room for a notion of negation, an operation that can be applied to any complete content (and perhaps some incomplete contents as well). Applied to a complete content, negation is unique (there is just one negation) and it reverses truth value, turning a truth into a falsehood and a falsehood into a truth. Although *ad hoc* conventions can relate aspects of a picture to negative facts, there is no standard way of effecting this, no operation that can convert a complete picture into 'its negation'. There is no such thing as the negation of a picture.

Although I shall assume that perceptual content is often propositional, assessable as true or false and having a unique negation, I shall not assume that it is conceptual. For example, a creature might be in a state with (propositional) perceptual content without possessing concepts capable of expressing this content. The perceptual content even of a creature richly endowed with concepts may be richer and more

[12] A contrary voice is Travis (2004).

detailed than can be expressed by means of these concepts. Within these assumptions, the question to be addressed is whether any perceptual content is singular. I shall argue that some is. I raise problems for the alternative purely generalist approach (§ 7.3.2), and argue that perceptual singularity is best described in the RWR style, according to which a content can be genuinely singular yet have no referent, rather than in the directly referential (DR) style, according to which empty singular content is impossible (§ 7.3.3).

In perception, objects appear a certain way: this tomato looks *red*, jays sound *raucous*, and so on. From such platitudes, an incomplete content (as italicized) can be extracted, a content which cannot as such be assessed as true or false, though it can generate a conception of veridicality. For visual perception, if something looks a certain way to a subject, the experience is veridical iff the object is that way. Generalizing, for any object x and any way an object may seem, F, if x is experienced as F, the experience is veridical with respect to x and F iff x is F. (We must doubly relativize the definiendum, for a perceptual experience of an object may be veridical with respect to F but not with respect to G, and a perceptual experience of one but not another object which seems F may be veridical.) Now suppose that whenever there is such an incomplete content (being F) there is also a complete content. For example, suppose that a tomato can look red to me only if some state of mine possesses a content, containing *is red* as a predicative element, but complete in the sense that it can be evaluated as true or false thanks to containing an element which somehow corresponds to the tomato. Such a content might be '*There is something* red' or '*That* is red'.[13] This permits a move to a

---

[13] What restrictions are there on English sentences fit to express propositions which can be perceptual contents? We must exclude propositions which state theoretical or mathematical facts. The details of the rest of the answer are well beyond my present scope. The answer needs to be neutral on the topic of main concern, namely whether there is singular as well as general perceptual content. I will use the following rule of thumb. Start with the schema for incomplete content:

    i.   ...look(s) (to be a/an) F to S (likewise with 'feels', 'sounds', 'tastes', 'smells', etc.).

A proposition fit to be a perceptual content is specified by an instance of

    ii. It looks to S as if... is (are) (a/an) F

only when (ii) is made true by a state of affairs expressed by a corresponding instance of (i). This allows contents like 'That orange is round' and 'There is an orange' to count as perceptual, for it can look to S as if that orange is round or as if there is an orange (satisfying (ii)) in virtue of some orange looking round to S or looking to S to be an orange (satisfying (i)). However, it excludes from perceptual content 'My neighbours are away', even when it looks to me as if my neighbours are away, if my neighbours look no way to me at all (I cannot see them) but I judge that they are away, and express the judgement by 'It looks different conception of veridicality, in terms of the truth of such complete contents. A given experience may be associated with more than one complete content, so we should take as definiendum *veridical with respect to a complete content p*; the definiens is just that *p* is true. Normal perception requires a match between veridicality for complete contents and veridicality for incomplete ones: if in a case of perception some experience has *p* as a complete content which registers *x* to be *F*, then the experience is veridical with respect to *p* only if it is veridical with respect to *x* and *F*. The move from 'only if' to 'iff' faces the difficulty that an experience which is veridical with respect to *x* and *F* might have a complete content in which the element corresponding to *x* is in some way unsatisfactory. For example, it might be that a hare seems lively, and it is, but the '*p*' in the schema is replaced by the subject's complete content 'A/That rabbit is lively'.

There is a third mode of ascribing perceptual content, corresponding to what I earlier called the scene/content ascription of linguistic content. In the first part we set a perceptual scene, for example by saying that the subject was perceiving a certain object, or some object of a certain kind. In the second part we introduce a complete perceptual content using a singular pronoun anaphorically dependent on the object specification in the scene-setting part. Examples:

6. Seeing a hare, she had a visual experience of it being lively.

7. Seeing Jack, she had a visual experience of him being tall.

In these ascriptions, the singular referring expressions 'it' and 'him' introduce a complete singular content in an unspecific way: no information is given about how the subject's experience represented the object. But the truth of these ascriptions requires that the experience did represent the object in a singular way.

The platitudes (that in perception objects seem a certain way) contain singularity, though not in the ascribed content; we can call it *external singularity*, marking the fact that it lies outside the ascribed content. It is natural to expect that there is a corresponding singularity in the content possessed by the perceptual states of any

to me as if my neighbours are away', on the basis of their car not being in the driveway, their blinds being drawn, and my remembering that they were soon due to take a vacation.

such subject. Inferences like the following seem to be valid in both directions:

8. The tomato looked *round* to her.
9. Seeing the tomato, it looked to her that *it was round*.

Whereas the singularity in (8) is external, we can say that (9) ascribes *internal singularity* in the scene/content way: the singularity ascribed is said to lie in the perceptual content. An opponent might say that sentences like (9) are not literally true, but are imperfect ways of gesturing towards states with only general content. Since sentences like (9) are pre-theoretically accepted as true, this opponent would need to offer some deep theoretical reasons for rejecting them.

We are now in a position to offer the first of two arguments for the conclusion that some perceptual content is singular:

10. For most perceptions, the platitudes apply.
11. The platitudes ascribe external singularity.
12. External singularity entails internal singularity.
13. Hence most perceptions involve internal singularity.

(12) is controversial. Its truth is supported both by examples like (8) and (9) and by a general consideration: it is hard to believe that a content-generating mechanism would produce external singularity, yet be incapable of producing internal singularity; hard to believe that though there are individual things which the system can represent to be a certain way, it cannot represent the individual things themselves (in a way which does justice to their being individual objects). A cognitive mechanism with the capacity for external singularity, but lacking the capacity for internal singularity, would be inexplicably handicapped.

There is a second argument for the thesis that some perceptual experiences have singular contents:

14. Perception induces belief.
15. In the normal case in which a belief is immediately based on perception, there is a content which is shared by the perceptual system and the belief system: the move is from its experientially seeming that *p* to believing that *p*.

16. Some perception-based beliefs, for example 'That tomato is red', have singular contents.
17. Hence the perceptions on which they are immediately based have singular perceptual contents.

To suppose otherwise is to leave entirely mysterious the source and justification of the singular contents of perception-based beliefs.

Although I find these arguments convincing, I have to admit that they are not completely decisive. It would not be contradictory to hold that the perceptual system trades in non-singular contents (or contents with only external singularity) whereas the belief system trades in singular contents as well (or contents with internal singularity). Part of my defence of the singularist position is to show, as I attempt in the next subsection, how difficult it is to sustain non-singularist, that is generalist, positions.

7.3.2 Problems for 'generalism' (the view that all perceptual contents are general)

The main argument for generalism with which I am familiar runs as follows (see, for example, Davies 1992: 26; McGinn 1982: 51; Tye 2000: 62):

1. Indistinguishable experiences have the same phenomenal character.
2. Experiences with the same phenomenal character have the same content.
3. If experiences had singular contents, there would be indistinguishable experiences with distinct contents.
4. Hence the content of experiences is never singular.

Support for (1) and (3) could be supplied as follows. Suppose objects α and β are distinct but indistinguishable, and in one of two experiences α is the only thing visibly G and looks F, while in another β is the only thing visibly G and looks F. These experiences have the same phenomenal character: what it is like to be the subject of one experience is just what it is like to be the subject of the other. The general content 'There is a unique G and it is F' is common to the two experiences. If the experiences had singular contents, these presumably would be (or entail) that α is F (in one case) and that β is

F (in the other), and these are different contents (since α and β are different objects). So if the experiences did have singular content, they would have distinct contents despite being indistinguishable.

The contentious premise is (2), and it would take us too far out of our way to review the reasons for which one might hold it or reject it. Here I merely inquire why one should accept it rather than something weaker: for example, that experiences with the same phenomenal character have indistinguishable (but possibly distinct) perceptual contents. Like many current theories, RWR carries no commitment to any kind of infallibility in judgements of sameness or difference of contents, so indistinguishable contents, like indistinguishable anything else, may differ. A thesis which allows this is more likely to accord with externalist accounts of content: arguably, my twin and I have experiences with the same phenomenal character when we perceive, respectively, H_2O and XYZ, yet with different content, mine to the effect that water is wet, his to the effect that twater is wet.

Generalism comes in three varieties which can be formulated according to how the complete content is specified:[14]

5. Using an indefinite with no uniqueness condition, e.g. It looks to Jack as if *something* is red. (Existentialism.)

6. Using a definite description containing none but general terms. (Pure Russellianism.)

7. Using a definite description which contains singular terms for a narrow range of special entities, e.g. self, directions, places, times etc. (Impure Russellianism.)

A problem for existentialism (and some other varieties of generalism) comes to the fore in perceptual tracking. It is perceptually given that it is the same object which was at one moment in one place, at another in another. This cannot be represented by a repetition of the same existential generalization (for example, 'There is an

---

[14] In this part of the discussion, it is not easy to maintain my official neutrality on the question whether perceptual content is conceptual or non-conceptual. I assume that non-conceptual content is not ineffable: at least some of it can be specified linguistically, as required by the versions of generalism given here. (Specifying a content might be different from expressing it.) The non-conceptualist position that harmonizes most readily with the discussion is one according to which non-conceptual content is intrinsically conceptual, but can characterize states of creatures lacking the relevant concepts. It might be that a more robust conception of non-conceptual content, according to which it is a distinctive kind of content rather than a distinctive way of possessing content, cannot make sense of the distinctions this discussion requires (for example, between singular and general). This would be as antithetical to the views I am here opposing as to those I am defending.

orange'), for these could have distinct witnesses, whereas movement requires a single witness. Merely allowing places to be referred to in perceptual content is not enough. 'An orange is *there*', 'An orange is *there*' ('there' referring to a different place each time) still loses the fact that it is given as the same orange. So one might try something like: 'An orange is *there*. Now it is *there*.' The 'it' is a singular referring expression (see Chapter 4 above), so generalism has been abandoned.

Russellian versions of generalism attempt to mimic singularity by means of definite descriptions (regarded as quantifier phrases). To suppose that pure descriptions were available would be to suppose that for every object of perception there is some purely general content, given in perception, which uniquely individuates it. No one would take this idea seriously. It is more plausible to consider just impure versions of Russellianism, ones which permit certain 'special' objects to be referents of perceptual contents; for example, places, directions, the experience itself, or the subject of the experience.

Impure versions must be judged on their merits, and there is no general response. Let us suppose that singular contents specifying directions are allowed within a Russellian description, so that a possible content could be expressed by 'There is at least and at most one orange *over there*, and it is round'. We have a primitive capacity to identify places relative to ourselves, a capacity that does not depend upon a prior identification of objects around us. In complete darkness, we can differentiate the thought that there is something dangerous to our left and the thought that there is something dangerous to our right.[15] However, the approach does not deliver the right veridicality conditions. Suppose two oranges are indistinguishable in the following sense: necessarily, two experiences of two environments have the same phenomenal character if the environments differ only in that one orange in one environment is replaced by the other orange (in the same orientation) in the other. Intuitively, two such experiences involve different veridicality conditions: veridicality in one case involves one orange being as it looks, whereas in the other it involves the other orange being as it looks. This fact cannot be registered by an impure Russellian whose impurity consists in including contents referring to places. In each of two experiences,

---

[15] It does not follow that every differentiation of place is primitive: perhaps very fine spatial discrimination does depend upon a prior discrimination of objects occupying the places.

one with one orange, the other with a different orange in the same place, the relevant content is that there is at least and at most one orange *over there*, and it is round; this content is the same in both cases. Both or neither experience is veridical relative to this Russellian content, which is insensitive to the individuality of perceived objects. By contrast, on a theory which allows there to be singular contents referring to perceived objects, the two experiences will have different contents, and so it might be that one yet not the other is veridical with respect to these singular contents. Even if both or neither are veridical, they owe their veridicality or lack of it to different facts, which intuitively is as it should be. This is the natural way to align veridicality about incomplete contents with veridicality about complete contents: if orange$_1$ seems round, the experience is veridical with respect to orange$_1$ and *being round* iff it (orange$_1$) is round. If the experience is indeed veridical with respect to orange$_1$ and *being round*, we expect the experience to have a complete content whose veridicality marches in step, and this can only be a content which says, of orange$_1$, that it is round; in other words, a singular content.

Matthew Soteriou (2000) has provided an example which nicely illustrates the present claim. Suppose two oranges are before you, one at about two o'clock and one at about five o'clock (see Figure 1). You are wearing displacing lenses which shift apparent positions to the right. As a result, the rightmost orange is not visible. The leftmost orange looks to be at about five o'clock which it is not, so this is a case of misperception: the world is presented as other than it is. The impure Russellian of the kind being considered will suppose that the

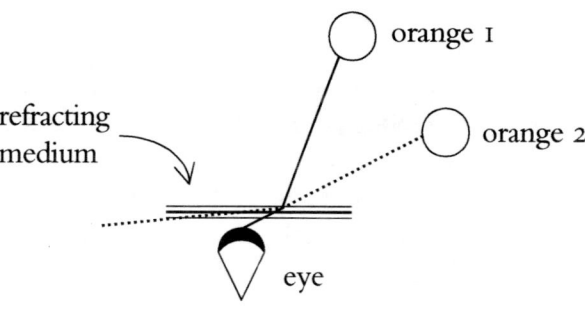

Figure 1

content of your experience is something like *there is exactly one orange at five o'clock*. The content is true, so the experience is veridical in this respect, but you do not see the orange which makes this content true. We need to find a false content. Otherwise the veridicality of incomplete contents is out of step with the veridicality of complete contents. Given that the complete content *there is exactly one orange at five o'clock* is supposed to register an orange at two o'clock seeming to be at five o'clock, the experience is veridical with respect to this content only if it is veridical with respect to the leftmost orange and *is at five o'clock*, which it is not.

The argument and example work against a specific form of impure Russellianism, but one should not rush to generalize.[16] Consider another version, for which the special entities, those which may feature as referents within the overall general description, include places and also experiences themselves. On Searle's version of this view, the content of any experience includes reference to that experience. This enables a different kind of fix on objects, as causes of this very experience. Instead of the content expressed by 'There is exactly one orange at five o'clock', this version of generalism can use one expressed by 'There is exactly one orange which is causing this very experience and it is at five o'clock'. In the case imagined, the responsible orange is in fact at two o'clock, so we have a false perceptual content, which is the desired result.

The pattern of content specification in terms of a unique cause is unsatisfactory since typically there is no unique cause of an experience. Even if there is only one orange, patterns of light on the retina, or the sun as a source of illumination, are candidate causes of the experience. If more than one orange is seen in a single experience, it is plain that neither can count as *the* cause of the experience. The general idea behind the approach might be better implemented if the range of special objects (those which can be referents of perceptual contents) is further expanded to include the perceiver. This makes available contents of the form *object-perceived-by-me* (a notion which no doubt requires causal analysis) in place of *cause of experience*. The view takes for granted the not implausible, though certainly contentious, opinion that objects are presented in perception as perceived

---

[16] Thanks to Nick Shea for stressing this.

by the perceiver.[17] In the problematic case of the two oranges, a content of the experience might be expressible as 'There is just one orange-seen-by-me at five o'clock', and this is false, as desired. The view can treat cases in which many objects of the same kind are seen by exploiting their different locations: there is just one orange-seen-by-me at five o'clock, just one at two o'clock, and so on. These locations may be a little coarsely described conceptually, but presumably one role of non-conceptual content is to supply finer grained contents.

It seems to me that this generalist view is both capable of meeting the kinds of difficulties raised by examples like Soteriou's, and is one which does not appeal to any highly implausible content. In this last respect, it contrasts with Searle's appeal to the concept of *cause* as a constituent of every perceptual content, an appeal which has contributed to its unpopularity (see Soteriou 2000). However, it has two features which make the search for an alternative worth the candle. One is that it is mysterious what distinguishes the special objects (those capable of being referents of perceptual content) from all others. The other is that it conflicts with a brute singularist intuition about veridicality.

One must accord some respect to the empiricist view that since the senses are sensitive only to qualities, perceptual content must be purely qualitative. On the other hand, we have seen that purely general accounts of perceptual content are completely inadequate. On the face of it, this shows that there is something wrong with the empiricist view, or at least with the consequences that have been drawn from it. No doubt at some level the information processed by perceptual systems is purely qualitative or general. This does not show that perceptual content, which supposedly stands at some remove from the early stages of processing of sensory information, it also purely qualitative or general. The need for 'special' objects in an account of perceptual content is a recognition of the falsehood of the conclusion, and so of the failure of the inference. The question immediately posed is why the particularity of perceptual content should be confined to these special objects. Once there are contents with particulars as referents, why not allow any perceived particular to

---

[17] Logical space for views of this general kind is highly populated. I have set up for discussion what I happen to think is a plausible variant.

be such a referent? It may be that the special objects are demon-proof: the Cartesian demon could not remove or fake them without the subject noticing. In the present climate, this would not serve as a special recommendation: it needs to be explained why non-demon-proof objects cannot be referents of perceptual content, given that these are the objects we typically perceive.

The brute singularist intuition is this: experiences of different objects cannot have all the same veridicality conditions. On a generalist view, scenes may involve different objects, without there being any difference in complete content, and so without there being any difference in what it takes for the experiences to be veridical with respect to those contents. In this respect, there is a lack of harmony between the veridicality condition for complete and incomplete contents. Two experiences could have the same veridicality conditions with respect to all complete contents, yet, for some object, x, and some way F that an object could seem, it might be that one but not the other of the experiences is veridical with respect to x and F. The original idea was that the complete contents would in some way do justice to the incomplete contents of experiences. This failure of harmony between the veridicality conditions shows that this has not been achieved. One would want to know why this should be so. It would betoken an inexplicable cognitive incapacity.

These considerations show that it is worth exploring singularist positions.

7.3.3 Hallucination and two kinds of singularism: DR (direct reference) and RWR

Assume that some perceptual contents are singular. The question arises what kind of singularity is involved: the directly referential kind, according to which every singular content has a referent, or the RWR kind, according to which this is not so. The approaches will agree in their verdicts for non-empty cases. The issue that divides them concerns hallucination, understood as perceptual experience in which no object is perceived. The DR theorist must say that there is no singular content in hallucination, since for this theorist every singular content requires an object, and hallucinatory experiences are ones in which no object is perceived. By contrast, the RWR theorist can allow singular contents in these cases, since some singular content is without a referent.

I offer three arguments in favour of the RWR approach. The first begins with the premise that two-part reports of hallucinatory content, using the scene/content structure, truly ascribe internal singular content, for example:

1. Hallucinating a little green man, it looked to her as if *he was bald*.

The ascribed content is singular (and, of course, not itself true); yet no one could deny the truth of such ascriptions. Perceptual content thus requires the RWR approach. This makes for a satisfying unification of mental reference and linguistic reference.

The second argument is this:

2. For every hallucinatory experience, there could be an indistinguishable veridical one. For example, if one hallucinates a pink rat, it is possible to see a pink rat while being in an indistinguishable mental state.

3. All actual or possible veridical experiences with possible indistinguishable hallucinatory counterparts have singular content. For example, in seeing a pink rat one is in a perceptual state with a singular content, perhaps expressible as 'That rat is pink', and this veridical experience has a possible hallucinatory counterpart in which a subject hallucinates a pink rat.

4. Indistinguishable experiences, actual or possible, have the same kind of content. More precisely: if an experience has content of kind C, and it is possible for there to be an indistinguishable experience with content of kind C', then $C = C'$.

5. Therefore hallucinatory experiences have singular content. For example, in hallucinating a pink rat one is in a perceptual state with a singular content, perhaps expressible as 'That rat is pink'.

The argument does not rely on the claim that indistinguishable experiences have the same content. This premise would deliver the conclusion that the empty content in the hallucination is identical with the non-empty content in the perception. By contrast, according to RWR non-empty singular content is essentially non-empty, and empty singular content is essentially empty, so no singular content could be common to perception and hallucination.

The most contentious premise in this argument is (4). One will accept it if one accepts a close connection between perceptual content and belief content. It is highly plausible that indistinguishable experiences immediately give rise to the same kind of belief contents, singular or general as the case may be. If perceptual belief arises simply by slotting the perceptual content into belief content, (4) follows.

The third argument is this. Not only does attributing singular content in cases of hallucination provide the appropriately false content to explain the deceptive nature of hallucinations, this content also meshes appropriately with explanations of actions induced by hallucinations. He hallucinated a pink rat, and so formed a false singular belief: that it was pink. In terror, he reached for his baseball bat to defend himself from it. That is why he reached for the bat. The DR singularist must say either that there is no content in these cases, or that it is general. The first option defeats both the goal of explaining the deceptive nature of hallucinations and their role in explaining actions. The second option does not harmonize with the stance of a singularist: if general content is good enough in cases of hallucination, why not also in cases of perception? Moreover, it does not fit with the quasi-singular character of the explanandum: according to the hallucination, there is a particular rat which is the object of the swinging of the baseball bat. We need to know 'about this rat' (for example, where *it* seemed to the subject to be) in order to explain the action.

A singular perceptual content is to be identified by its functional role: it issues from a mechanism designed to produce singular contents with perceived objects as referents, and is available to the mechanisms which guide perceptually based action. A singular content which, through some malfunction, fails to have a referent is still a singular content, just as a malformed heart, incapable of fulfilling its pumping function, is still a heart.

References

Almog, J. (2004). 'The proper form of semantics', in Anne Bezuidenhout and Marga Reimer (eds.), *Descriptions and Beyond* (Oxford: Oxford University Press), 390–419.

Bealer, G. (1998). 'Propositions', *Mind* 107: 1–32.

——(2004). 'An inconsistency in direct reference theory', *Journal of Philosophy* 101: 574–93.

Bostock, D. (1997). *Intermediate Logic* (Oxford: Clarendon Press).

Burge, T. (1973). 'Reference and proper names', *Journal of Philosophy* 70: 425–39.

——(1974a). 'Truth and singular terms.' *Noûs* 8: 309–25.

——(1974b). 'Demonstrative constructions, reference and truth.' *Journal of Philosophy* 71: 205–23.

——(1991). 'Vision and intentional content', in E. Lepore and R. Van Gulik (eds.), *John Searle and his Critics* (Cambridge, MA: Basil Blackwell), 195–213.

Campbell, J. (2002). *Reference and Consciousness* (Oxford: Clarendon Press).

Chastain, C. (1975). 'Reference and context', in K. Gunderson, (ed.), *Language, Mind, and Knowledge* (Minneapolis: University of Minnesota Press), 194–269.

Davidson, D. (1967). 'Truth and meaning', *Synthese* 17: 304–23. Repr. in D. Davidson (1984), *Inquiries into Truth and Interpretation* (Oxford: Clarendon Press), 17–36.

——(1968). 'On saying that', *Synthese* 19: 130–46. Repr. in D. Davidson (1984), *Inquiries into Truth and Interpretation* (Oxford: Clarendon Press), 93–108.

——(1969). 'The individuation of events', in N. Rescher (ed.), *Essays in Honor of Carl G. Hempel* (Dordrecht: Reidel), 216–34. Repr. in D. Davidson (1980), *Essays on Actions and Events* (Oxford: Clarendon Press), 163–80.

——(1970). 'Reply to Cargile', *Inquiry* 13: 140–8. Repr. as 'Action and reaction' in D. Davidson (1984), *Inquiries into Truth and Interpretation* (Oxford: Clarendon Press), 137–48.

——(1973). 'Radical interpretation', *Dialectica* 27: 313–28. Repr. in D. Davidson (1984), *Inquiries into Truth and Interpretation* (Oxford: Clarendon Press), 125–39.

Davidson, D. (1976). 'Reply to Foster', in G. Evans and J. McDowell (eds.), *Truth and Meaning* (Oxford: Oxford University Press), 33–41.

—— (1977). 'Reality without reference', *Dialectica* 31: 247–53. Repr. in D. Davidson (1984), *Inquiries into Truth and Interpretation* (Oxford: Clarendon Press), 215–26.

—— (1986). 'A nice derangement of epitaths', in R. Grandy and R. Warner (eds.), *Philosophical Grounds of Rationality* (Oxford: Clarendon Press), 157–74. Repr. in A. P. Martinich (1996), *The Philosophy of Language*, 3rd edn. (New York: Oxford University Press), 465–75.

Davies, M. (1981). *Meaning, Quantification, Necessity: Themes in Philosophical Logic* (London: Routledge and Kegan Paul).

—— (1992). 'Perceptual content and local supervenience', *Proceedings of the Aristotelian Society* 92: 21–45.

Donnellan, K. (1966). 'Reference and definite descriptions', *Philosophical Review* 77: 203–15.

Dummett, M. (1973/1981). *Frege: Philosophy of Language* (London: Duckworth).

—— (1978). *Truth and Other Enigmas.* London, Duckworth.

—— (1983). 'Existence', in D. P. Chattopadhyaya (ed.), *Humans, Meanings and Existences*, Jadavpur Studies in Philosophy 5 (New Delhi: Macmillan, India), 221–51. Repr. in M. Dummett (1993), *The Seas of Language* (Oxford: Oxford University Press), 227–307.

Evans, G. (1977). 'Pronouns, quantifiers and relative clauses (I)', *Canadian Journal of Philosophy* 7: 467–536.

—— (1982). *The Varieties of Reference* (Oxford: Clarendon Press).

Foster, J. (1976). 'Meaning and truth theory', in G. Evans and J. McDowell (eds.), *Truth and Meaning* (Oxford: Oxford University Press), 1–32.

Frege, G. (1892). 'On sense and meaning', in B. McGuinness (ed.) (1984), *Collected Papers on Mathematics, Logic and Philosophy* (Oxford: Basil Blackwell), 157–77.

—— (1906). 'Introduction to Logic', in H. Hermes, F. Kambartel, and F. Kaulbach, (eds.) (1984), *Posthumous Writings* (Oxford: Basil Blackwell), 185–96.

—— (1918). 'Logical investigations: thoughts', in B. McGuinness (ed.) (1984), *Collected Papers on Mathematics, Logic and Philosophy* (Oxford: Basil Blackwell), 351–72.

Graff, D. (2001). 'Descriptions as predicates', *Philosophical Studies* 102: 1–42.

Grice, H. P. (1969). 'Vacuous names', in D. Davidson and J. Hintikka (eds.), *Words and Objections: Essays on the Work of W. V. Quine* (Dordrecht: Reidel), 118–45.

Heim, I. (1982/1988). *The Semantics of Definite and Indefinite Noun Phrases* (Ann Arbor: University Microfilms International).

Henry, D. P. (1984). *That Most Subtle Question* (Manchester: Manchester University Press).

Hespos, Susan J. and E. Spelke (2004). 'Conceptual precursors to language', *Nature* 430: 453–6.

Hilbert, D. and P. Bernays (eds.) (1939). *Grundlagen der Mathematik*, vol.2 (Berlin: Springer Verlag).

Hirsch, E. (1997). 'Basic objects: a reply to Xu', *Mind and Language* 12: 406–12.

Jackson, F. (1998). 'Reference and descriptions revisited', *Philosophical Perspectives* 12: 201–18.

Kamp, H. (1981). 'A theory of truth and semantic representation', in J. A. G. Groenendijk, T. M. V. Janssen, and M. B. J. Stockhof (eds.), *Formal Methods in the Study of Language*, I (Amsterdam: Mathamatisch Centrum), 277–322.

Kamp, H. and U. Reyle (1993). *From Discourse to Logic* (Dordrecht: Kluwer).

Kaplan, D. (1973). 'Bob and Carol and Ted and Alice', in J. Hintikka, J. Moravcsik, and P. Suppes (eds.), *Approaches to Natural Language* (Dordrecht: Reidel), 490–518.

Kaplan, D. (1977). 'Demonstratives', unpub. ms, UCLA Philosophy Department. Repr. in J. Almog, J. Perry and H. Wettstein (eds.) *Themes from Kaplan* (Oxford: Oxford University Press), 1989: 481–614.

—— (1989). 'Afterthoughts', in J. Almog, J. Perry, and H. Wettstein (eds.), *Themes from Kaplan* (Oxford: Oxford University Press), 565–614.

King, J. (1992). 'Unbound anaphora'. Unpublished ms.

Klima, G. (2001). 'Existence and reference in medieval logic', in E. Morscher and A. Hieke (eds.), *New Essays in Free Logic. In Honor of Karel Lambert* (Dordrecht: Kluwer), 197–226.

Kripke, S. (1972/1980). *Naming and Necessity* (Oxford: Basil Blackwell).

—— (1979). 'A puzzle about belief', in A. Margalit (ed.), *Meaning and Use* (Dordrecht: Reidel), 239–83.

Lambert, K. (1991). 'A theory of definite descriptions', in K. Lambert (ed.), *Philosophical Applications of Free Logic* (Oxford, New York: Oxford University Press), 17–27.

—— (2001). 'Free logic and definite descriptions', in E. Morscher and A. Hieke (eds.), *New Essays in Free Logic. In Honor of Karel Lambert* (Dordrecht: Kluwer), 37–47.

Larson, R. and G. Segal (1995). *Knowledge of Meaning: an Introduction to Semantic Theory* (Cambridge, MA: MIT Press).

Lehman, S. (1994). 'Strict Fregean free logic', *Journal of Philosophical Logic* 23: 307–36.

Leisenring, A. C. (1969). *Mathematical Logic and Hilbert's ε-symbol* (New York: Gordon and Breach Science Publishers).

Lewis, D. (1979). 'Scorekeeping in a language game', in R. Bäuerle, U. Egli, and A. von Stechow (eds.), *Semantics From Different Points of View* (Berlin: Springer Verlag), 172–87.

—— (1986). *On the Plurality of Worlds* (Oxford: Basil Blackwell).

Linsky, L. (1963). 'Reference and referents', in C. E. Caton (ed.), *Philosophy and Ordinary Language* (Urbana: University of Illinois Press), 74–89.

Mates, B. (1950). 'Synonymity', *University of California Publications in Philosophy* 25: 201–26.

McDowell, J. (1976). 'Truth conditions, bivalence and verificationism', in G. Evans and J. McDowell (eds.), *Truth and Meaning* (Oxford: Clarendon Press), 42–66.

—— (1977). 'On the sense and reference of a proper name', *Mind* 86: 159–85.

—— (1984). '*De re* senses', *Philosophical Quarterly* 34: 283–94.

McGinn, C. (1982). *The Character of Mind* (Oxford: Oxford University Press).

McKay, T. (2003). *Plurals and Non-Distributive Predication*. Draft version available on McKay's page at <http://philosophy.syr.edu/>.

Mendelson, E. (1964). *Introduction to Mathematical Logic* (New York: Van Nostrand Reinhold Company).

Mill, J. S. (1843). *System of Logic* (London: Parker).

Millikan, R. (1984). *Language, Truth and Other Biological Categories* (Cambridge: Cambridge University Press).

—— (1991). 'Perceptual content and Fregean myth', *Mind* 100: 439–59.

—— (2000). *On Clear and Confused Ideas* (Cambridge: Cambridge University Press).

Morscher, E. and P. Simons (2001). 'Free logic: a fifty-year past and an open future', in E. Morscher and A. Hieke (eds.), *New Essays in Free Logic. In Honor of Karel Lambert* (Dordrecht: Kluwer), 1–34.

Neale, S. (1990). *Descriptions* (Cambridge, MA, London: MIT Press).

—— (2004). 'Pragmatism and binding', in Z. Szabó (ed.) *Semantics and Pragmatics* (Oxford: Oxford University Press).

Oliver, A. (2000). ' "Ghost writers" (with Alexius Schmeinong)', *Analysis* 60: 371.

Parsons, T. (1980). *Nonexistent Objects* (New Haven: Yale University Press).

Plantinga, A. (1974). *The Nature of Necessity* (Oxford: Clarendon Press).

Quine, W. V. O. (1956). 'Quantifiers and propositional attitudes', *The Journal of Philosophy* 53: 177–87.

—— (1960). *Word and Object* (New York: Technological Press of MIT and John Wiley and Sons, Inc.).

Recanati, F. (1993). *Direct Reference* (Oxford: Blackwell Publishers).

Roseveare, N. T. (1982). *Mercury's Perihelion from Le Verrier to Einstein* (Oxford: Oxford University Press).

Russell, B. (1905). 'On denoting', *Mind* 14: 479–93.

Russell, B. (1912/1959). *Problems of Philosophy* (Oxford: Oxford University Press).

—— (1913). *Theory of Knowledge*. First pub. in E. R. Eames and K. Blackwell (eds.) (1984), *The Collected Papers of Bertrand Russell, vol. 7: Theory of Knowledge, The 1913 Manuscript* (London: George Allen and Unwin).

—— (1918–19). 'Lectures on the Philosophy of Logical Atomism'. *Monist* 28: 495–527, 29: 32–63, 190–222, 345–80. Repr. in R. C. Marsh (ed.) (1956), *Bertrand Russell: Logic and Knowledge; Essays 1902–1950* (London: George Allen and Unwin), 177–281.

—— and A. N. Whitehead (1910–13). *Principia Mathematica*, Part I repr. 1981 (Cambridge: Cambridge University Press).

Sainsbury, R. M. (1983). 'On a Fregean argument', *Analysis* 43: 12–14.

—— (2002). *Departing From Frege: Essays in the Philosophy of Language* (London: Routledge).

—— (2004). 'Sameness and difference of sense', *Philosophical Books* 45: 209–17.

Salmon, N. (1986). *Frege's Puzzle* (Cambridge, MA: MIT Press).

—— (1998). 'Nonexistence', *Noûs* 32: 277–319.

Sawyer, S. (2002). 'Abstract artifacts in pretence', *Philosophical Papers* 31: 183–98.

Schiffer, S. (2003). *The Things We Mean* (Oxford: Clarendon Press).

Sharvy, R. (1980). 'A more general theory of definite descriptions', *Philosophical Review* 89: 607–24.

Simons, P. (2001). 'Calculi of names; free and modal', in E. Morscher and A. Hieke (eds.), *New Essays in Free Logic. In Honor of Karel Lambert* (Dordrecht: Kluwer), 49–65.

Soames, S. (2002). *Beyond Rigidity* (Oxford: Oxford University Press).

Sosa, D. (2001). 'Rigidity in the scope of Russell's theory', *Noûs* 35: 1–38.

Soteriou, M. (2000). 'The particularity of visual perception', *European Journal of Analytic Philosophy* 8: 173–89.

Spelke, E. (1988). 'Where perceiving ends and thinking begins. The apprehension of objects in infancy', in A. Yonas (ed.), *Perceptual Development in Infancy* (Norwood, NJ: Ablex), 197–234.

Spelke, E. and G. Van de Walle (1993). 'Perceiving and reasoning about objects: insights from infants', in N. Eilan, R. McCarthy, and B. Brewer (eds.), *Spatial Representation: Problems in Philosophy and Psychology* (Oxford: Blackwell Publishers), 132–61.

Sperber, D. and D. Wilson (1986/1995). *Relevance. Communication and Cognition* (Oxford: Blackwell Publishers).

Strawson, P. (1950). 'On Referring', *Mind* 59: 269–86.

Tarski, A. (1933). 'The concept of truth in formalized languages', originally pub. in Polish as 'Pojecie prawdy w jezykach nauk dedukcyjnych' ('The concept of truth in languages of deductive sciences'), *Prace Towarzystwa Naukowego Warszawskiego, Wydzial III Nauk: Matematyczno-Fizycznych* 34 (Warsaw). Repr. in A. Tarski: (1956), *Logic, Semantics, Metamathematics* (Oxford: Clarendon Press), 152–278.

Travis, C. (1996). 'Meaning's role in truth', *Mind* 105: 451–66.

—— (1997). 'Pragmatics', in B. Hale and C. Wright (eds.), *A Companion to the Philosophy of Language* (Oxford: Blackwell Publishers), 87–107.

—— (2004). 'The silence of the senses', *Mind* 113: 57–94.

Tye, M. (2000). *Consciousness, Color, and Content* (Cambridge, MA: MIT Press).

Van Inwagen, P. (1977). 'Creatures of fiction', *American Philosophical Quarterly* 14: 299–308.

Wiggins, D. (1980). *Sameness and Substance* (Oxford: Basil Blackwell).

—— (1995). 'The Kant–Frege–Russell view of existence: toward the rehabilitation of the second-level view', in W. Sinnott-Armstrong, D. Raffman, and N. Asher (eds.), *Modality, Morality and Belief. Essays in Honor of Ruth Barcan Marcus* (Cambridge: Cambridge University Press), 93–116.

Wynn, K. (1992). 'Addition and subtraction in infants', *Nature* 358: 749–50.

Yourgrau, P. (1987). 'The dead', *Journal of Philosophy* 84: 84–101.

Index

Abelard 197
acquaintance (knowledge by acquaintance) 63–4, 99, 101, 185–6, 240–2
actually 29, 40n, 75–7, 79–80, 178
Almog, Joseph 110
Ammag 114–15, 117, 120–3
anaphora 55, 125–53, 155, 160–3, 168, 232, 244
Anselm 91
Aristotle 1, 67n
Asher, Nicholas viii
austerity (in truth theories) 39, 41–3, 45, 47, 74

Babinet, Jacques 68n
Ballerin, Roberta viii, 77n, 107n, 139n
Bealer, George 62n, 97n
Bedeutung (reference/meaning) 8–9, 12, 17
Berkeley, George 147
Bermudez, José viii
Boethius 91
Bostock, David 65
Buckner, Dean viii, 1n
Burge, Tyler viii, 47, 66, 139, 158, 179

Campbell, John 62, 63, 239n
categories, semantic 46, 94, 95–6, 202
Chastain, Charles 31, 127n
cognitive value 8, 44
connotation 5–6, 33
Copeland, Jack viii
Crowther, Tom viii

Davidson, Donald 33, 34, 40, 41, 48, 49, 51–5, 59, 40–1, 128, 158
Davies, Martin 49, 246
demon-proof 63, 101, 252
demonstratives 7, 54–8, 62–3, 83, 122n, 125, 153–69, 175, 189, 206, 226, 230
denotation 2–8, 85, 204
descriptions, definite
  description theories of names 24–32, 98–105, 204
  rigid 28, 152
  theories of descriptions 132, 174–94
Dever, Josh viii
direct reference theories
  of names *see* names
  of individual concepts *see* individual concepts
Discourse Representation Theory (DRT) 145–6
Donnellan, Keith 51, 72, 177, 179, 187–91
Dummett, Michael 7, 15n

ϵ 128–9
Eigenname 17
E-type pronouns 133–6
Evans, Gareth 17–18, 20, 22, 41, 62, 68, 70, 79–81, 94–7, 102, 109, 113, 114, 119–21, 132–7, 139, 141–3, 145, 147n, 150, 155, 163, 166, 167, 187, 201, 222, 223n, 226, 227, 233, 237
existence 19, 22–3, 27, 46, 48, 51, 64–75, 77, 87, 90, 98, 183, 195ff, 237–8
existential generalization 65, 75, 82, 130, 138, 143, 200
Ezcurdia, Maite viii

fiction 7, 17, 67, 75–6, 87, 152, 195, 202–15
  fictional characters/entities 48, 97, 209–15
File Change Semantics 145
fission 122–3
Foster, John 34
frame problem 56
Frege, Gottlob 1, 2, 8–18, 22, 27, 30, 33, 42, 43, 45, 73, 91, 92, 97, 166n, 185n, 204, 232
Fregean free logic 66–9, 72

Goodman, Victoria viii
Grice, H. P. 235n, 236n

hallucination 167, 239, 252–4
Heim, Irene 145, 147
Heller, Mark viii, 69n

262 INDEX

Henry, D. P. 91, 196, 197
Hespos, Susan 221n
Hilbert, David 128–9
Hirsch, Eli 221n
homophony 40–1, 43, 46–7, 52, 54, 56, 168, 177, 202, 237
Hopkins, Jim viii, 116n
Hossack, Keith viii
Howell, Robert 77n

I 15, 58, 125, 154, 166n
identity 6–8, 9–12, 15–16, 19, 23–4, 63, 66, 69, 98, 103–4, 129, 156–7, 175, 179, 228, 229–341, 233
indefinites 125ff, 129–30
indexicals 54–6, 77n, 153ff, 166n
individual concepts 146–50, 155, 169, 217ff

Jackson, Frank 100–1

Kamp, Hans 145
Kempson, Ruth viii, 141n
King, Jeffrey 140
Klima, G. 64n, 197n
Kölbel, Max viii
Kripke, Saul 2, 11n, 16, 27–32, 38, 74, 76, 81, 106, 112–13, 151, 161n, 177n, 182, 183, 185, 224

Lambert, Karel 66, 175, 178
Larson, Richard 53n
Le Verrier, Urbain 68n, 89, 104, 110, 198, 201, 214, 236–7
Lehman, S. 66
Leisenring, A. C. 129
Lescarbault, Dr. 88–9, 198
Leverhulme Trust vii, viii
Lewis, David 76, 138
logic
  classical 46, 64–5, 72, 73–4, 82–3, 131, 172, 199, 200, 237
  negative free (NFL) see NFL

MacBride, Fraser viii
Macdonald, Cynthia viii
Macdonald, Graham viii
McCabe, MM viii
McDowell, John 16, 33–46, 47, 48, 49, 51, 52, 74, 84–5, 96, 97, 98, 237
McGinn, Colin 246
Meinongian views 74, 75, 237
Mendelson, Elliott 48
Mill, John Stuart 2–8, 22, 75

Millian see names, Millian theories of
Millikan, Ruth 16n, 216n
modal profile 27–8
mode of presentation 8–10, 12, 14, 16, 17
Montague grammar 62
Morscher, E. 64n, 67n
mouse example 21, 45, 63, 242

η 129
names
  common 3
  connotative see connotation
  denotative see denotation
  descriptive 95–6, 109
  direct reference (DR) theories of 3, 64, 81, 83–4, 94, 98, 165, 169, 229, 240, 252
  empty (bearerless) 43–4, 48, 64–5, 67, 72–3, 86–90, 93, 95, 97–8, 103–6, 108, 122–4, 153, 196, 199, 208, 236N, 237–8
  in fiction 7, 67, 75, 87, 97, 169, 195, 202–15
  logically proper 19–24, 84
  Millian theories of 2, 3, 8, 44–5, 64, 74, (see also: Mill, and names, direct reference theories of)
  ordinary proper 24–7, 92, 101, 154
  Russellian 94–7
name-using practice 15, 86, 87, 90, 93, 96, 103, 106–24, 232, 233
Neale, Stephen viii, 49, 127, 134n
Neg 67
negation
  scope of 69, 71, 85, 138n, 195, 196–8, 205–6
negative existential sentences 26, 69, 81, 135n, 195, 199
NFL (negative free logic) 45, 46, 47–8, 64–75, 80, 93, 98, 138n, 178–9, 199–201
non-detachability 160n
non-existent things 75, 97, 200, 237
object-dependent 163
object involving 81, 83–5, 93, 94, 96, 164, 180–2, 188–9

Ockham, William of 46, 65n, 80, 130, 131, 132, 133, 152, 173n, 196, 197

P (Evans's reference principle) 79–81
Paderewski cases 11n, 12n, 14, 15, 67, 103–4

Papineau, David viii
Parsons, Terence 75
perceptual content 242–54
phlogiston 89–90, 168
Pickard, Hanna viii
plural terms 45, 46n, 79, 80n, 170, 172–4, 191–4, 215n, 222, 234n
propositions, Russellian 22, 47, 60–3
Proudfoot, Diane viii

R (rigidity) 77–9, 81, 84
really 199, 202
Recanati, François 26n, 83n, 151
reference condition 46, 53, 95, 131, 133, 140, 143, 144, 150, 176, 177
referential intentions 164, 179–82, 184–6, 188–9, 194
Reyle, Uwe 146
rigid designator 28–9, 46, 74, 77n, 83, 169, 179, 182
 de facto/de jure 29, 151
Roseveare, N. T. 68n, 88n
Russell, Bertrand 2, 19–27, 32, 45, 60, 61–2, 70, 75, 84, 91, 94, 99, 101, 175–6, 182, 203, 235, 239, 240–1
RWR (reference without reference)
main theses listed, 45–6

salience 136–9
Salmon, Nathan 3n, 7, 8, 12n, 83n, 87, 209, 210, 211, 212
Savile, Anthony viii, 115n
Sawyer, Sarah 212
scene/content attributions 55–7, 155, 160–3, 165, 166, 167–9, 190, 244–5, 253
Schiffer, Stephen 60, 101, 102, 209–10, 211, 213, 214
Segal, Gabriel viii, 53n
semantic referent 114–22, 126–7, 130, 136–7, 164–5, 189–90
semantically complex vs semantically simple 17, 29, 46, 62, 66n, 79–83, 95, 170–94
sense data 19, 21, 60, 63, 240
sense 7–18, 27–30, 33, 35, 40, 66n, 146, 199, 201, 216, 232
 de re 33, 41–9, 81, 85, 96
Sharvy, R. 193
Shea, Nick 250
Simons, Peter 64n, 67n, 178n

singular terms, 17, 20, 67, 79, 95, 98, 161, 174, 201n, 213, 237, 247; *see also* names
Soames, Scott 211
sortals, 89, 221n, 224–6
sortal-subsumption theses 116n, 225
Sosa, David viii, 29
Soteriou, Matthew 249–51
speaker referent 114–18, 120, 130, 136–9, 164, 189, 190
Spelke, Elizabeth 219–21
Sperber, Dan 49, 154
Stanley, Jason viii
Strawson, Peter 46, 80, 85, 129, 132, 173n, 185
Sturgeon, Scott viii

Tarski, Alfred 33, 53
Textor, Mark viii
Thau, Michael 110n
Travis, Charles 49, 50, 242n
truth condition(s) 22, 25, 26, 28, 33, 34, 46, 47, 50, 51, 53, 59, 61, 65n, 70, 72, 79, 85, 127, 129, 130, 133, 135, 139, 142, 143, 144, 145, 150–3, 154, 165, 171, 173, 176–7, 179, 185, 200, 229
 conditional 131n, 158–63, 169
 Ockhamist vs Strawsonian 46, 65n, 85, 129, 131, 132, 133, 152, 173n
 singular 81, 83, 131n, 151–2
truth theory, 33–5, 38, 40, 46, 48–59, 61, 82n, 83
 axioms of 35–41, 42, 49, 53, 55–6, 58, 74, 95, 105, 122, 176–9, 202
 interpretive 33–7
T-theorem, 33–5, 40, 53, 55, 61, 83, 177
 canonical 40, 53
 singular 82.
Turner, Mark viii
Tye, Michael viii, 246

van de Walle, G. 220, 221
van Inwagen, Peter 209n
variable binding 126–7, 132

Wiggins, David viii, 69n, 74, 196, 198–202, 214, 224, 225–6
Wilson, Deirdre 49, 154
Wynn, K. 219

Yourgrau, Palle 75n